Leap of Faith

You have changed my mourning into dancing for me. You have unfastened my sackcloth and wrapped me in Joy.

Psalm 30

LEAP *of* FAITH
My Dance through Life

SHONA DUNLOP MACTAVISH

Longacre Press

Acknowledgements

I wish to thank Longacre Press, Christine Johnston, Fiona Clark,
Peggy Gallagher and Hilary Dunlop. Also Jennifer Shennan and
the New Zealand Dance Archives for its financial assistance.
I am especially grateful for the loving support of my daughter Terry.

ISBN 1 877135 04 6

First published 1997 by Longacre Press Ltd.,
P.O. Box 5340, Dunedin, New Zealand

Cover and book design by Jenny Cooper

Printed by Brebner Print Ltd, Auckland

For my children, Terry, Dugald and Catriona,
my grandchildren,
and Louise.

And to the memory of my husband, Donald.

Chapter One

Suddenly Shona Dunlop became the centre of attention.
I discovered the power of holding an audience and according
to my mother, gave an excellent performance.

In 1926 my father owned the only steam car in New Zealand. He had purchased two Stanley steamers in quick succession and in the early 1930s drove one of the last steam-driven cars to come off the assembly line, the Doble. Father's pride and joy in his steamer was matched by his children's extreme embarrassment. We hated to be seen stuck halfway up one of Dunedin's steep hills, and the car's loud reports as it left the garage shamed us. Once underway the car was considerably quieter than contemporary petrol-driven cars – its chief attraction as far as my father was concerned, but this was no compensation to us children.

The sight of flame and smoke belching from the rear of the car startled the unenlightened – once a cyclist sped alongside the driver crying, 'Your car's on fire!' – and on one memorable occasion even brought out the fire brigade with hoses at the ready. The tale of Professor Frank Dunlop and his family emerging from their car dripping wet soon became a stock item of the annual Otago University Capping Concert.

We had many adventures in that car. Overtaking a truck on the Taieri Mouth Road, Dad drove the steamer too close to the side of the road. The left wheels spun uselessly in the air, and because the engine was low-slung, we remained perilously perched, the beach and rolling breakers a few feet away. I was in tears, wedged behind some large trunks. A farmer with a team of six draft horses was persuaded to pull the car back on the road. Jocelyn and Wallace, my teenage brother and sister, sat an embarrassed distance off, wishing for the hundredth time that their father drove a *petrol* car like everyone else.

My father's passion for steam had become the chief diversion of his life and steam-engine drivers were among his closest buddies. In his bookcases pamphlets and books on steam vied with those on philosophy, religion, literature and languages.

*　*　*

My father's father, John Dunlop, was born a farmer's son in Ayrshire, Scotland in 1837. He was educated at Glasgow University and Theological Hall, ordained as a Pastor of the Free Church of Scotland in 1880 and served the parish of St David's in Dundee.

As a boy of five, my father, Francis Wallace Dunlop, severely injured his left leg while playing. When the injury became infected with tuberculosis, he was confined to bed for a year, during which time he developed a great love of reading. The injured leg however remained shorter than the other. In 1887 his parents emigrated with their five children to New Zealand where John Dunlop became Professor of Theology at the University of Otago and subsequently Moderator of the Presbyterian Church of New Zealand.

Frank was twelve when the family settled in Dunedin. After attending Otago Boys' High School, he went on to Otago University, gaining an M.A. in Mental Science in 1899. Two years later he graduated with First Class Honours from the Theological Hall. He would follow in his father's footsteps as a minister of the Presbyterian Church. Frank Dunlop further distinguished himself by studying for a Doctorate of Philosophy at the University of Jena in Germany under the famous philosopher, Professor Rudolf Euken. His dissertation which was written in German earned him the commendation *magna cum laude*. Upon his return to New Zealand in 1904 he took up his first parish position as minister at Knox Presbyterian Church in Invercargill. It was there that he met his surprising future wife.

Maud Giller, the daughter of a Southland farmer, was training to be a nurse at Invercargill Public Hospital. Unlike the other members of the Knox Church Invercargill Bible class, Maud teased the handsome young minister and even questioned his teaching. To everyone's surprise and the disappointment of several, Doctor Dunlop's engagement to this charming but surely unsuitable young woman from Lumsden was announced.

If attendants of Knox Presbyterian Church were surprised, no less were Maud's student colleagues at the Invercargill Public Hospital.

'You'll see,' they warned her when she told them the minister had invited her to accompany him on a trip to Riverton beach. 'When he gets you behind the rocks, it'll only be to read you a sermon.'

'Nothing in the world,' my mother confided to me years later, 'would have led me to confess to them that he had done exactly that!'

My parents were married in Invercargill in January 1909. While travelling by train to Bluff where they were to spend their honeymoon, Maud was embarrassed to discover that the young man sitting opposite was a former boyfriend. To make matters worse he kept winking at her!

Unfortunately, their honeymoon was interrupted by the news that Frank's father had died at the age of 72.

My mother came like a breath of fresh air into the scholarly, ecclesiastical Dunlop family. Her reputation for being a rather scatty young lass gave her husband's family some sleepless nights. Determined to prove herself a dutiful and model wife she bought a sixpenny pig's head from the market and proudly announced to her sceptical in-laws that from this purchase she had made no less than two brawn shapes and a stew, as well as a delectable soup. It was true – as a daughter of the land she understood how to make a penny go a long way. Southland farmers who had to break in their land by the slow process of felling bush and draining marshes found it difficult to feed and clothe their families. Their children had known few luxuries.

After my sister Jocelyn was born the following year, my parents moved to Sydney where my father was inducted as minister of the Presbyterian Church in Glebe. It was there that my brother Wallace was born in 1912. The family was not to remain in Australia long, for in 1913 Frank Dunlop, aged 39, succeeded Professor Salmond as Professor of Mental and Moral Philosophy at the University of Otago in Dunedin. In 1916 my brother, Bonar, was born and four years later on 12 April 1920 Maud Dunlop was delivered of a second daughter - Shona Katrine Dunlop. My brother and I were born at home, at 121 Clyde St on the hill behind the University.

Mother took her role as professor's wife very seriously. At laburnum time, when the two laburnum trees in our garden were in full bloom, she had her garden party for wives of the University staff and friends. Mother liked doing things on a grand scale and would walk her guests the short distance to the Rhododendron Dell of the public gardens, which were then at the height of glory. Her manner indicated that this magnificent display of rhododendron was simply an extension of her own garden.

Mother was President of the Free Kindergarten Association, was a regular church attender and took part in various church-centred activities, but she did have a problem with punctuality. During a period when my father was minister at Knox Church in Dunedin and living in the manse next-door, one of the more famous of Mother's misdeeds took place. My father had gently reminded her that it was customary for the minister's wife to be seated at least five minutes before the commencement of the service. As she had failed to meet this expectation on various occasions he asked if she would make a special effort to do so that morning. The fashion of the time dictated that she wear a long train and as Mother shut the door behind her, she found herself caught fast. By the time she struggled free the church bell had ceased ringing, and the shame-faced lady of the manse slipped into her pew, earning a reproachful glance from the pulpit.

The one supreme embarrassment experienced by us children was the Sunday each year when the clocks were put forward for daylight saving. The Dunlop family unfailingly filed into Knox Church not as the first hymn was being sung, but to the last hymn. The amused eyes of the congregation had us cowering in our pews.

Our house in Clyde Street (now the extension of the Arana Hall Hostel) was lined from floor to ceiling in every room, including bedrooms, hall, and landings, with books of every size and colour. Along with my mother's red silk lampshades with black fringes, and the old prints in the breakfast room – 'First Love', 'The Elopement' and 'The Quarrel', the books are part of my first memories. I was drawn to them from the start, and loved to move from shelf to shelf, touching each volume with my finger, despite stern warnings from my parents.

Regular consignments of the latest publications in philosophy and religion, both in English and in German, came regularly from the renowned Thin's Bookshop in Edinburgh. One of my mother's stock complaints regarding the hundreds of books she was obliged to dust was that within three years of marriage they had shifted houses four times with five tons of books.

My father's admiration for German philosophy and the German people had caused him some difficulty during the 1914-18 war. After preaching against the obscene custom of smashing all German-made pianos, my father was labelled collaborator by some, and received vicious threats. He remained an admirer of German music and literature all his life. One of the few occasions I saw him angry was when I accidentally sat on a stack of his recently purchased 78rpm German records. I broke the lot.

The duty-doing Dunlop family felt that play was quite incompatible with true Christian living, but my mother taught my father how to enjoy life. During the steamie years, he developed the habit of taking drives or picnics on lecture-free days. However, his responsibilities to his students always came first. Night time seemed the best hours for his work. Sometimes I would hear him thumping up the stairs with his stiff leg as the birds began their morning chorus. This meant that he was not at his best in the mornings. I recall our maid Evelyn bringing up the breakfast tray, just as my brother Bonar and I were clamouring for tramcar money from the foot of the bed.

'Hand me my breeks,' Father would say and, fumbling about in the pockets, he would draw out a couple of pennies. 'And dinna lose them now!' He loved resorting to Scottish expressions and would recite verses from Robbie Burns.

Mother loved people and was a popular hostess. She was particularly good to those she called her 'lame ducks', lonely people or invalids. Almost every Sunday after attending service at Knox Church, people were invited back to the house for a good sing-song. We younger children found these occasions pretty boring, and some of the guests who played piano or sang, hard to endure. But my father singing 'Come into the garden Maud' in a pleasant tenor never failed to send shivers of delight down my spine. He was very musical and acquired an impressive collection of records. On long summer evenings as I lay unwillingly in my bed, strains of the *Cavaliera Rusticana*, Bizet's *Carmen* or Offenbach's *Orpheus in the Underworld* wafted up the stairs.

*   *   *

When the summer days lengthened and Dad's lectures were finished for the year, we packed up the steamie and headed off on holiday. Travelling even the few miles to Taieri Mouth was a delight, and sometimes we ventured as far as Pounawea in the Catlins, or to my favourite place of all, Stewart Island.

White House, the cottage we used for our holidays on the beach at Pounawea, was hardly first class accommodation. We arrived on one occasion to find rats had gorged their way through every mattress, and then died on the kitchen floor. As both rain water tanks were empty, our resourceful mother organised all the children to fetch buckets of sea-water which were thrown with wild enthusiasm throughout the cottage. As far as we were concerned these primitive conditions added to the charm of the holiday.

University papers were marked in the lupins of the Pounawea estuary. A sudden gust of wind would send me and my brother chasing papers along the beach. At night I could hardly stifle my excited giggles as we all set forth with lanterns to spear flounder for the next day's dinner. We spent the balmy summer days swimming, boating and tramping through the native bush. Often we'd find penguins nesting in flax bushes above the beach.

It was at Butterfield Beach on Stewart Island that we had our happiest holidays. Rakiura, the island of the glowing skies, was then and remains the most magical unspoilt island. We would travel by steamie to Bluff, visiting Mother's relatives on the way, and cross the turbulent Foveaux Strait on the *Teresa Ward*.

I remember fairy huts in the bush, exploring the forbidden cave at the end of the beach, stockings bulging at the end of my bed on Christmas morning. Dismal, washed-out campers were offered hot soup and blankets, and a dry piece of floor in the passage of our cottage, to throw down a blanket. Once my brother Wallace and his girlfriend set forth with their baggage in a flimsy dinghy for Oban Bay in order to catch the *Teresa Ward*, sailing for the mainland. Swamped by a huge breaker, they had to return to the house, dry out and hope for calmer surf the following day. There were no vehicles on the island, dinghies providing the most common means of transport. In the charming little church standing on the hill above Half Moon Bay I heard Dad preach a sermon to a congregation of happy holiday-makers who were more than ready to sing their praise to the creator of this beautiful island.

George Turner, a well known Stewart Island identity, had become a good friend of my family over the years of visiting the island. At his invitation we spent a day on his launch , discovering the beauty of Paterson Inlet. Some of us fished, others knocked luscious oysters off the rocks and we children swung out on the red flowering rata trees to plunge into the sea below. Heading home, we became engulfed in a thick fog and Mr Turner, who had suffered a head injury during the war, lost all sense of direction. We were utterly lost. General agreement among the adults was to find a beach and camp there overnight, otherwise we might strike a rock, or run aground.

Two of Jocelyn's friends manned a dinghy and found a small beach to which we were taken in turns. A large fire was built, and I soon fell asleep to the sound of song and laughter. As dawn broke we began climbing through heavy bush until eventually we came to a clearing where we discovered a whaling station, run by Norwegians. We were graciously, if a bit dubiously, welcomed and sat down to a generous serving of whale steak. After this unusual breakfast we were returned to safety.

Back at our cottage at last, our maid Evelyn met us weeping at the gate.

'I packed all the clothes and cleaned the house,' she cried, 'but I didn't know what I was going to do with the corpses.' She collapsed into further loud weeping and could not be consoled for some time.

Most university professors kept at least one maid in the 1920s. In our eleven-room, double-storey brick house with a household of six, a general domestic had plenty to do. Over the years we had several maids called Evelyn. The one I remember best had spent most of her early life in an orphanage, and adopted the first family she had ever known with the same love and loyalty with which we adopted her. On Sundays I would sometimes be invited to walk out with Evelyn and Tom, her patient boyfriend, along the cinder track to the Botanical Gardens to feed the ducks and to hear the Scottish pipe band play in the rotunda. My mother arranged the wedding breakfast when they married, and I was excited to be chosen as their flower girl. I was dismayed however to see Evelyn tearful throughout the exchanging of vows and came to the sad conclusion that marriage could not be the romantic affair I had thought. Later I learned that at the time of her marriage Evelyn was pregnant with another man's child.

A hole in the fence dividing the Dunlops from the neighbouring Cree-Browns grew ever larger over these years. Of the Brown children, Johnstone was by far my favourite. The large chestnut tree in our back garden was difficult to reach, but Johnstone and I persevered and climbed far into its leafy branches to hide from the world. We discussed marriage there and decided one day we would buy the dairy at the bottom of our street and sell lollies and serve afternoon teas! Sadly the Cree-Browns' strict religious beliefs interfered with many of our games. They did not approve of fancy dress parties – and on Guy Fawkes' Day their children were punished and I was sent home in disgrace for taking a Guy from door to door.

My parents did not fully endorse the puritanical ethos of the time, but we children were expected to obey without question. My older brother and sister both experienced pain and humiliation from the stick to which Dad sometimes resorted in times of desperation. Jocelyn displayed a defiant streak as she reached adolescence and felt the need for greater freedom. Wallace, who was quite a gentle boy, suffered in his teenage years from becoming very tall and temporarily outgrowing his strength. His lethargic ways became a source of great irritation to his father. Otherwise, I consider our parents to have been tolerant and open-minded for their time.

My brother Bonar who was four years older than me, was clearly my father's favourite son. He was a solitary child but his good looks and early artistic ability won him much admiration, especially from the girls. Together with the artistic streak came a darker side. He used to boast that he had fought every boy in his class and took delight in removing the wings from flies. Bonar never allowed me to think that I deserved affection or praise. One night he was left to baby-sit me. Lying in bed I heard the sound of Mother's Triumph revving up in the drive and I suddenly realised that I was to be alone in that great shadowy house. I lay frozen with panic beneath the blankets until, much later, I heard the sound of the car returning.

Seldom did a Saturday go by without my asking or being asked by a little friend to play. On very special occasions we might even spend the night in one bed giggling together. Esperance, Joy, Kathleen – most of them lived at St Clair or Andersons Bay which meant a long tram ride down to the other side of town. On one of these occasions a cyclist stopped me to enquire the way to Clyde Street. Pulling me up on the cross bar, he rode off. As his hand began travelling up the leg of my bloomers I realised that I was in danger. Fortunately as we turned into hilly Clyde Street, he had some difficulty pedalling. I jumped off and tried to run, but he grabbed me and exposed himself. Luckily our house was only a few yards away and I broke free and ran sobbing into the house and into my father's arms.

My shocked parents hastily called the police. Sitting up in bed, I was questioned by a detective. Through tears I recall recognising the situation as a new and exciting event. Suddenly Shona Dunlop

14

became the centre of attention. I discovered the power of holding an audience and according to my mother, I gave an excellent performance.

* * *

Starting school at Archerfield, a private girls' school in Lees Street, was a huge thrill for me. From the beginning I adored my school years, throwing myself into all physical activities with zest. My sister Jocelyn, a good student, was a sixth form prefect the year I first attended Archerfield School. It must have caused her some irritation as she hurried up from the Princes Street tram stop, dragging a seven-year-old. More than once she incurred 'unpunctuality marks' because of my slow pace. Waiting outside the dining room each day, Jocelyn tried to smarten me up. My hair was hurriedly brushed and my droopy brown woollen bloomers given a hitch. I didn't mind. Jocelyn was a senior, and my friends all admired her and her grown-up friends. School seemed a much less exciting place when Jocelyn and her companions turned their sights upon that formidable institution, the University.

Clubs and secret huts loomed large in those years and I was the leader in all of them. My Christian Endeavour badge was usefully transformed into Captain Earwig and if we grew tired of him, I became King Sos, ruling over my subjects. Our favourite meeting place was behind the toilets where a fallen tree became the inspiration for many games. I would stand on the highest point and make my friends line up and salute me as they passed.

Our standard one and two teacher, Mrs Ferguson, adopted strange methods in order to control her class. Her favourite punishment was to make us crouch beneath her table beside her stockinged feet. Sometimes four or five of us would meet each other in that distasteful spot. Mrs Ferguson also suffered from severe dandruff, which clung to her hair and coated her shoulders. As we returned to our seats we would turn to touch the hand of the girl behind. 'Ferg's fleas,' we would mouth, 'pass it on.' Learning took a turn for the better when I reached standards three and four under the remarkable Mrs Yetti Bell who introduced literature, music and history. I fell under their spell.

In 1931 my father suffered a heart attack and was granted a year's leave of absence, while Bonar and I were enrolled as boarders at our respective schools. Bonar attended John McGlashan College.

Our parents enlisted the services of Major Astley Campbell as assistant driver and undertook a leisurely journey throughout the North Island.

The dormitories of Archerfield were spartan and we suffered dreadfully from sleeping on open scrim-netted verandahs with only a canvas blind to drop when the rain reached the foot of the bed. My chilblains became the talk of the school. They developed on every finger and as the winter developed burst and suppurated. Those on my toes and heels inflamed to such an extent that I filled my water bottle with cold water instead of hot each night. When I became a member of the A basketball team I caused much amusement, jumping for goals, encased in white bandages, looking like a traffic policeman on duty.

The boarding department consisted of one long senior dormitory and a number of ten-bed dorms intended for the juniors. Our dormitory was considered a naughty one, but it was also a very happy one. Between bells and prying matrons, we managed to create a little world for ourselves. Our pranks were harmless but regular, and required enough daring to make us feel brave and superior to the others. Our favourite pastime was 'double-dares'.

The best night-time double dare involved hiding under the dorm teacher's bed while she undressed and then creeping back to bed when she began deep breathing. One night I had to hang from a fire escape in freezing weather for what seemed hours, before a whistled all clear released me. We had a secret floor board under which pears, chocolate and biscuits were smuggled and replenished after each exeat. We wore stays over our singlets to help keep up our thick brown stockings. While not very sexy, they were at least useful for attaching our O.B. club button. The Old Brigade club ran its own magazine each month, but like all such independent endeavours, it lapsed just before exam time.

The matron believed in spartan training for the young and stood over us each morning, as we took our compulsory cold water plunges regardless of season. To be 'in the cupboard' meant your monthlies had arrived, for the cupboard was the place the napkins were stored.

All of us would have confessed to having a pash on Miss Margery Black, the Australian Principal. She was a charismatic figure and considered advanced in her views on education. Miss Black believed in the honour system, exhorting her pupils to confess to any wrongdoing, rather than waiting to be found out. I seemed to carry a great measure of guilt about with me, till the moment of acquiring sufficient courage to confess that I'd broken bounds or the silence hour. My worst offence was tossing butter balls onto the dining room ceiling, which later melted in the warm atmosphere of the senior ball, dripping butter onto the fine dresses and suits of the dancers.

In those depression years many parents could not pay their school fees and the school was plunged into a financial crisis. Severe measures were taken to balance the school budget. When the ancient heating system proved inadequate, we were issued with grey blankets to wrap around our legs in class, and five minutes skipping was introduced between lessons. Squares of newspaper replaced toilet paper until the drains clogged up.

There were some fine teachers on the staff. Along with my interest in literature, music and history, Miss Black's classes in geography and social science fascinated while mathematics remained my bête noir. As a day girl I had been introduced to Greek dancing and a creative dance class was started at Archerfield, but my family decided that music and speech or 'oral training' were sufficient extramural subjects for me. Miss Helen Black offered to take me into her dance class free and I cherish this memory as the first sign that some dance talent was identified.

Acting was encouraged in the school. The production which excited me the most was a play written by Form IV enthusiasts and based upon the parable of the 'Wise and Foolish Virgins'. The role of a foolish virgin appealed to me. When the bridegroom arrived, those wise virgins who had tended their lamps and stayed awake were ready to greet him. The foolish virgins had fallen asleep and as the temple doors closed upon me and my slothful companions, we hammered upon it with such vehemence that we split the wood.

'Open up,' we cried, 'open up!' but to no avail. In an outpouring of expressive realism I sank sobbing to the floor in my first improvised solo. The emotional power of this experience frightened me no less than it undoubtedly startled my audience.

Apart from a few homesick moments after a quarrel with a friend or a twinge of jealousy when I was unexpectedly beaten in the twenty yard dash, my boarding days were very happy. However in 1932 when I was twelve years old my life changed forever.

While my father was on sick leave from the University, staying in the home of friends in Tauranga, a massive heart attack struck him down. He died at the age of 57. I was informed of his death and allowed to visit my sister, Jocelyn, who was by then married to Rev. Hubert Ryburn and lived in William Street, close by. Throwing myself into her arms, I found comfort as we wept together. It was hard returning to face the sympathetic eyes of the school where privacy was unknown.

My father was buried in Tauranga, his tombstone most fittingly an open book. Major Campbell drove my grieving mother back through the rain to Dunedin.

Chapter Two

I have met several English girls here. The parents of one
live in China & another is Lord Asquith's grandchild,
& her cousin a Princess of Rumania, or something.
So I move in pretty high company, nicht wahr?

Number 121 Clyde Street was let, so Mother put up elsewhere, while Bonar and I remained at our boarding schools. Wallace had completed his Agricultural Science course at Lincoln College and was eager to start farming, so it was decided the family would purchase a sheep farm in Southland that would become a home base for the five of us, including Major Astley Campbell. From then on 'Majie' as he was known, became a member of the family.

By the early 1930s the worldwide depression had the country in its grip and land had never been cheaper. For the unbelievably low figure of four thousand pounds, Mother was able to buy two hundred and eighty-three acres of excellent arable land in Southland, five miles from the little village of Centre Bush and thirty miles from Invercargill. The price included sheep and horses. Wallace with his agricultural training would farm 'The Gree', named after the original Dunlop farm in Scotland. Major, who had been a supervisor of a coconut farm in New Guinea, and involved with cattle farming in the North Island of New Zealand, would become senior adviser. Mother would cook the meals and tend the flower garden. Bonar and Shona would return to a wonderful home when school holidays came around. It proved ideal.

Mother was a spirited woman and when relations and friends found Major's continued presence in the family improper she stood up to them. Some remained hostile and disapproving, refusing to meet Major, but others less conventional took my mother's part, agreeing that Major's devotion and selfless attention to my sick father deserved recognition.

I was intrigued by 'Majie'. For a school essay upon 'The Most Interesting Character I Know' I wrote a truncated biography of this unusual man. Major Robert Louis Astley Campbell's lineage could be traced back to King William IV. His father was a colonel in the British Army, later British Consul General to Portugal. Major had become an Officer of the Seaforth Highlanders, travelled widely and fought in the Boer War. A tall, impressive-looking man, fastidious about his appearance and reserved in demeanour, he was constantly urged by us to tell of his adventures. My favourite story was that of Majie as a young lad being sent by his parents with an urgent message to the King and Queen of Portugal to warn them not to travel on a certain day because a plot had been discovered to assassinate the pair during their journey. I included in my essay the amusing tale of how, one day, walking along a jungle path in Africa, Majie had come face to face with a lion sedately walking the same path. Majie and the lion turned and made off in opposite directions! Although colourful, most of the essay was true, but I suspect my teacher believed Major to be a figment of my imagination.

Perhaps the telling of such adventures affected my mother too, for after a couple of years living in the country she decided overnight that Bonar, who had completed his schooling, must be given the chance to develop his exceptional artistic talent overseas. The Slade School in London had been warmly recommended. What was she to do with his younger sister, only halfway educated and showing no specific skill except an adolescent adoration of the stage? I was not initially impressed by the suggestion that I leave my school and my friends and set forth with my mother and brother to foreign parts. I had definite hopes of rising to the enviable rank of school prefect. That was about the extent of my ambition, despite a longing, common to most girls of my generation, to act in the movies. The plan formed, however, and the decision was made. Mother in characteristic fashion moved with great speed.

It seemed clear that Major with his knowledge of languages and general worldly acumen should accompany us. In April 1935 we boarded the SS *Viminale*, a Lloyd Triestino line vessel in Sydney, which became our home for the next seven weeks. It was principally a cargo ship, carrying fewer than thirty passengers. By the end of our journey we all seemed to know each other pretty well. It says a lot for the Italian crew that the passengers could still speak to each other after such close enforced living.

Although I had celebrated my fifteenth birthday in Sydney before we departed, I was very young for my age. The thought of growing up had little appeal to me. As the youngest on board I spent most of those shipboard days playing shuttle board and deck tennis or, as the equator loomed, cooling off in a rather small canvas swimming pool. Crossing the equator, King Neptune forced us to walk the plank blindfolded with the traditional watery end. Otherwise the monotony was broken only on the days we dropped anchor at one of the exotic ports.

Colombo was our first sight of the east, and chiefly memorable for the rickshaw ride and the bedraggled Indian youngsters who ran alongside us calling 'Baksheesh, baksheesh!' Port Said is remembered for the repellent 'gooly-gooly' man who produced live chickens out of his mouth and coins from his nostrils. Mother was so entranced by the hordes of hawkers who clambered aboard offering baubles, trinkets and cheap leather goods that Bonar and I felt obliged to take matters into our own hands. We locked her in her cabin and giggled from a safe distance while we watched infuriated hawkers pounding on her door.

At the Suez Canal I had my first sight of a camel and rider etched against a fiery sunset, and in my mind's eye a picture which had hung in our family breakfast room came suddenly to life. Piraeus and the famous Acropolis became a recurring passion and a place I was to return to several times.

As we approached the Bay of Naples, my mother began to question the wisdom of our original plan which was to disembark at Genoa and from there continue directly to London. The wonders of classical Rome and Florence lay before our very feet! Her son was to be an artist, was he not, and her daughter aspired to a career on the stage. How foolish to pass by Italy and ignore an opportunity of seeing some of the world's greatest art. So we four New Zealanders bounded down the gangplank at the Port of Naples to the astonishment of our shipboard friends.

Certainly we were naive, taken in by guides of Pompeii and Herculaneum who pressed small pieces of charcoal upon us as genuine relics of the original bread, ostensibly found in the ruins following the eruption of Mount Vesuvius. A visit to the blue grotto on the Isle of Capri in row boats delighted me but the small village of Ana Capri on the island, the inspiration for Axel Munthe's prize-winning book *The Story of San Michele* excited me even more.

I thought Rome less beautiful but far grander than Naples. St Peter's Basilica was incredibly impressive. Michelangelo's *Pieta* made religion a reality for me but I could not understand why so many relics of the cross and locks of Mary Magdalene's hair were to be seen in the treasury of St Peter's and then replicated in a further dozen churches of the city.

As Major had high ranking military connections it was not difficult for him to acquire passes for us to attend a private audience with Pope Pius XI. For this 'private' audience, forty people gathered outside the Vatican to be granted entrance by members of the colourfully costumed Swiss guards. Required to wear black clothing and having none, I had to wear my mother's petticoat. It was a relief to hide my embarrassment somewhat by adding a black net veil to cover my face. For two merciless hot hours we stood waiting for His Holiness to appear. When he finally arrived we sank to our knees as he moved between us murmuring in Latin, and offering a ringed hand to be kissed. We Protestants were not so much impressed by this, as delighted by what seemed an example of historic theatre. Afterwards, once again consumed by self-consciousness at my strange attire, I persuaded Mother to allow us a taxi back to our hotel.

Bonar and I haunted museums and galleries and wore ourselves out traipsing over the cobbled streets. The heat and cobblestones wrought havoc with Mother's and my feet. When a heatwave struck, we lost no time in heading for Lake Garda, one of Italy's most appealing lakes, but not before experiencing another exciting piece of local theatre.

On the day before leaving we found ourselves caught in a huge crowd which had gathered to see Mussolini and King Victor Emmanuel reviewing the troops. We squeezed our way to a vantage point on the Victor Emmanuel Monument, spellbound by the proud display of Mussolini's army. Certainly it presented a colourful sight. Light horsemen on spirited steeds, Bazigleri storm troopers on the run, and infantry, goose-stepping with marvellous precision. Filled with awe, we saw Mussolini, a frozen figure in the distance, his body laden with medals.

Afterwards, we had to fight our way through a mass of sweating humanity, trying not to faint in the heat. This experience has often returned to me as a nightmare. We made our journey to Lake Garda where we cooled off, avoiding the washerwomen to one side of us, and the fishermen, gutting fish on the other. An English woman we got into conversation with advised us to move north to the Dolomite Mountains, which she declared were both cool and extremely beautiful.

My mother's extroverted and gregarious nature led to many spontaneous decisions. A friendly tourist took our fate in hand, advising Mother; 'Take your children to Austria. The Austrian Schilling is in your favour, and Vienna is one of the most highly cultured cities in the world.' Then, noticing our worn shoes, 'And you can purchase shoes there for only thirty Schillings a pair!' The beauties of the Dolomites notwithstanding, we headed for the Austrian border.

On our way to Vienna we stopped off at several small Carinthian villages, staying in pensions and small hotels, one of which I described in my diary:

Well our hotel, the Alpenrosen, is just a scream. It is the dearest, funniest little place imaginable. No carpets, but spotlessly white boards, funny little windows with wooden bars like a jolly prison. The funniest rickety little stairs over which we have nearly killed ourselves dozens of times already.

At Millstatt am See, our next stopping place enroute to Vienna, decisions were made which shaped our futures. Bonar felt this pleasant lotus-eating lifestyle was beginning to lose its appeal, and decided to study German at a summer language school being held at nearby Schloss Heraldeck. I was also aware of a lack of direction in my life and wrote in my diary in August 1935:

We are all getting very well tanned but more & more Bonar & I realise how we would love a bit of work again, even smelly old Arithmetic would be met with outstretched arms. We do our best to pick up the language, but one can't really learn a new language without a bit of a grounding first.

Frau von Musil, the owner of the castle, had a rather fierce military bearing which made it easy to believe that she was a descendant, as she claimed, of the great Prince Bismarck, First Chancellor of the German Reich. Her English mother had given her excellent English, and soon we had become daily associates. This very determined woman made up her mind to take our hapless family in hand, and she persuaded us to take a good look at the opportunities the great city of Vienna could offer us, culturally, linguistically, and educationally.

Frau von Musil was as good as her word, and when we arrived in Vienna in the autumn of 1935, she acted as guide and interpreter with tireless enthusiasm. A house was found for us to rent and Vienna became our home. We drank in the beauty of its architecture and steeped ourselves in learning of its glorious past. I described our new home to my diary:

23 October 1935

We have now shifted into the Haas's home, & we love it. Mother's and my room is a darling little bed sitting room with a bed sofa surrounded by orange curtains. Everything is orange & green & so cosy. There is a piano in the drawing room, & Major sleeps in the nursery, Bonar in the study with a wireless, & I in the sitting room.

The great sweep of history which we suddenly found ourselves part of did inevitably cause a sense of culture shock. But once we had mastered the language, we could appreciate all that Austria had to offer.

Frau von Musil introduced Bonar to Professor Heischmaster, the Professor of Art at the Vienna State Academy, where he was immediately accepted. His two principal subjects were sculpture and drawing, and his teachers were impressed by his talent.

It was decided that I should attend a Vienna Gymnasium to complete my studies. I was horrified to discover this Jewish School, situated on the fourth floor of a city building, had no sports fields or open space of any kind. For exercise we were marched around the block. I was expected to translate French, (which I had previously studied from English) into German. My German was very shaky, and my mathematics woefully backward, and so I became desperate to leave. A new plan evolved.

An American friend of my mother's would give me private lessons in English and European History. German lessons would be given by Fraulein Koblishka, and later Frau Gesternberger. I took piano lessons with a wonderful elderly woman, Marianna Frey. She had once lived at Windsor Castle as piano teacher to the Princess Royal, sister of the Prince of Wales (later Duke of Windsor). An excellent, but strict piano teacher, she insisted on three to four hours' piano practice daily.

Unimpressed by a brief taste of life in a Mädchen Gymnasium,

I persuaded my mother that my true vocation was the stage and we set off for the renowned Reinhardt Seminary in Schönbrunn. Max Reinhardt, celebrated dramatist and producer, showed much sympathy, but made it very clear that until I acquired a good grasp of the German language, he could not accept me as a pupil. 'Go, study German, dance, and fencing, and return to me in one year's time,' he advised. I left, my tail between my legs and immediately began seeking out the best dance schools in the city.

The school of Vienna's Waltz Queen, Grete Wiesenthal, was my first stop – a lovely gracious lady, who must have despaired of my gawky movements and slow perception, as much as I despaired of ever being able to achieve the soft lyrical movements she asked of me. My next attempt was more successful. Frau Professor Gertrud Bodenwieser, the first professor of dance at the Vienna State Academy for Music and Dramatic Art, who also taught at the Reinhardt Seminary, held classes in her private school below the Academy. She enjoyed an enviable reputation with students coming from many parts of the world to study under her. Her classes were full of energy and excitement, and I liked her style.

As I nervously changed into my 'Kittel' for my first Bodenwieser lesson, I spotted Hilary Napier. She seemed so cautious and reserved, I guessed that she was English. Finally I plucked up enough courage to ask her. Yes, she said, she was English. Hilary had preceded me by one year, and was well ahead of me in both dance and language. I was delighted to discover her, mainly because I felt so vulnerable constantly struggling with my poor German, but also because I immediately liked the look of Hilary. She and I were to become fast friends.

December 1935

I am not going to Wiesenthal any more but to Bodenwieser. I like it much better because there are so many more girls and I don't feel half such a duffer. I have met several English girls there. The parents of one live in China & another is Lord Asquith's grandchild, & her cousin a Princess of Rumania, or something. So I move in pretty high company, nicht wahr?

Frau Gerty, as she was known by her students, was a small erect figure who, when not demonstrating, examined her class through an intimidating lorgnette. On that first morning I curtsied to my teacher like the others and stammered 'Küss die Hand' (*I kiss your hand*). Although very nervous at first, I began to relax and enjoy myself, as it appeared she was taking little notice of me. Soon I was swept up with the rest of the class – a mass of whirling bodies with ecstatic faces. Before long these expressive dance classes under Frau Gerty became highlights of the week. As my interest developed, so did the number of daily classes I took: Classical Ballet (for technique purposes); Tap (to sharpen the footwork); Acrobatic (for greater flexibility); Gymnastik (so called in German, but actually a strict technique class accompanied by percussion); Spring (for elevation); as well as Rhythm (Dalcroze) and folk and ethnic classes.

The expressive dance classes were always the most exciting. I began to understand the method Bodenwieser used. A sequence of movement would commence with floor or barre exercises, which motivated and stretched the part of the body central to the sequence she had in mind. The different parts of the body were used separately at first, and eventually brought together in natural instinctive development. Once this was achieved, the tempo might alter, and the stress points change. The movement would be executed either lyrically, or raised on toe, or sharply. The body might be taken into the air, or flung to the ground. Sometimes a middle section was left for each dancer to create themselves. At times it was done with a partner, in opposition, in a group, or in a round. Again the sequence might be given varying expressions: grotesque, syncopated, comic, tragic, angry etc. Bodenwieser appeared to possess endless pedagogic ideas, and I don't believe she ever came to the end of them.

Bodenwieser's eclectic view of a dancer's education came from her own association with artists from many walks of life. She attended salons where foremost artists congregated to discuss the new ideas and beliefs of the time. Writers and producers such as Arthur Schnitzler, Thomas Mann, Stefan Zweig, Frank Wedekind, Hugo von Hoffmansthal, Rainer Maria Rilke, Franz Werfel and Max Reinhardt gathered regularly. Also present, and considered the most radical painters of the Vienna Secessionist school, were Oskar Kokoschka, Felix Albrecht Harta, and Wolfgang Born. Bodenwieser collaborated with a number of celebrated musicians and composers, particularly Fritz Kreisler and Hugo Wolf. She was related to the eminent psychologist Sigmund Freud, whose work inspired her early ballets.

Bodenwieser encouraged her students to broaden their vision of life and art by attending concerts and visiting art galleries, to immerse themselves in art in order to extend themselves as dancers. Most followed her wishes, some becoming successful costume designers as well as accomplished dancers. Our teacher encouraged in us a sensitivity to injustices to the poor, and the dangers of power-hungry politicians and autocratic leaders lusting for war. Bodenwieser's style shrugged off the old conventions, encouraging us to express through movement the responses of the mind and heart. We began thinking of ourselves as being in the forefront of a new wave in dance.

Bodenwieser was an awe-inspiring figure, greatly respected by her professional colleagues, her public and her students. The force of her personality, and the obvious mastery she demonstrated in her teaching, left us in no doubt as to her genius. I was not the only one who was nervous in her presence. There was a hushed silence in the dressing room as Frau Gerty descended the stairs leading to the dance room, wearing the black silk trousers and small kid slippers she always wore to teach.

I rejoiced in the anonymity in the big classes under Bodenwieser. It was only when my teacher called 'England, England, rechte Fuss' that I could no longer bask in obscurity. Despite a Kiwi accent, and although I had never set foot on English soil, I remained unquestionably English in her eyes.

Born Gertrud Bondi in 1890, the second daughter of a Jewish stockbroker, she and her sister received their education from French and English governesses. Gertrud and Franzisca were enrolled under the celebrated Carl Godlewski, the first ballet master at the Viennese State Opera, a choreographer and teacher who was influenced by modern trends.

Three dance revolutionaries – Isadora Duncan, Ruth Saint Denis and Loie Fuller performed in Vienna between 1898 and 1908. In 1910 Gertrud adopted the name Bodenwieser to protect her family, who were not enthusiastic about her chosen profession, and devoted herself to the modern dance movement. She gave her first solo performance in 1919 at the age of 29. She developed and adapted the ideas of Francois Delsarte and Emile Jaques Dalcroze, but her most highly regarded 'guru' was the distinguished Hungarian dance educationalist Rudolf von Laban. Gertrud Bodenwieser began teaching at the Convent of Sacre Coeur, but went on to teach mime and dance at the Vienna State Academy of Music and Dramatic Art and in her own private studio.

In the 1920s Bodenwieser developed her skill as a choreographer, devising over a hundred pieces, the most enduring of which is probably

The Demon Machine, and several full length ballets. She used the music of well known composers, or commissioned works by her accompanist Marcel Lorber and other contemporary composers.

Like Grete Wiesenthal, Bodenwieser had emerged dissatisfied with the traditional forms of ballet still practised at the Vienna Opera Ballet. The new physical language she and Wiesenthal promoted was a development from Isadora Duncan's active opposition to the conventional classical technique. They believed classical ballet hampered the dancer's search for free expression. These highly intelligent, emancipated Viennese women between them wrought the changes to enable the Central European dance genre to align itself with the other revolutionary movements in contemporary art. Central to Bodenwieser's approach was her concern for the human condition and commitment to poetic realism.

At fifteen, as a member of Bodenwieser's beginners' class, I was not capable of understanding the true value of her vision and the originality of her technique. I only knew that I found her classes fascinating and could not wait for the next one. In following Bodenwieser's encouragement to dance every emotion known to me, I also discovered myself. At the same time my muscles received an intense training which slowly began to take effect. Physical, creative, and musical qualities were stressed in Bodenwieser's classes but they always worked together as a harmonious whole. Her style, though beautiful and lyrical, also favoured strong dramatic, even grotesque, movements. All of these she found necessary in order to express the contemporary themes she felt inspired to choreograph.

We made the most of the opportunities Vienna provided enjoying concerts, opera and theatre, and at the same time I kept up with the latest American and British films. I adored Greta Garbo, loved Ginger Rogers and Fred Astaire. I was impressed by the palatial beauty of the opera houses and although I usually bought the cheapest ticket – 'Stehplatz' or standing place, I enjoyed all the more the rare occasions when we were seated in a box. I preferred Tannhaüser to Lohengrin. To my diary I confided that 'Rachmaninoff fully came up to my expectations though I rather wished he had played a few more of the very popular sonatinas.'

(Letter to friend in Dunedin)

Our friend Mrs Musil was given a box for the Burgtheater & she invited us to join her. Imagine it, a box. If you saw that picture Anna

Karenina, you will remember they took a box. It was just like that. We dressed up in our glad rags & sat there, you know, as if we had done it all our lives, & it was such fun staring up at the people in the standing place (where I usually abide). The play was Lady Windermere's Fan, & I had not heard a German play before & was frightfully thrilled, cos I understood practically everything! Who do you think we saw also in a box? None other than Richard Tauber, with the British film star he wants to marry but can't cos his wife won't divorce him, eyeglass & all. All the opera glasses were focused on him very shortly, & she blushed. Very charming really, but surely audacious. Tauber can't clap anyway, he only knows how to be clapped at. I put a special daub of powder on at interval in hopes that in the promenade I might see him, but I had no such luck. It is a magnificent building, & Hilary dances in it in a play & she has only been learning 1 year...

I was horrified the first time I saw a beggar, standing with outstretched arms by the Stadtbahn while commuters poured past without a sidelong glance. My compassion however, did not hold up against the hundreds more to be found begging at nearly every street corner in the city. Seventeen years after the end of the First World War, the Austrian economy was still struggling. In 1935 the splendour and affluence of the nineteenth century Hapsburg Empire was a thing of the past. Only a very few could enjoy the traditional Viennese lifestyle of frequenting coffee houses and restaurants for hours during the day, followed by concerts and the theatre at night. However there were still the friendly cafes in the Kärtnerstrasse, where you could find daily newspapers in a dozen different languages. For even the poorest customer, a one Schilling coffee would be generously replaced by continuous glasses of water as long as you remained seated.

The numerous beggars and vendors on every street corner made us aware that many Austrians were on the bread line. For several months, a small, pale seven-year-old boy shared our main meal. It must have been nourishing for Hansi, and a relief for his parents, but I often wonder what he made of the strange English food and that rather bewildering home.

The owners of our apartment in Baumgarten Strasse, in the suburb of Hietzing, Professor and Mrs Haas, proved to be among the few far-seeing Jews who predicted early the future downfall of Austria, and the likely extermination of its Jewish citizens. The

Haas family departed for the United States, leaving the renting of their furnished apartment to a most kind and conscientious sister, the same Frau Gesternberger who taught me German. The chief fly in the ointment in this arrangement proved to be the two maids who went with the apartment!

23 October 1935

Our two maids are a bit of a handful, & Fräulein takes Mum's hat off & would put her to bed if she could.

Mitzi the cook, and Fraulein the lady's maid, both found great difficulties in understanding the funny foreigners' ways, and their taste in food. Communication proved a difficulty as well and my mother, who had never known the obsequious flutterings of a lady's maid, found the situation quite intolerable. Following Mitzi's tearful outbursts in the kitchen, Frau Gesternberger was hurriedly called in to help solve the dilemma. An agreement was finally reached, we and our maids parting company without acrimony. From this time on we engaged no further live-in help. Major seemed to enjoy sharpening up his German at the market, and mother relished being mistress of her own kitchen once more.

We went regularly to the Anglican Church in Vienna.

30 September

Today we went to Church, for the first time for ever so long, and I quite enjoyed it. I had never been to a whole Anglican service before, but what a lot of singing etc. & what a short sermon compared with ours, but still I liked the simplicity of it all, after the R. C. Church. The minister was very nice, but I nearly expired when he asked me to join the choir, & go every Thursday for a practice.

17 November

Today was oh! so bitterly cold, but we dressed up & went to Church. I doubt if we will go again, as Mr Grimes is the most unusual kind of Minister I have ever met, never mentioning the name of Christ or God, & certainly he does not inspire us to much.

I learnt to ski that winter and enjoyed it immensely. Although the snow lay thick on the ground I wrote in my diary:

I don't think Vienna is half as cold as at home & neither I nor Bonar have got a single chilblain. When I think of my hands last winter, it makes me very joyful.

Bonar and I spent every day at our various studies in the city. Travelling half an hour each way by Stadtbahn proved ideal for learning my German vocabulary, although in midwinter when the car filled with unwashed garlic-eating passengers, it became difficult even to breathe. Evenings were taken up with piano practice, and in the winter weekends we frequently put on skis and plunged straight into the snowy Wiener Wald. Bonar brought his artist friends, and Hilary and other dancing colleagues seemed eager to join in on the fun. I did not believe that I alone was the attraction – I benefited from having such a good-looking brother. Bonar's Bohemian friends with their unkempt appearance and grubby clothes did not seem a fair exchange for my charming, dancing friends. Once again I was deeply indignant that one of my friends was getting interested in Bonar. This time it was Hilary Napier.

After Christmas we accompanied some Austrian friends on a brief skiing trip into the Tirol, and tried to persuade Mother to come too. She declined with a 'No my dears, I'd break my bally leg'. Upon our return we found her in plaster from ankle to hip. It was a Pott's fracture and she did it without even moving out of the house!

As Mother felt it unlikely she would ever master the language sufficiently to find friends amongst the Viennese, she joined the British Club, where she soon found more than enough friends. The Club met in the renowned Bristol Hotel on the Kärtner Ring. Mother's notoriously bad sense of direction saw her step out of the building, and invariably head in the wrong direction. This kept occurring until we told her, 'Decide which way you think you should walk – then walk in the opposite direction.' That seemed to work. Two English women, whose names I knew only as Mollie and Quitty, befriended Mother, and came frequently to our flat, especially after Mother's accident. Their past was never revealed, but their present partners were both Austrian. Although never said openly, and not even perceived by us at the time, Mollie and Quitty obviously believed Mother and Major's relationship to be the same as their own. They were not great intellectuals, but lots of fun and often, as I dragged myself home with sore muscles from a taxing dance class, I would hear laughter ringing out from the house and know they were visiting.

25 January 1936

I am coming on at dancing & feel much more at home, & have started taking Acrobatic. So twice a week I stand on my hands, turn cartwheels & all sorts of things.

One night Bonar and I returned home late from a marvellous production of *Guidetta* – an opera by Lehar, who conducted, with Richard Tauber in the leading role, to find Major *'anxiously listening over the wireless for news of the King who was dying & who died at two o'clock. Austria is intensely interested in the King & black flags are being flown on every important building. All sorts of celebrations are going on also for our new King Edward VIII who really isn't frightfully keen to be King...'*

29 January

On Tuesday a Funeral Service was held in the English Church for King George. Grimes should have hired a hall for the occasion, as it was, they had two services, one for the Austrians and all the Diplomats, & the next for the English people. I arrived just in time, to see the diplomats drive away. I saw Schuschnigg,[1] Dr Dollfuss's widow,[2] & hundreds of others all dressed most marvellously & I saw the Egyptian delegates with their snappy red Fezzes... The service was played quite well but the Funeral March was played very badly & they only played one verse of 'God Save the King' while we were all left with our mouths wide open ready for the next.

The Prince of Wales visited Austria quite frequently. We had seen him outside the Bristol Hotel during our first week in Vienna. I wrote:

My word he is a little man, & he wore a grey suit, & carrying a little dog in his arms.

April 1936

On Sunday 12th I was sixteen years old. My last was in Sydney, this one in Vienna. I wonder where the next will be? I certainly did very well with presents. Major gave me a stunning stamp album, Bonar a magnificent brush, Mrs MacPherson a manicure set, Hilary 'Golden

---

[1] The Austrian Chancellor.
[2] Widow of the Austrian Chancellor assassinated by Nazis in 1934.

Treasury' & Mrs Musil a rather overawing cake, with 'Three Cheers for Sweet Sixteen,' inscribed in pink letters on the icing. Mother's present I haven't got yet, as it is to be a second hand bicycle, & a new spring outfit.

Just as we had been confronted by a fascist display in Rome, increasingly we became aware of the Nazis' influence. On 14 March 1936 I wrote:

At this minute we are all very excitedly listening to a speech of Hitler's over the wireless from Munich. It is very clear & Hitler seems to be getting pretty excited himself & has several frogs in his throat already. Bonar is pretending he understands it, but I don't know.

19 May

One day while returning from dancing class, I saw a number of young students going along, singing 'Heil Hitler' every now & then. The police were soon upon them though & attended to things.

Early in June I went on a three-day cycling trip with Hilary and two other friends. We set off at three in the morning.

We met Susi at the appointed place & off we set. We felt very hilarious to begin with, & tore down the streets waving our arms, & unable to show all the joyous feelings that bubbled out of us. Before long we crossed the Danube, & rode its banks. Young birches were growing to the right of us, & as we rode on the sun, like an airship, rose in the heavens. Gorgeous... It was so interesting passing through funny little villages with old hand pumps & statues of Saints, & angels...

We struck a few hills, but the funniest thing was the look on the old peasants' faces while coming back from Church to see us in our shorts. Some were really shocked, others amused & some even wondering if we hadn't forgotten our skirts. We decided we would like a bathe and another meal at about 3, so chose a lovely grassy spot on the side of a stream only to find that here it was verboten... We had really gone a long way, so decided to look out a Bauern Haus, as the girls' idea was to sleep in a hay shed...

...A peasant suggested that though he as well as the other peasants had no hay at present, we could have a little room he had... Then it began to rain. We had to wash out in the rain under the pump, one washing while the other pulled the pump...

We wrapped up as best we could, & set off like warriors through the rain. We had done 100 kilometres which is roughly 66 miles, & hoped to do as much again… After a pretty satisfactory meal, we once more took to our bicycles & just fled. I don't know what happened to Hilary, she just couldn't stop, so we couldn't either & flew past village after village.

22 July

Wednesday I spent with a German lesson in the morning. In the afternoon Mother, Major and I went to the American Women's Club where I helped to hand round the tea, which was followed by a most magnificent concert given by the Viennese Boys Choir. They sang like angels & nearly reduced me to tears. They sang all kinds of alleluias in four parts, & finally ended with Dixie which they sang in English. When they had finished I went up to them & asked in German, if they had been to New Zealand & sure enough, they were the very group that had even been to Dunedin. I was so thrilled I nearly hugged them.

Both our Academies closed for six to eight weeks over summer. This proved a great opportunity for further exploration of the Continent. My Aunt Ada, and Joan Thompson, my sister's friend, had joined us from New Zealand, and they too had to be squeezed into our old Fiat. More often Joan took the train and we met up at our destination and found lodgings.

One fine morning, the hood down, and some cases strapped to the running board, we headed away. No actual plans had been made, and we had no idea where we would lay our heads that night. But that was my mother's way and none of us thought to question the wisdom of it. 'Where are we going?' inquired Aunt Ada. 'Oh out into the blue,' replied my mother gesticulating vaguely, quoting from J.B. Priestley's *The Good Companions* which she had just finished reading.

18 July

We passed a wonderful old castle, once a monastery & finally crossed the Danube to Krems. We drove alongside the Danube through a number of little villages till we reached Dürnstein & there we stayed the night. It was the most marvellous little village I have ever seen in my life. It was over a thousand years old & was the place where Richard the Lionheart was imprisoned by the Austrians and ransomed by his servant.

We arrived in Salzburg just in time to see an impressive piece of German medieval theatre. To play in a Max Reinhardt production of *Jederman* (Everyman) was the dream of every good actor, and many young hopefuls such as myself. This production was staged in Cathedral Square with the magnificent stone Cathedral as a backdrop. I was to find the allegorical theme of the play repeated later in painting (Holbein) and music (Saint-Saens) as well as the subsequent theatre of Strindberg and Wedekind, but that first encounter with *Jederman* could never be surpassed.

The spine-chilling cry from Death as he called across the vast stone arena to Jederman first from one parapet, and then from the next, raised the hair on the back of my neck. I watched rapt, as Jederman's friends, Strength, Beauty, Knowledge and Fellowship, all refused his plea to accompany him to the other world. It is Good Deeds alone who stays by his side. The beauty of the setting, the power of the acting and the tragedy of the play all made a lasting impression on me.

Oh! But the play was good. It was held outside the Cathedral, & though our seats were nothing more than boards with backs to them, our eyes were so glued to the stage, that we felt no discomfort... So thrilled were we that Mother, Bonar and I determined to walk off steam somehow, so we found a path that led up from the town. Here we got such a magnificent view of the whole town & the towers, & spires of churches rising up into the sky, with the most glorious pink sky, & coloured feathery clouds in the background. The little inn with the loud voices of men and the clatter of dishes contrasted rather jarringly with what we had seen before.

Goethe's *Faust* held in the famous open-air rock theatre (Fausthaus) was a production of a very different kind. Paula Wessely, a popular Viennese actress, in the role of Marguerite won my heart. This was our first experience of 'Stehplatz' where we were compressed so tightly and held upright against a sea of vertical bodies. These two wonderful productions served to convince me that I too wished to be part of that world.

It was Munich and the medieval towns of Regensburg, Rothenburg ob der Tauber, Ingolstadt, and Dinkelsbühl, which charmed my mother and aunt most. We stopped off only at guest houses with catchy or humorous names. One porter flaunting the name 'Elephant' on his peaked cap seemed irresistible, but Gasthof 'Black Bear', or 'Red Hen' were equally appealing.

After visiting Munich we drove north to Nuremburg.

21 August

We didn't arrive in Nürnberg till quarter past nine, when we put up with quite a nice inexpensive buffet meal. Had a little difficulty in procuring rooms being the last day of Olympia. We did finally, but the noise was so terrific, we hardly slept a wink, what with picture theatres just across the road.

In Oberammergau we found ourselves guests in the home of the actress who played the part of Mary mother of Jesus in the Passion Play for which this village was renowned.

On Sunday morning we went to mass, an awfully nice mass, the nicest I have seen or heard, and on watching the congregation disperse, I noticed many interesting looking men with long hair & beards, apparently in preparation for the 1940 Passion Play. I bought a little wooden crucifix as a keepsake.

And so, over the Brenner Pass to Venice, the city of canals. Bonar and I were becoming more and more bewitched by the art and culture we experienced daily, yet a visit to the Lido in order to cool off made us very indignant. Accustomed to the great open beaches of our own country, the sight of deck chairs strung out across the sand as far as the eye could see and splendid hotels lining the shore seemed quite offensive. Little men in blue uniforms demanded lire every time we sat on a chair. We paid again for a cabin to change into a swim suit, and instead of the refreshing cold waters of the Pacific, we hurled ourselves into a warm flat sea, and never a wave! So we disregarded all physical temptation and made for the Doges' Palace, Palazza Venezia, galleries and museums till we teetered with tiredness.

Aunt Ada was a humorous companion, but she could be stubborn too. 'Look Ada, look!' cried my mother constantly as the Fiat took us along some particularly beautiful village lane, or mountain pass. 'I prefer the view on the other side,' replied Ada perversely. When we reached Fiume on the Italian side of the Adriatic Sea, we learned we must buy the steamer tickets we required to reach the Dalmation coast in the neighbouring town of Susak. Aunt was tired and chose to remain in the car. The task of finding the ticket office took us much longer than we expected. Upon arriving back at the car we found a tearful lady still sitting tightly on her purse in the front seat, wondering if she would have to sit there for ever! Italian officials had apparently harassed her and not one of them *spoke English!*

We were relieved to find the Adriatic a lot bluer than the Danube.

We left [the car] in a garage in Italy... & came on to the Dalmatian Coast by steamer. She was a gorgeous boat, & though we began first class we changed to second at meal time which we felt not a scrap sorry for, as we received an excellent meal. Crowds of young cadets in red pants with swords in their scabbards came on board & sang, just wonderfully. I enjoyed the trip thoroughly but my sorrow at leaving the ship was quite forgotten in the excitement of landing in Rab. Crowds of people stood round watching us pull in, & no sooner had our feet touched the ground, than we were rushed at by crowds of men with the name of their Hotel on their caps, begging us to come to them. One man said one took a boat to get to his & Mother jumped at it. In a few minutes we were all in a yacht, & off we went.

'Twas a great adventure, with not the foggiest idea where we were landing ourselves. All was pitch dark, we could barely see each other, & to add to the excitement our rower was suffering a little from drink, & making an awful caboo. It seemed just miles that we rowed before we spotted a lantern waving in the darkness, & we jumped on land & proceeded to examine our new abode. There were two separate houses. Mother & I slept in the main one & the others shared rooms in another house. Everything was simple, but looked clean enough. Besides we were just too sleepy to bother about anything, only too thankful to be able to sle-e-e-e-p.

Pension Keko was no four star hotel. Instead, we found our lodging primitive – hard iron beds, sparse furniture, and a fare of black bread and grapes for every meal. But it *was* romantic. We walked straight into the sea out the front door. Grape vines clung to the arid soil around us. Donkeys were the chief means of transport, and we were given a choice of dinghy to row out into the sunset.

One day we clambered up to a nearby habitation where grapes were being trod in large wooden troughs. Mostly young men and women, naked to the waist, tramped with their bare feet and sang as they tramped. Their limbs were stained purple and as we watched one was lifted out having fainted from the fumes. Juice from the grapes was poured into skins, and carried on their shoulders to waiting boats on the shore. Life on this little island was like a big step back in time.

Our final adventure in Rab might well have been our last anywhere. Having spent an afternoon exploring the life of the village, Joan and I thought it time to row back to our pension (Mother and Major having already left). We soon realised our two little crafts were heading into a storm, and we struggled to make progress against the lashing waves. Ahead of us Mother and Major brought their dinghy safely to shore, but Joan and I were not so fortunate. We broke an oar and were washed onto the rocks which fortunately were not too far from land. In the growing darkness we salvaged a few possessions and scrambled in the direction of Keko. I was immensely relieved to hear the anxious voice of my mother from the end of the pier: 'Cooee, Shona, Joan, are you there?' and she, no doubt, to hear my reply. All Keko, armed with dry blankets and fearing our demise had gathered on the wharf to welcome us. Alas, it was still only black bread and grapes to appease our appetites!

Aunt Ada returned to Britain with Bonar as companion as far as Vienna where he was to enrol at the Graphische Schule. A few weeks later as we headed to Vienna for the start of my new dancing term, we drove over the Semmering mountains. The first snowflakes reminded us that our carefree summer break had ended.

Chapter Three

I've been practising here in my bedroom alone tonight,
& I've come to the inevitable conclusion that I cannot &
could never give up dancing lightly. I love it – passionately –
vehemently – it's grown a very part of me, & four days
without work for the body has been most disagreeable.

Our home for the next three semesters was a flat at No 11 Starkfriedgasse Potzleinsdorf Bezirk on the edge of the Wiener Wald. In the apartment below us lived our landlady, the severe Baroness Rokitansky. We met only on Mondays, when we took our washing from the attic where it hung most of the week, and she hung hers in its place. Later we learned that her husband, Baron Rokitansky, was serving a prison sentence concerning a Phoenix Insurance scandal in which he had been implicated.

New Year's Eve 1936 found Bonar and me in the Austrian Alps, enjoying the skiing.

1 Jänuar 1937

Skiing is a great sport. I'm getting along a little better now, my third day, but have still a great deal to learn. Bonar is really good, but when he does fall down, he does it properly, completely covering himself in the snow. Last night, being New Year's Eve, we waited up to see the New Year in. We lit up the Xmas tree, & the postmistress arrived with a wireless, so we danced a little, & Frau Arnold (a terribly generous woman) gave us punch & fasching buns. Nobody seemed to know the correct time, but having decided it must be twelve, we clinked each others glasses & cried 'Prosit Neujahr'. No sooner had we seated ourself again at the table than a voice from the wireless cried 'Achtung Achtung, ist schon zwölf Uhr'. Then we had to do it all over again.

Life was full. I worked hard at my classes, and we travelled during the holidays. My diary entries at this time describe my days:

8 January

On Thursday we had Gymnastic, & I don't like it. A dreadfully boring lesson without even music, but undoubtedly good for one. I'm terribly worried about what I am going to do & so is Bonar. I'm no genius at dancing & sometimes I get very fed up.

18 January

On Saturday I put my music lesson off, & we had three dancing lessons one after the other, Gym, Ballet & Spring. I didn't unfortunately take enough wadding with me, & find it very hard to walk.

7 February

I went to my Step (Tap) Class. I like it very much indeed, & Herr Max is a splendid teacher...

Yesterday I had Gymnastic, Ballet & Spring. In ballet every girl for once had ballet shoes, so we did nothing but standing on our toes, & as the cotton wool in my shoes had shrunk a little I got nasty blisters as did Hilary & a few others I fear. We were a very small class in Spring, but I was told I was making progress. I limped home to a late dinner.

15 February

In dancing this morning Trudi Dubsky the marvellous dancer said 'Shona you have improved tremendously.' I was so bucked. It was a marvellous lesson. Everyone's very soul was in it & Marcel accompanied beautifully. I wish I had joined the Academy now, I really do adore dancing.

19 February

I have been dancing a lot, & getting so terribly keen, & everyone is saying how much I have improved. I just live for it in fact.

23 February

We heard Hitler speak for two and a half hours over the radio on Sunday and he caused much comment. Oh! Austria if you too become a centre of brownshirts... you are done for! ...No, it's quite impossible, it just couldn't be!

24 February

On Monday I had a dancing class. On my way in I saw about a thousand young students marching through the town, crying Hitler Hitler Heil!! & waving their arms about & causing such a commotion. A minister from Germany had arrived, & the town was swarming with people. My tram that usually takes ten minutes to get round the Ring took nearly half an hour. People in the tram were returning the Nazi salute to the swarms of people that lined the Ring Strasse. Some in their excitement nearly fell out of the tram. Crowds & crowds of police kept rolling up in buses, & did their best to keep the crowds back. Numbers were on horseback & veritably drove the crowds back. It was really quite a thrill.

Major dined with the Duke of Windsor at the Beefsteak club & came home radiant, professing him a man with a very great personality & plenty of charm.

4 March

On Sunday morning Major, Mrs L & I went to Church. To tell you the truth we had hopes the Duke of Kent would be there as he is in Vienna at the present. We were disappointed. Perhaps it was as well he wasn't there though, because Grimes spoke about divorce, rather a tactless subject surely in front of the Royal Family. Hilary was there too, I made her go.

13 March

On Friday I had a dancing lesson. We had to interpret a story in dance. It was the first time I had ever done such a thing, & it was most exciting... I played truant from Tap & went shopping with Mother. We spent a lovely time trying on new Spring hats, coats & frocks. I had an early meal at Mary Burlingham's & then we went to Greta Garbo in Kameliendame at the Opera Kino. I adored it and Mary cried the whole way through. She is a magnificent actress, what I'd give to be such a one too.

28 March

Easter Friday broke clear & glorious & it is a day they don't hold as a holiday in Austria. We had a great argument at first whether we should drive to Budapest or not. After a decision to the contrary we just couldn't sit at home, so rang up H & Joan rang us to say she was back from skiing. We went on a most heavenly drive through Mödling to Heiligenkreuz. We stopped on the way to gather baskets full of wild flowers growing profusely all over the fields. We had the hood down & the air smelt good.

We lunched at the back of a farmhouse up on a hill, lying on dead leaves overlooking pretty undulating country. Then we drove to the wonderful old Monastery at Heiligenkreuz...

This morning was sunny again. Mother & Major went off early to the St Stephan Kirche for High Mass, & Bonar & I met them at [the English] Church after the service. When we arrived there were no more seats to be had. We waited outside with numbers of others, until the Duke of Windsor arrived...He looked healthy but a little... embarrassed. Then we squeezed in after him & stood at the back. Edward read the lesson. I hardly heard a word of the sermon, my thoughts being centred on an Austrian man beside me who was so fidgety, wore an expression of such anxiousness that I felt sure he was up to something. As the Duke came out, I stood in front of him & was preparing to snatch a pistol from his hand, but there was no need. I was terribly close as the Duke of Windsor passed & he looked right at me. I wonder if I should have curtseyed?

15 April

Well I'm 17 now, & don't feel a scrap wiser...

Yesterday...we had a ripping class & more improvisation. I got great praise for that. Bodenwieser said, 'Shona I had no idea you could do any thing so marvellous.' I was greatly bucked. Ballet was rather boring. I got a fit of nobleness in the afternoon and practised piano three and a half hours.

23 April

Mother & I went to see the Jooss Ballet. The school is in England, the head man a Swede & nearly all the pupils German. They were splendid. The style of dancing is of course very balletish. They danced 'Der Verlorene Sohn', 'Der Grüne Tisch', & 'Ball in Alt Wien'...

8 May

Well aren't I a duffer, I have bust up my foot. Yesterday in dancing I came down on my foot the wrong way, & it gave me for a moment excruciating agony. The girls bandaged it up quickly & I proceeded to dress. Little Eva helped me to the tram stop & came all the way home with me... Major motored me to the hospital. It's really a hospital for babies as you are well aware on entry when greeted with their crying. I had my foot X-rayed, & they discovered a small bone broken in the foot. It's not bad though. They say I shan't be able to dance again for 3 or 4 wks, so it looks as though it's the end of my lessons with Bodenwieser because we leave in 3 wks. The most torturing thing about it is, that I was to have danced the part of an angel at the Burg Theatre with other girls. Now of course it's impossible.

On Sunday 31 May we left Starkfriedgasse 14, but not happily. The Baroness had presented us with a large bill for a new 'offen' (a porcelain stove) which she declared we had cracked. We were in fact not guilty of the deed but realised that to allow this affair to go to court would lead to a long drawn-out battle which would ruin our vacation plans. My artful mother decided to fox them all by leaving in the dead of night. We lunched at Kreuzenstein. The country was very pretty & we thought as we crossed the Czechoslovakian border, that the Austrian country was the prettiest... We were hugely delighted to note that every peasant woman characterised her country by wearing vermillion stockings...

At midday next morning we found ourselves in Prague. The hotels are amazingly expensive & we were forced to take rooms & have our meals out. We went very off Prague consequently although I admit it is a very fine city with wonderful architecture... We left the following day & had dinner at a little Czech village not far from the German border. Our host who had been imprisoned for 3 years in Russia gave us a jolly nice meal, even if he was a little slow about it. We wrote a few letters while waiting. We passed through the Ertz mountains & some very fine country. We found Pensions etc. much more reasonable in Germany. We loved Dresden at first sight...

In the afternoon Mother, Bon & self went to a big 'Haus und Garten Schau'... We wandered through a lot of dull rooms as well as some very interesting ones propagandising Germany. The whole Show was really put up to show the people what a fine country Germany is, & what a great deal has been done for it since the latest Government has been in power. Also maps & pictures of all the old Colonies Germany once possessed, & all the goods they produced. Huge placards adorned the walls saying 'Deutschland wo sind ihre Kolonien?'... (Germany where are your colonies?)

On Friday Mother & I took the tram out to Mary Wigman's School & made arrangements to go again that afternoon. We drove in the tram up to the Weisse Hirsch where we beheld a wonderful panorama of Dresden, from a very posh hotel.

After dinner returned to Wigman School & watched one of her classes. It was intensely interesting. The first five minutes were spent in toe exercises, & the rest of the lesson in walking round the room. Towards the end they all got very lashed up, & Mary herself was like a mad woman chasing them, shooing them, clicking her teeth & waving her arms around, her hair waving, while the rest of the pupils doubled up in the corner in convulsions of laughter. We also. The lesson over, Mary Wigman came up to us & spoke very nicely. She has a wonderful figure for a woman of 54 & though you would never call her beautiful, she has a very interesting face...

We also saw all over a big Porzellan shop full of the most exquisite Dresden China & many things I wouldn't give a hairpin for as well... In the evening Mother & I went to an open air serenade concert in the big Barok square, one of the world's masterpieces in Gothic architecture... The Philharmonic was playing in front of the steps of a lovely building. All along the balustrade running round the square, above us, stood people silhouetted against the slowly darkening sky. Fountains played behind us & the tall towers & spires stood up against a pink sky from the city. It was awe inspiring...

As the first notes of the orchestra broke the air, swallows and blackbirds flew from their nests in the buildings & circled round, chirping loudly against the injustice of it.

Mary Wigman's girls danced to Gluck. Tripping down the steps in orange and blue garments ankle length, they danced between the pillars. Parts of it were good, but I noticed none of the dancers for one moment stood with her head & shoulders up. While they danced, while they turned, they always gave the impression of a cramping of the upper part of the body. The whole evening was a great success, & will always leave an impression on my mind....

By eleven o'clock next morning the car was packed... Halfway through our journey we developed a leak in the radiator, & at the first garage stopped to have it repaired. The day was hot & we felt sticky so Mother & I ambled along till we found a Gasthaus. We ordered a bottle of lemonade & a dunkles Bier all for 35 pfennigs. We told the host we had come all the way from N.Z.

'Ah so,' he said meekly. We knew by that he didn't know where N.Z. was, but was ashamed to admit it, so we helped him by suggesting Australia.

'Australien, um Gottes Willen. So weit! Und sind Sie den ganzen Weg mit der Elektrische gehfahren?' [1]

We suppressed a smile, & told him that we had needs mussen 8 wks with the ship. That was too much for the poor man, so he called in his wife, who went into even greater ecstasies... She told me with great pride

---

[1] 'Australia, for God's sake. So far away! And did you travel the whole way by tram?'

that she had a cousin in Australia whom perhaps I might know. I suddenly remembered the car & dashed to the window only to see it that very minute sailing past. I shrieked to Mother who was enjoying herself immensely admiring the pet rabbits & puppies.

Together after bidding a hurried farewell to the two still open mouthed admirers we scurried down the road after the retreating car. We caught up on her much to our relief & went on our way filled with lemonade, & the excitement of recent appreciation, The two men sat biting their finger nails, hoping the radiator would last till we reached Berlin.

We passed a very large aerodrome, one of many we had spied in Germany. Numbers of huge military lorries packed with soldiers & tanks passed us. Everywhere in Deutschland one is reminded of the Militär. At last we steamed into Berlin, that huge city...

B & I set off in the Stadtbahn for the Olympia Games Stadium. We were quite flabbergasted with its greatness. Apart from the tremendous main Stadium are three more & then the swimming pool & the open air theatre... B & I surveyed with pride the name of Lovelock, N.Z. in black letters on a tablet. The whole establishment is devastating & stupendous. It must have been quite unspeakably grand last year...

Up early next morning in most unbearable heat, the hottest day Berlin has experienced for 18 years...

Not very far out of Berlin we stopped at a tiny place at 3 o'clock and ate quite a good meal. For the next 4 hrs all the way to Stettin, we drove at a great old rate along the new Reichsautobahn... At Stettin we caught the first whiff of sea air.. It urged us on dishevelled & tired as we were, just one whiff of sea air. Arrived in Göslin in darkness, where we spent a hectic night in a room just above a pigsty, where the pigs made a terrific row. The beer house was also 'in die Nähe' [nearby] & noisy men also made a row. To add to this, it attracted flies. Can you blame us for getting up very early next morning?...

The Polish Corridor is narrow, so much so, that we didn't realise we had come to the end of it, & went flying into Danzig. We backed the car, to an irate official who didn't like being ignored...

We didn't drive into Danzig but stopped at a house in Zoppot, a place right on the sea which had been recommended. We procured two rooms & after a cup of tea, changed into our suits & ran down to the beach. It is a lovely beach, & one doesn't have to pay to enter. That is what flabbergasted us. The water was rather cold, but very bracing. I became quite drunk from its effects, & cart-wheeled & turned somersaults all up the beach...

Bonar & I gathered quite a lot of amber on the beach. Nearly enough for a necklace! We were terribly thrilled to taste flounders again, but cold smoked eel we rather turned up our noses at...

The town of Danzig is ...the quaintest, most old-world little town I have ever set eyes on. Full of the quaintest little peek roofed houses, grand old churches & picturesque steps & squares..

On the day when Hess & thousands of Hitler's very first men passed through Danzig the town was in a tremor of excitement. German flags flew from every house, every window, every tree, every branch, and even every twig. Never have I seen such a profusion of flags anywhere. Not even in Germany. One thing was missing though. Their own flag.

We went into a little café house on the main street, & ordered coffee, & waited there watching all the Hitler Jugend girls & men lining up in their various uniforms. Then as Hess came marching along the crowds cheered & yelled, enthusiastically giving the Nazi salute. We at this exciting moment stood on our tables...

On Monday the 28th of June [1937] we left Zoppot... The day was very hot but we drove on through Elberg to Königsberg, now in East Prussia... We bought some of Königsberg's world famous marzipan, which doesn't appeal to me nearly as much as that I used to buy in Dunedin... The amber works were very interesting, & I think I could tell echt Bernstein from false now...

Things were raging rather hotly against the English again while we were in Königsberg, because England remains so stubbornly neutral about the Spanish business.

After an early lunch on Thursday we packed the car, all threw ourselves into rather bad tempers & left Königsberg in this frame of mind. We were terribly thrilled to see storks' nests built precariously upon the highest objects, chimneys and church spires. Mother stork always sits in her nest, while Daddy keeps watch. They fly gracefully for such heavy birds...

A bridge only, & we were in Lithuania. What thrills or horrors did this country hold? In Germany no longer, the good hard bitumen roads changed to bumpy dusty ones. Fortunately we scarcely passed a car, & whenever we passed a haystack travelling on the road, the horses shied, & their drivers cursed us bitterly, frantically trying to keep the horses in control, & to keep the dust off their own persons. What pigs we were - we laughed!!...

Breakfast in bed next morning, a visit to Cooks, & the Bank, & by twelve o'clock we were on board a small ship on our way to the 'Kurische Nehrung', a... curious narrow strip of land [which] reaches from Memel (where the sea breaks through at the mouth of the river) right down to Danzig... In three hours time we pulled in at a tiny place called Schwarzort, inhabited entirely by Jews... A grey haired old 'Pfarrer' whom we stopped on the road conducted us to Hotel Eicher, which I would never recommend as scrupulously clean. There we procured rooms of sorts, with low ceilings & hard mattresses, but blissfully quiet...

The next morning we spent on the other side of the Nehrung, bathing and lounging in the sun. We had intended returning to Memel by the two o'clock boat, but somebody had suggested driving to see the moose, & it sounded attractive... Our mode of travel was a trap & two horses, with a tremendous leather arrangement to help us against the dust. The journey was long & rather tedious, until we branched off into the half forest area, where all eyes were set to work in search for moose. Twelve we saw in all, & what graceful fine beasts they are...

A tiny hut hardly visible from the road represented the Latvian border, & while the business was being attended to Mother & I walked through the forest, picking the last of the wild strawberries.

That night we arrived at Libau, the second largest town in the whole of Latvia, but not very exciting all the same... We stayed at the Hotel Petersburg, quite the poshest place we have ever stayed in. Mother & I were given a 'Suite' no less, bathroom, bedroom & sitting room, & very grand... Precisely at 11 o'clock the sunset faded, & for 2 hrs it remained dark. By two next morning it was light again. Latvia is very near 'The Land of the Midnight Sun'. Our Suite lay exactly over the orchestra which played until all hours. Bonar & self exhilarated with the thrills of travelling & new countries nothing daunted, practised dance steps in our private sitting room till the band condescended to allow the guests a little slumber, which was mighty little anyway seeing by 4 o'clock it was broad daylight...

Riga looked very fine as we crossed the bridge over the Daugava, her tall spires & steeples against the sky... Riga is a devastatingly interesting place, & full of the weirdest characters. Well dressed women, gypsies with wide eyed curly headed babies in their arms, deformed old peasant women (one I saw with 3 legs), Russians in black boots, frock shirts, & Russian hats, & figures that look as if they had stepped straight out of the Bible with long hair past their shoulders, long beards, & robes sweeping past their ankles, all parade the streets together.

The women sweep the street, drive the tramcars, the 'druschkas' & even carry stones & work on the roads.

The Russian Church I find very beautiful. B & I entered one

morning while a service was in progress. A priest in cream & gold vestments stood at the altar, & worshippers who bought prayers at the door, gave them to him with a coin, & he read the prayers aloud for them. They all crossed & recrossed themselves, kneeling & bowing their heads to the ground. Others walked round the church kissing every painting of Christ, Mary or the Cross.

A large Friede Denkmal [2] towers in the middle of the town by the side of which stand two soldiers like clockwork, night & day.

After two or three days in Riga we motored to one of the local holiday places. It was one hour away set on the edge of a glorious beach, edged with forest. We stayed at 'Schloss am Meer', & because of a shortage of rooms, B & Major slept in a tiny cottage next door. Three days later we had hired that very same cottage, & here we are still two and a half months later.

On the first morning, Bonar came rushing from the beach which was a few yards from our back door. 'Mother, don't let Shona go on the beach – it's full of naked men!' Later in the day, I returned from the same beach also alarmed. 'Mother, don't let Bonar go to the beach – it's full of naked women!' The rules of the beach were soon made clear to us. Men mornings, women afternoons, and in the weekend mixed bathing. On a hot Saturday afternoon Mother and I marched down to the beach wearing bathing suits. I never felt so conspicuous!

We made some real friends in Riga, particularly among the English community. Chief among these were Mr and Mrs Addison, who had been in the Baltic timber business for many years. We were fascinated by their tales of living in Riga through the Russian Revolution. Their *dacha* or villa home which was set in a large garden had been commandeered by the Bolsheviks, their drawing room parquet floor ruined when it had become a stable for horses, their possessions broken and looted. I was intrigued to discover that Mr Addison's elderly mistress lived with them without, it appeared, any hostility from his wife.

Of their two attractive granddaughters, Lorna Addison-Hall became our special friend.

Charming, pretty, tactful, she is quite the... nicest girl I think I have ever met, & for all her 24 years she is extremely nice to me. After that

---

[2] Peace Monument

Family home at Clyde Street,
Dunedin.

Shona, two years

Professor Francis Wallace Dunlop

Mother and Shona at
Warrington, 1927.

Shona at seven, the Greek dancer.

With friends at Archerfield,
Shona centre.

Below: A holiday picnic. From left –
Jocelyn, Ada, Mother, Bonar, Dad.

Shona and Bonar on board the
SS *Viminale*.

Centre: Port Said. From left – Bonar,
friend, Major, Mother, Shona.

Bottom: With Mother at Florence.

At the Acropolis, Athens.

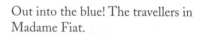

Shona at 15, a dance student in Vienna.

Out into the blue! The travellers in Madame Fiat.

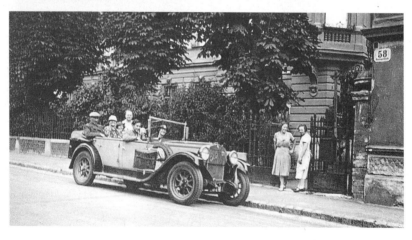

The Rink family, in the Tirol.

Bonar and Shona in Dresden, 1937.

Off to church in Paris. From left – Shona, Mother, Wallace and Bonar.

Skiing in the Wiener Wald.

Reading letters from home, before watching *Jederman*, Salzburg 1936.

Pension Keko, Yugoslavia.

On the boat to Rab with Mother and Joan Thompson (sitting)

Above: With Russian friends
in Riga, Latvia. Shona and
Mother sitting left, Major
and Bonar standing.

Slovakian peasants

Lorna

The crowds give Rudolph Hess the Nazi salute, Danzig 1937.

Faces in the Jewish ghetto, Warsaw 1937.

first meeting about 3 or 4 wks ago, we have seen each other constantly...

One day Lorna took me on the back of her motor bike (with which she has practically been all over Europe by herself) along the beach right to the furthermost peak. For 2 breathless moments while we tugged & heaved we thought we had lost the bike when we landed in quicksand.

Another night she surprised us by marching in at half past eight in the evening with Ira, another young girl. We walked down to the beach in the pitch dark, lay on the sand gazing at the stars while she played the Balalaika. Lorna is teaching me to play & also helping me make a Russian Costume.

I sought out a teacher at the Riga Opera School, and began studying Russian National Dance. Great use is made of the knees, and both strength and elasticity are required. In an effort to impress my handsome Latvian dance teacher I made fifty knee bends nightly, hanging desperately onto the bedpost for balance.

Lorna and I found old Russian lace in a shop, and both a blouse and an apron were exquisitely embroidered by her Latvian friends. In a tiny shed on the side of the road, a little man made me a pair of soft red leather boots. They had hearts sewn into them and for dance purposes not a single nail was used. They cost only 30 Lats and I was ecstatic.

Mother, Major, Bonar and I all fell under Lorna's spell, for she was equally charming to us each in turn. Certainly her seductive charm began to work on my usually detached brother. As well as striking good looks, Lorna possessed great linguistic skills, which got us out of a number of awkward situations. She spoke fluent Russian, Latvian, French, German, and English. When time came for us to leave, Lorna suggested taking the fifth seat in our car. Paris was our goal. Bonar had decided to venture into new areas of his art, this time to study painting. The best teachers were said to be found in Paris, so to Paris we must go.

4 October 1937

We stopped the car at a small Lithuanian village. A church service was just over & numbers of poor old figures stood round & came out of church... Huddled figures crouched just inside the door, counting their beads, & mumbling... Others sat on the path leading to the door singing & praying with mournful faces. We noticed how very small the people were, & how very sad. What an existence to eke out! What poverty! What misery. On our return to the car, we were amused to find a crowd of curious people collected round it. We in our 'Gypsy Camp' with luggage tied to every side present a much more interesting subject even than a 1937 Rolls Royce. The mob was as amused with us as we were with them. They looked at us & laughed, & I think they had plenty of reason to do so, as dressed in our motoring clothes we do look rather odd.

By the time we reached Tilsit, on the German border, it was almost dark & there again while changing money at a garage, within a couple of minutes, another large crowd had collected round us.

We planned our return journey via Poland, as Polish friends we had made in Zoppot had offered us hospitality and the chance to show us the attractions of their land.

Frau Fischer, whose family owned the largest chocolate factory in Poland, invited us to her imposing home in Warsaw for dinner. Across the table, shimmering with crystal, silver and glowing with candles, passed conversations in several languages – Polish, Russian, German, French and English. For me, it was the height of culture. White gloved waiters constantly refilled our glasses at table. How was I to know the drink was not lemonade – but vodka! Halfway through the meal I was carried comatose to a bed and I have no further recollections of that night. The family fortunately treated the occasion with humour, although I was given a grave warning about the dangers of strong drink.

Eager to see more of the city we made our way to the Jewish ghetto.

The characters were vastly interesting, producing much work for our cameras. At once the people knew we were strangers, & within minutes a crowd of thirty had collected around us...

It seemed to us like walking back in time. The streets teemed with ultra-orthodox Jews who wore long black coats, broad brimmed black hats, and flowing locks. Scarcely a woman was seen but many inquisitive youths and small children gathered round our car, amused by our strangeness, as we ourselves were by their dress and style. We could not know then how short a time would lapse before this very ghetto would be razed to the ground by the Nazis and all its occupants killed or incarcerated in concentration camps.

In Krakow we walked through the Jewish quarter.

After a little difficulty we managed to see the inside of a small synagogue. Bonar was not allowed in bareheaded, so a small black velvet cap was produced... We were then led into a very ancient cemetery, where lay the bones of men of thousands of years ago.

We moved on to the lovely city of Budapest, where word was awaiting, informing us that a police summons by a Baroness Rokitansky had been laid for a certain Maud Dunlop should she attempt to cross the border into Austria. This news threw us into confusion as our plans had been to return to Vienna, collect our belongings then proceed to Paris. Mother could not risk returning to Vienna now, so after journeying to Bratislava on the Austro-Czechoslovak border, the family reluctantly had to break up. Mother and the Fiat remained in Bratislava, and Bonar, Major, Lorna, and I caught the train for Vienna to collect our belongings. I was very excited about getting back to my 'Lieblingstadt' and seeing my dancing friends again. Hilary would be one of them.

We travelled into Vienna & as chimneys, spires & roofs became visible a great excitement filled me, but it was not until I saw again the familiar old Opera & Ring Strasse, & Schwarzenburg Platz that my whole being sang with jubilation, my eyes filled with tears & I sang 'Home, Home'. It had been my home for 2 years, & I loved it & still do with a passion only equalled by that for New Zealand.

For Bonar, having now two girl friends in the same city must have presented some problems. When Hilary and Lorna were introduced to each other even my untrained eyes could sense the atmosphere.

Upon our return to Bratislava, bearing many bags and boxes, we received a tremendous welcome from a delighted Mother. But I was not happy to be pulling up our Austrian roots and moving to France. I had to remind myself that this whole European experience had been planned for Bonar's sake, not mine. My sorrow in finishing my studies with Professor Bodenwieser was somewhat mollified when I heard a Viennese dancer friend Magda Brunner was also coming to Paris for dance and language studies.

A few hundred miles of further travel brought us finally to our new home in Paris. My mother could not abide the idea of living in the noise and bustle of a great city, so after a short orientation period we finally settled for a rather dilapidated but appealing villa in the village of Sevres on the outskirts of the city. This three-storeyed pink and white building set in a wild unkempt garden suited us ideally. We and 'La Miche' seemed to understand each other from the very beginning, sharing the tribulations and exulting in the happy times.

La Miche (according to my French teacher 'a wasps' nest') became a refuge for many lonely students, friends and down-and-out artists. Many were sent to us through Reverend Donald Caskie, the minister of the Scots' Presbyterian Church of Paris. Donald Caskie took particular interest in the young people in his congregation – *au pair*, language and music students.

It was customary for those of us attending his services to appear in kilts if we had them, and for us all to wear stout walking shoes. We brought our cut lunch and laid it on an empty back pew until the service was over, when young people of various nationalities gathered to be led by our parson into the French countryside, for a rare day free of French language, dance or art classes. He led us on exciting expeditions to Chantilly, Fontainebleu, and other such places of romance and history. Waiting for trains on the platform of the Gare du Nord, we would dance Scottish reels and in the carriages frequently exchange Scots songs – 'Ye Banks and Braes of Bonny Scotland' and 'I'll take the High Road and Ye'll take the Low Road and I'll be in Scotland Afore Ye' – with groups of young French travellers who tried to out-sing us with songs of their own. Caskie allayed the homesickness of many young people exposed to the 'abroad experience' for the first time.

Years later I read his book *The Tartan Pimpernel* and learned of his courageous exploits during the German occupation of France in the Second World War. Having assisted many allied airmen to escape back to England, Caskie was eventually and inevitably caught and then subjected to some unspeakable and inhumane treatment. His wonderful faith kept him alive, but his health was impaired and never fully regained.

Bonar was immediately enrolled in a leading art studio, and I began language study at the 'Cité Universitaire'. It took longer to find suitable dance training. Lorna, who continued to live with us, accompanied me to several teachers of modern dance. I made a start with Irene Poppard, but was quickly disillusioned. In only my second lesson Mademoiselle Poppard stretched my leg against the wall in an effort, she explained, to make me more supple. She then pushed me with such force that I collapsed to the floor in considerable pain, having pulled my hamstring. I never returned to that studio, but for months to follow, I would receive notes written in flowing green ink: 'My dear little English pupil, when are you coming back?'.

My next experiment met with greater success. Magda and I met up and managed to find the address of a modern dance teacher, who was well known in Vienna. Ellen Tels Rabeneck who was of Russian extraction and married to a German, declared herself happy to hold daily classes for Magda and myself. Ellen Tels had been a child pupil of the famous Isadora Duncan School in Russia. Her style was lyrical, offering a good, but not over-strict technique. Magda and I found her a very sound teacher though not nearly as inspirational as Bodenwieser. The classes were held in a studio off the Trocadero, started with just two students, but gradually numbers increased. I was astounded to learn that Marie, the young dancer in our class with blue eyes and rosy cheeks was actually the granddaughter of the notorious Russian monk Rasputin!

23 February 1938

We are a large class at the Alliance Française now, & a great mixture of races. I'm finding very little opportunity to exercise my French. Far too much grammar.

I'm satisfied with my dancing. Not the way I dance – far from it, but with the work I am given. A few days ago, Madame Tels Rabeneck didn't turn up, so Magda, Manja & I practised tap together & later Magda played & I improvised. I felt I did well, but were I to spend too long with Rabeneck my originality, & my own ideas would be almost stamped out. I've learnt a great deal... technically, & one receives more individual attention than ever was the case with Bodenwieser.

Ellen Tels was not given to fulsome praise, but an occasional grudging word from her brought fresh heart, and strengthened my resolve to become a great dancer! I complained in my diary:

4 March

Dancing goes on as ever, & sometimes it is very 'forte'. We have a great deal of repetition, & little colour throughout the whole lesson. Frau Rabeneck is usually very cross and 'unsympatisch' & when annoyed falls into a kind of Esperanto, of French, Russian & German. Magda & I have trouble keeping straight faces. But we wouldn't laugh. Not for worlds!

4 April

I love Monday mornings for the first time. It brings me dancing again. Frau Rabeneck who has been simply a pig for the last week was suddenly quite charming today & praised me an inkling. That is a lot from her.

20 April

Oooh! I'm going to be the most brilliant dancer the world has ever known. How I can dance, & how marvellous, how perfectly divine a thing it is to produce in movement, in lovely in unutterably lovely movement.

The dance I saw in Paris in 1938 was restricted almost entirely to the classical ballets of the Opera, where Serge Lifar choreographer/dancer, the last of Diaghilev's protégés and a member of the famous Ballet Russes, reigned supreme. The French in the thirties had not yet become followers of the New Dance so I saw only a few examples of modern dance. I realised how advanced Vienna was in understanding where dance was heading, and what it had to say for our time. However, Lifar created some fine ballets during his years at the Paris Opera Ballet, and the great Chaliapin in his famous role of Boris Godunov was quite unforgettable.

Several times a week I had lunch with a French family in the hopes of improving my spoken French. And although my days were filling rapidly, I did not want to give up my piano studies. My teacher was a Scots music student, Edgar Curtis, who was studying with a foremost piano teacher in Paris. Edgar suggested that he come straight from his own lesson, and practise the lesson he had just received on me. In lieu of payment, he enjoyed large meals in our home and often accompanied our family to hear famous pianists perform. I developed a crush on Edgar and was distraught when he had to return home and my delightful piano lessons came to an end. Over and again I played Beethoven's 'Moonlight' and 'Appasionata' sonatas seeing Edgar's shock of blonde hair and serious blue eyes before my own.

Between my studies, I diligently began to visit as many historic sights, concerts, and theatre as I could fit into a heavy schedule, and my attachment to Paris grew daily. Magda joined me and we strolled in the Bois de Boulogne, climbed to the top of the Eiffel Tower, played with children in the Tuilleries Gardens, gazed at the fashionable shops in the Rue de la Paix, and for fun, tried to count the number of cars as they circled the Etoile. We would then wander through the Louvre and the Latin Quarter to end up sipping coffee on the sidewalk of the Champs Elysees, as we admired the elegant Parisians passing by.

The relationship between Bonar and Lorna was causing my mother some concern. Lorna had originally intended taking a position as governess, but this did not eventuate, and Bonar's studies were clearly beginning to suffer. Beautiful Bohemian Lorna was several years Bonar's senior, and Bonar showed no immediate means of supporting himself, let alone another. Mother decided the time had arrived for Lorna to leave. For three days following Lorna's going Bonar remained locked in his room, with only the kitten Lorna had given him for company. We shoved food under his door. All of us were miserable at Lorna's going. I cannot speak for Bonar's true reaction, but I cried for days!

Meanwhile in Austria the situation was becoming quite desperate.

27 February

Schuschnigg spoke amazingly well over the wireless, & was given great applause & cheering. He said the Government in the last 4 years had made prolific strides & that without outside help (meaning Germany) they would continue doing so. The Väterländische Front is flourishing, & is to be the only movement allowed.

Good for you Schuschnigg, old Man, & I'm sure you'll win through yet. Hurrah!

11 March

The Austrian Government has resigned, & German troops are mobilising on the frontier. Good bye Austria! I'm afraid you're gone, & Schuschnigg – a broken man after 8 years fighting. I'm sorry, oh! & how.

On 12 March 1938, the German army invaded Austria. We gathered nightly around the radio learning of the increasing pressure being applied to the Austrian Government. Chancellor Schuschnigg, already a prisoner of the Germans, resigned his post in a hopeless last ditch stand to save his country. Magda was inconsolable over the turn of events, returning to Vienna immediately with her mother. It was now obvious to all that the Germans were about to break up the uneasy peace of Europe.

18 March

Madga looks white & unhappy... ever since the terrible dying of Austria... The misery that has followed! & poor Bodenwieser, she being a Jew can't possibly continue teaching. I guess she will just have to scoot, as will thousands more. Ooooh! I could kill that man Hitler, he is such a swine... Dollfuss's monument is to be replaced by that of Hitler!!... Why is the world so feeble?

The anguish I felt, arising from my own strong ties to the city of Vienna, extended to my Jewish friends who faced the advancing holocaust. Hitler had made his convictions very clear in *Mein Kampf*, and there seemed no grounds to believe that now, as Chancellor, he would revise his policy of eliminating all 'undesirable elements'. This included not only Jews, but also gypsies, homosexuals, black people and all mentally and physically impaired people. Hitler was determined to be the Führer of the 'pure' German race.

Everyone was unsettled and weighing up their options. Bonar's artwork had won him a scholarship to the Royal Academy in London and Mother had itchy feet again.

April 1938

What shall I do? Stay on here in Paris in a French family & continue with Rabeneck or go with Mum to Austria for a month & then go on to England. I would adore to go back to A(ustria). There is nothing in this world I'd love more, but dare I sacrifice even one month's dancing for the sake of it. Je ne sais pas.

In early April my brother Wallace, who ran the farm, joined us in Paris. After a two year separation, we had all changed and a little readjusting was called for.

5 April

I am beginning to realise how very changed things will be when we return to N.Z. It can't possibly be the same, after 3 years continental living. I have a horrid hollow little feeling that I will feel estranged, almost as a stranger in a strange land. Wallace made me feel that way. We noticed Wall's slow way of talking, his accent, his ways of looking at things, either he had changed or we had? – & I s'pose it must be us.

If only I had confidence in myself, confidence of making a success of a dancing school in N.Z... I feel so ignorant, so young.

11 April
It's ten-thirty at night, & my last few hours of sweet seventeen are fading before my eyes. Up till now I have always wished to be older, now I begin to regret for the first time stowing away another year in the past.

It was coincidental that an old girlfriend of my brother's was also living in Paris at the time and a frequent visitor in our home. This caused some embarrassment when Wallace and Edith met again for the first time. When my mother told Wallace that she had invited Edith to join us on our forthcoming journey through France and Switzerland, he said with some heat, 'Mother, it's time you understood. Three times I have proposed marriage to Edith MacDonald, and three times she has turned me down. You put me in an impossible position.'

However Edith did take the vacant seat in the Fiat, because Bonar had already left for London, where for the next two years he would pursue his studies. To begin with one felt a strain between Wallace and Edith, but it wasn't long before Edith was sitting beside him as he drove, with Mother relegated to the back. The atmosphere improved greatly from then on.

We began packing our bags and getting ready to depart on a slow journey which would bring us at last to Britain. Britain had been our intended destination originally, but despite the circumstances I was excited that at last I was about to step on English soil.

1 May
Three years travel has not made us the tiniest bit wiser. We still never make up our minds until the very last minute. We never make previous arrangements, still change our plans if we can find the smallest excuse to do so, & above all remain tied to nobody & nothing.

The Gypsy Dunlops, we are called, & nobody could reform us. We are very happy to remain so. Concerning our approaching journey, we know little more than that Austria is to be one port of call, & because of Wallace's imminent departure & our desire to 'discover England' & Scotland, we will not have more than a month to be wandering through Europe.

13 May
The last week before leaving on a trip is always a busy one, but never have I been dragged off my feet to quite such an extent as has been the case

this time. Actually things are very exciting... A telegram arrived from Bodenwieser in quaint English: 'Come to Paris in next days'. I have kept very quiet about a very big secret, which has been the cause of much anguish, many a heart break, & no little joy. Bodie suggests opening a school for dancing with me in N.Z. Did you ever hear of anything more fantastic, more baffling? An offer to join in with Frau Professor Bodenwieser the world famous dancer & teacher of the same? Why it's a simply topping chance, a golden opportunity!

Permits, money, everything is going to be difficult to arrange but what fun... Marcel, Bodie's pianist, being a Jew with an extremely long nose, is also very anxious to clear out of Austria... He by the way is a perfect genius of a man. He understands music & dancing to an almost uncanny degree, & he plays his own inventions beautifully. As a man though I'm not sure how I'd like him, but then that's a secondary consideration...

Today at my last dancing lesson at Ellen Tels I fairly purred. A teacher of dancing was looking on, a woman who had been there once two months before. At the end of a ripping lesson, having been given all the things I relish most, this woman said to me, with a serious look on her face, 'Mademoiselle, you must not give up dancing. You were born to be a dancer. Go ahead, dance.' She added that the improvement I had made in the last 2 months was stupendous, that she could hardly credit I was the same person. Ellen Tels was very sweet too & kissed me goodbye & I bet she is sorry to lose her oldest pupil. I'm ever so glad I went to her, I've learnt just heaps, stuff I'd hardly have learnt anywhere else & certainly not with Bodenwieser.

I began to get the wind up, after receiving various letters from Hilary stating that Magda was helping Bodenwieser to get to America...

My next trouble is – will she be here before we leave on Monday?

15 May

No news of Bodenwieser, things remain anxious. I have such a pain in my back because of the ceaseless stooping & packing, & I have such dirty fingernails & I'm very tired. Well old sleepy head, I wonder where you will be laying your weary head this time tomorrow night?

Unfortunately, we had not taken into account the likelihood of trouble from our devious house agent. We were presented yet again with a large bill of trumped up charges for such items as frayed carpets and torn curtains. I retain memories of camping out on the front lawn while Major was sent to iron out the problem with a lawyer. It was nightfall before we crept out of the city. Our final impressions of Paris could have been pleasanter ones, but could do nothing to change our feelings of admiration for that grand city.

18 May

I'm so very keen to make a success at the dancing for which I'm prepared to sell my very bones. I've been practising here in my bedroom alone tonight, & I've come to the inevitable conclusion that I cannot & could never give up dancing lightly. I love it - passionately - vehemently - it's grown a very part of me, & four days without work for the body has been most disagreeable.

Actually, I'm exceedingly worried about Bodenwieser. We left Paris without hearing from her, & now I have no means of finding her. She will think on finding me gone, Oh! Shona doesn't appear very interested & then let things slide. I couldn't bear that. The more I think of the Bodenwieser plan the more impressed I become & the deeper grows my decision to make it happen 'at any cost'. I think she'll be in Paris in 4 wks when we return. Of course had Bw. arrived in Paris before our departure, & she had asked me to stay on, & work with her I should have jumped at it. Wonderful as travelling may be, dancing is a deal more wonderful still.

Travelling via Orleans, Mother insisted we inspect the historic Museum Jeanne d'Arc. I found the Maid's life, outlined by documents, portraits and sculptures spell-binding. From then on, I snapped up any material, biographies or plays about Jeanne d'Arc which I could find.[3]

Further along the Loire Valley, we came at last to the Chateau Nicolas Vernelle. A Count and Countess, fallen upon lean times, had opened their home to guests and this delightful place was etched in our memory because here a significant family event took place. We were relaxing in the large sitting room which I shared with Mother, when Wallace and Edith announced their engagement. Majie produced a bottle of champagne from nowhere. Before we drove off next morning the Count and Countess, their friends and a number of strangers gathered around the car to wish the joyous couple God Speed.

---

[3] My unusual interest in her life led Bodenwieser to create a solo dance trilogy on Jeanne d'Arc for me some years later.

Our excitement seemed to affect Madame Fiat, who as my mother expressed it, flew like a bird. We made good time, reaching Lausanne first, then over the Jaun Pass where the spectacular mountain scenery made us homesick for New Zealand. We continued on through Interlaken, Aigle, Sion and over the impressive Simplon Pass. Our spirits soared until we came to rest once more at the small village of Pallanza on Lake Maggiore.

Two memorable events took place on Lake Maggiore. Firstly, Mother made a disastrous plunge into the lake, fully clothed, as she tried to step off the Island of Isola Bella. A sympathetic signora of the ristorante lent her a complete outfit of Italian national dress – long black woollen stockings, black skirt and black shawl. She returned by boat again to Pallanza where, badly shaken, she made straight for her bed. And secondly, came a sensational invitation from Frau Bodenwieser in Paris.

Pallanzo, Lake Maggiore – 30 May

Such excitement! Today our mail arrived from Milan, & amongst it was a letter from Bodenwieser suggesting I go with her & her Group on a Tournée to Colombia in S. America for a one month engagement. She said I must ask Emmy, her assistant in Vienna first, if there was still room for me. Quick as thought I sent off a telegram & tonight, a few minutes ago, received the answer: Platz frei, Hilary fährt, abschluss unentschieden!! [4] *That is a wonderful reply & funnily enough, just because things appear so very serious, I feel quite calm. I also heard from Magda, saying she was going, & Hilary also. They will make all the difference, & we shall be the three youngest. Bodenwieser says if I wish to join the group, I must go immediately to Vienna & begin studying up dances, with the others... Oh! Dear, I'll miss the wedding...*

We learned that the Bodenwieser Gruppe was being engaged for a three month season as a top overseas attraction on the occasion of the four hundredth anniversary of Bogota, the capital city of Colombia. Magda Brunner's father, the Austrian Consul to Colombia, had organised the tour. Although Professor and Frau Brunner were not Jewish, they readily came to the assistance of their daughter's celebrated dance teacher, who now feared for the safety

---

[4] Place available, Hilary going, date of departure undecided.

of her students and friends, as for her own family. It would have been naive to believe that Frau Gerty would have chosen me over far more experienced dancers. She felt it expedient to keep her options open. Her world was crumbling around her, and she could only guess at the future which lay ahead, and the land to which she might flee. It was not beyond the realms of possibility that the next Bodenwieser school would be in New Zealand.

We would be sailing within the month. The fact that two special friends of mine, (presumably with their parents' approval) were joining the tour made it increasingly difficult for my mother to say no. My brother Wallace was surprisingly supportive of my passionate wish to go on the South American tour. 'You have allowed Shona to study dance,' he said to Mother, 'and now at this chance of a lifetime you would turn it down!' Major on the other hand was less enthusiastic. 'Are you going to allow your daughter to throw up her legs before a bunch of savages on the equator?' he roared. Fortunately for me, my mother, who loved any sort of adventure herself, began to share some of my own excitement. Finally she agreed to let me go, providing Hilary (who was already a seasoned Group member) was going on the tour.

Alas, there was another obstacle. Mother could not risk returning to Vienna, for fear the Baron and Baroness Rokitansky were still seeking arbitration. She was convinced that she could never successfully combat them in a foreign country. By the time we reached Cortina D'Ampezzo in the Dolomites, we had decided upon a course of action. Wallace and Edith would accompany me to Vienna to make sure all was above board with the prospective tour, and help check all documents pertaining to contracts and such. The fact that neither of them understood German did not seem to occur to anyone, but I felt their presence would be a great support. We left an anxious-looking Mother and Major among the mountain wild flowers, and caught an overnight train which brought us wearily, but excitedly, back to my favourite city.

I was in for a rude shock. From the moment I stepped from the train, I noticed the change. Red and black swastikas hanging from every building announced that the *gemütlich* (lively, music-and-pleasure-loving) city of Vienna was no more.

The renowned coffee houses in Vienna which have been described as representing an oasis in the desert of life, still played that role for many. People gathered for companionship or to discuss plans to escape the encroaching Juggernaut threatening their lives. The many varieties of delicious foods were still available in shops and restaurants. Die Fledermaus opera, most popular of all Austrian operas, still played at the Opernhaus, and expeditions could still be taken to outlying palaces and castles beyond the Wienerwald, but the fearful human dramas which were taking place behind locked doors defied description.

June 1938

We took a train to the old Hospiz[5] which had changed hands, & which had become loud in its swastikas, pictures of Hitler & Heil Hitler all over the place... I saw Emmy a couple of hours later & we all took a taxi... to Bodenwieser's manager, & discussed things...

There followed a very strenuous time, with lots of hard work. Every morning we had 'Proben'.[6] Between rehearsals I ran round looking up people, friends of mine & Mother's, tore around with the girls to Tourist Bureaus, & shopped. I spent an anxious time after signing the contract, wondering if Hilary would really come...

I spent an evening at Annie's [Rink] where I was told the most atrocious stories. The whole family is trying to get to Australia, & they were very keen to hear what life out there was like... Annie hates walking down the street for fear someone will spit in her face & scream 'Dirty Jew' as anyone has every right to do. She is also afraid to go to the Kino for fear of being turned out. No Jews are allowed into any of the municipal baths & no Aryan shops will sell goods to a Jew. Every Aryan shop pastes in large letters on the window that this is an 'Äerishes Geschäft' & their only greeting is 'Heil Hitler'... Unless the Viennese wear small Hakenkreuz [7] pins in their coat, they are liable to be under suspicion...

Oh! I wanted to cry. I felt my heart swelling with anger & pity for these folk...

The Rink family led me into their living room, and blocking the key hole with cotton wool, turned to me with despair in their eyes and dropped to their knees. In whispered tones they begged me to procure them New Zealand visas for their escape. As Jews they knew

---

5 Hostel
6 Rehearsals
7 Swastika

their days were numbered before they too would hear, 'Open up, open up!' in the dead of night when the S.S. would break in and drag them off to a concentration camp. I knew well that my chances of procuring visas for these people were almost nil. My mother and Majie were already pulling every string they could with the British Embassy to get visas for Frau Bodenwieser, her husband, her sister, nephew and Marcel Lorber, the company's brilliant pianist. These efforts would only be undermined should they add still further names to the list. Feeling wretched and racked with guilt, I stumbled from their home burdened with the weight of their lives on my shoulders.

It hadn't occurred to me that so many of my friends were Jewish, though I should have known, as they made up a very large portion of all artists and intellectuals of the city. Gathering just a few possessions together, Bodie and her husband Dr Rosenthal had escaped by virtually the last train to leave Austria for unoccupied France. For such a celebrated woman, this creeping like a whipped dog out of her own land was the supreme humiliation.

Bodenwieser was particularly anxious to see her sister and nephew out of Austria, as they had already been victims of Nazi brutality. Dr Hecht, Bodenwieser's brother-in-law, who held a high position in the Austrian Government, had been arrested and taken away by the S.S. Days later they returned to the Hecht apartment and, without comment, handed over a small casket of his ashes to a shocked widow.

My own British passport gave me security, but I also experienced a sense of guilt. Freedom to expect courteous treatment was something I had always taken for granted. I was now daily witnessing the lives of many who would never know freedom again.

I paid a visit to Dr. Appel, poor man, & I scarcely recognised him, his cheeks are hollow, & his eyes drawn, as if he hadn't slept for weeks... He told me that he only had another three weeks in Vienna, & then he & his wife would be forced to go, & the terrible criminal part of it is that it's almost an impossibility to procure an Einreise[8] to enter another country. Poor Jews... Very often these poor devils never return from Dachau (the political prison) & it is given out that they have committed suicide...

---

8 Travel permit

In fact, Dr Appel and his wife did commit suicide by jumping from a top floor window of the bank of which he had been manager.

Hilary's arrival from holidaying in Yugoslavia was a great relief to me. Wallace and Edith having rejoined the family, I was beginning to feel quite alone and traumatised by the daily tragedies I witnessed. We seven dancers threw ourselves into rehearsals and within a short time learned many roles in as many dances. We met in various venues, including the old familiar Hollander Saal where Bodenwieser had given her last lesson. It was a nostalgic and emotional experience returning to the place where my love of dance had blossomed. By the end of three weeks, Emmy had miraculously pulled together a mixed programme of Bodenwieser choreographies.

In my final week in Vienna I stayed with the family of my German teacher Frau von Gesternberger. It was an awful time, as I shared her fears for their youngest, intellectually-handicapped child, Crystal. Frau von Gesternberger was not able to fool herself that this child could be rescued. Hitler's aim for a pure and perfect Aryan race did not allow for imperfect children. There was no way little Crystal, who was part-Jewish, would be able to live under the Nazi system. The perfect irony of this tale, I later learned, was that the Aryan father had been a secret member of the Nazi Party for some time. Through the intervention of English friends Frau von Gesternberger received permits for all but Crystal, and she and two of her daughters were among the few Jews who escaped the gas chambers of Auschwitz, Dachau, and Buchenwald. For Crystal there was no escape.

Vienna was the home of many great artists of Jewish origin, who were forced to make ignominious departures. After the Anschluss, Hitler condemned the modern movement as 'decadent', which saw remaining contemporary exponents of most art forms emigrate to other countries. The modern dance teacher/choreographer, Rudolph von Laban, who had influenced Bodenwieser's ideas so profoundly, moved to England, and the Viennese Gertrud Kraus to Israel. The seed of modern dance which had flourished so successfully in Europe was scattered wide. Of the modern dance pioneers, only Mary Wigman, Grete Wiesenthal and Rosalia Kladek fell in line with the Nazi dictum, and remained in the German Reich. Most of those who could not leave in time were sent to the concentration camps.

Austria and Germany were almost overnight bereft of a large

portion of their intellectuals, paralysing the literary and artistic life of the two nations. Famous artists such as Gustav Mahler, Max Reinhardt, Arnold Schoenberg, Stephan Zweig, Franz Werfel, Lion Feuchtwanger, Richard Tauber, Arthur Koestler, Sigmund Freud, Franz Kafka, Otto Klemperer, Bruno Walter, Elizabeth Bergner were among those who escaped in time. Few of them returned after the demise of Hitler. Upon my return to Vienna in 1988 I was unable to find even one school of modern dance. The modern movement had been effectively destroyed.

After a series of horrid vaccinations and immunisations for cholera, typhoid and diphtheria, a twenty-strong company of dancers, singers, comedians, directors, managers and the inevitable few hangers-on assembled under the name *Revista Vienesa* at Westbahn Railway Station. We were destined for Amsterdam on the first lap of our journey to South America. An uncomfortable ten hours followed with all of us packed into two compartments. Some were suffering from vaccinations, and most were in great turmoil knowing that perhaps they were leaving their homeland forever.

I was indeed surprised with myself when we left by train, that I appeared to have no feelings of regret, only a great hatred for the man who has been the ruin of the most wonderful city in the world, & of thousands of people.

We had good reason to fear the moment we reached the Austrian-Dutch border town of Aachen, for there were Jews among our number. Several young blonde Nazi officers boarded the train, and flirted with us while they examined our papers. They then passed to the adjoining carriage where our non-Aryan colleagues sat paralysed with fear. After a few moments the doors burst open and they shoved two of our friends off the train. Gone were the smiling faces. They sneered at us and shouted, 'You should be ashamed to be travelling with such scum!'

Hilary immediately flung up the carriage window and waved her British passport at the soldiers. 'We will tell England,' she cried indignantly, 'we will tell the whole world of the crimes you Nazis commit!' To our astonishment the officers took notice of this. They grudgingly released the two Jewish men and watched grimly as they scrambled back onto the train.

Chapter Four

The women, scantily dressed in coloured rags and men's felt hats, held six lit candles above their heads, & glided through the mud, wet oozing through their toes.

Mother, Major, Wallace and Edith had managed to get to Amsterdam where we spent two days together, culminating in the series of dreadful photographs taken before our ship the *Costa Rica* set sail for South America on 20 June, 1938.

We had a bit of a rush to get to the ship on time & to find the right wharf. Then of course the goodbye. I felt strong, firm as iron until the whistle began to blow. I just couldn't shame myself in front of all the girls but then – the parting kiss with Wal, my mouth twitched, a kiss from Edith & my nose quivered, a kiss from Majie & my eyes stung, a kiss from Mother – & I was undone. Those wretched tears!!... Anyway, I just let them flow...

A few hours' stop at Dover gave Bonar a chance to bid Hilary and me farewell. As poor Hilary wept inconsolably in the berth beside me that night, I was made aware of the seriousness of their relationship. Neither of us could guess the many traumas and dangers the subsequent war years would bring Bonar.

It was with great relief we spied Frau Gerty, a brave little figure standing on the wharf as we docked at Boulogne. Frau Gerty took stock of the assembled dancers – three Austrians (Magda Brunner, Johanna [Hanny] Kolm, Poldi Peroutka), one Estonian (Hilja Luukas), and two English (Hilary Napier and me) – and quickly set to work. We were persuaded to give several concerts on board. Our first try-out was for the tourist-class passengers, which proved a hazardous experience for the dancers, but delightful entertainment for the audience. As the ship heaved and wallowed in a sudden storm, balancing became impossible. We slithered about the deck clutching at rails or each other, until both dancers and audience became helpless with laughter. A couple of spills and a shoe overboard finally brought the concert to an early end.

...it was very very exciting, especially for me, who had never danced before the public before. I had to do my Russian dance which was a great success, though I found the length & tilt of the ship a little difficult for the jumps. I was interested to see how dancing in public would affect me. I know what a perfect funk I fall into when I have to play the piano before people, but to my own surprise & delight I felt calm & cool-headed, with a flame of excitement burning inside me somewhere, but well checked.

The next three weeks at sea were spent in training class, and rigorous rehearsal. Any thoughts of a lazy shipboard life were quickly forgotten, for we were also launched into Spanish lessons and the standard Vienna State Academy subjects of Dance History, and Art History. The tight daily schedule was only broken upon arrival at the various West Indian ports of call: Madeira, Barbados, Trinidad and Curaçao.

Madeira is very charming. We took two cars & drove halfway up the hill where we saw an expansive view of the harbour, & our ship, a tiny fleck in the distance. The variety of growth was surprising. A gum tree & a banana & a coconut side by side... The town of Madeira is comparatively clean, & the park lovely, consisting of trees lavishly massed in red, blue, mauve and yellow flowers. One hears so much of Madeira wine, so we all trooped off to a Wine Keller, where we were cordially seated in amongst great casks & barrels of wine & given many excellent wines to taste. By the time we had finished the fifth glass we decided that we had had about enough...

Our first glimpse of the mixed Spanish, Indian and Negro polyglot society of South America took place during the day spent in the Venezuelan capital, Caracas.

The road was precipitous, steep, & overflowing with traffic. Our driver drove like a madman, making our otherwise thrilling journey a perfect misery... Caracas possesses a very grand park, with alleys of stately mahogany trees, but I think that the Governor's house about finished the 'fors' of Caracas City, the 'againsts' are too numerous to mention. Bodie talked with the theatre manager, & almost decided on taking her Group there when her other engagements are finished. God forbid..!

My first impressions of Colombia, though mixed, were more positive:

15 July 1938
So this was Colombia, rich in green grass, in undergrowth, in greenly leaved trees. It looked good, but unkempt.

Finally disembarking from the ship at Puerto Colombia, we immediately boarded a plane for Bogota which at 8900 feet, next to La Paz, claims to be the highest capital in the South American continent. For most of us, it was our first memorable experience of air travel. While crossing the Cordilleras we entered an air pocket and made a sickening plummet some thousands of feet. Passengers panicked as luggage was thrown about the cabin. We noticed our German pilot's unhealthy pallor as we disembarked in Bogota. All the same, at Frau Gerty's urgent request we stepped jauntily from the plane, turning angelic faces to the cameras and accepting exotic sprays of orchids with outward pleasure. Frau Gerty impressed us with the ease with which she addressed the press in excellent Spanish.
At Bogota our mail awaited us.

Poor BW [Bodenwieser] collapsed into a chair quite broken with bad news she had received from more than one quarter. I was terribly thrilled to get a letter from Mummy the minute I stepped on land too, it was comforting to know she has at last really reached England.

The following days and weeks were packed with activity – ranging from dance class and rehearsal, to press conferences, photographic sessions, and invitations and receptions from Festival Committees and the various Diplomatic Corp. Finding ourselves celebrities overnight was rather intoxicating and we played our parts with zest.

16 July
Ran round all the newspaper offices telling them what a marvellous journey we had had, how the people were really too charming, & how we

were all quite 'ravis'[1] about Bogota. We had our photos taken, going into each office, whilst in each office & coming out of each office. By the end of the day I felt like some parakeet being drawn round by a string... with all these other pretty parrots...

We were taken to watch a polo match in the outskirts of the town, which are very very lovely... We were rather surprised to see such a well dressed crowd of people, but the pedestrians in the street looked so utterly poverty stricken...

Changed after lunch, & were driven out to the Country Club. It's a clubhouse with a gorgeous verandah, & a fine golf course, & tennis courts. Numerous Colombian youths were introduced to us, I danced with a few, if one would call walking round in circles holding one at shoulder length, ballroom dancing. They all looked a little South American somehow, & smelt of whisky...

Bodenwieser was not altogether pleased to see Hilary and me making friends with the German community. We understood her attitude well, but could not share her suspicion that behind every German lay a hidden Nazi.

Frau Gerty prepared us gradually for our gala opening night in the Teatro Colon. Owing to Bogota's high altitude our rehearsal lasted only ten minutes the first day, building up to two hours by the end of the week.

22 July

On Sunday there was a most ghastly accident. During a military parade, an aeroplane looping the loop... crashed into the crowds of onlookers. The death toll was 85 & double as many wounded. The whole town is in mourning, our performance has been postponed. The funeral was a big sad affair, which we watched from our bedroom window.

It was my misfortune by the time the première arrived, to be prone in a hotel bed nursing a violent attack of quinsy. The Spanish doctor who attended me alone in my hotel bedroom, decided to lance my throat.

...when they had finished with me, I fell back onto the bed like an empty sack of potatoes, & cried. I couldn't stop crying, quite quietly, but I couldn't stop. Somehow, I felt they had wrenched my heart out!

---

[1] Delighted.

The première, & there I lay gargling, spraying my throat, swallowing pills & saying fiercely to myself, over & over again, that I didn't really mind a scrap – no not at all!

5 August

Such a relieved feeling. We have just heard that our pay for the new engagement which we were just about to take, has dwindled to a very small sum. So all the girls refused to go. The tournée was to be made through Colombia, spending a night or two in many small towns. The whole idea didn't appeal to me, the towns might be anything, may not even possess a moderately decent hotel, & then my greatest fear was the audience. Would people understand our dance? ...Frau Brunner, her husband & Magda were very much against it & Herr Prof refused bluntly to let Magda go with the Group. Last night a long conference was held in Hanny's bedroom, we all screamed at each other, feathers flew in all directions, & by twelve o'clock we didn't seem to be any further on. ...We have still but two weeks in Bogota & at the end of that time we are thrown into the streets so to speak. None of the girls wish to return to Vienna & all of us are badly off for money. It seemed if we didn't take that offer with a (at the time) very large salary, we may find nothing more...

Hilary really wished to go straight to China, especially now, if what the Bogota papers state is true, that war is raging between Russia & Japan, but being a sport, she refuses to leave the Group in the lurch... There is nothing left for me to do, other than accept the next offer, or else take the next ship alone to England, or possibly get Mother to cable me money & remain here till her arrival which I should hate above all things.

Bodie is a devil too, although in a state of complete breakdown, I don't feel I can trust her. She is as keen as mustard, to get permits for N.Z. just to put in her pocket, but if anything with better prospects came her way, she would grab it & drop me like a hot potato...

Well I have danced three times with the Group now... At first I only took the part of a page in the Ballet, but last night, in a rather important performance before the President, I danced in a South Slavian Dance with four others, in red flannel costumes. Effective & gay & the dance we only started the previous morning. It's rather fun making-up & discovering with experience just what suits one best...

The excitement before the curtain rises, the dash and flurry for a quick change, the hollow sinky sort of feeling... when one is not quite sure of a certain step, but when all mixed up together, they mix well, they spell the word FUN!

17 August

I must jump back to two weeks ago, when Albert, George & Otto took Hil, Poldi & Shona to a bullfight. I knew I was going to loathe it but I felt 'when in Rome do as Rome does' & an idea that it would make people's eyes open in far off NZ in the years to come...

All of a sudden without any warning a bull with bloodshot eyes & trembling badly rushed into the arena. Several men in gay attire brandished red capes at the poor beast, infuriating it to a maddening degree. One fellow would approach the bull slowly holding out two spears, the bull would dash at him, whereupon he would jump aside & at the same moment fling the arrows into the wretched animal's back. Then came the worst and most dastardly part of all when two horses appeared & the picadors on their backs proceeded to stick long spears into the maddened bull. The bull then made a rush at the horse, & gored him frantically, until half his inside was hanging out... The Torrero, the man chosen to kill the bull, plays & teases the beast further, & then produces his sword, & digs it into the neck, just behind the head...

After five bulls had been successively tortured, killed & dragged out, I felt pretty sick, & expressed my wish to leave. ...I just cannot understand the mentality of the people here...

The 4th & 5th of August were the four hundred years' Anniversary of Bogota. Big parades, lots of marching in the streets. It took us half an hour by taxi to get from our hotel to the theatre, a stretch which usually takes 5 minutes.

21 August

Heute habe ich wirklich etwas neues erlebt.[2] Never, never in my life before have I danced in a bullfighting arena until today, & it was truly funny. We were given an evil smelling sick room used for the wounded Torreros, as a dressing room, and had to use the dark muddy passage, where the bulls are led, to enter the stage which was erected in the middle of the arena. Thirty thousand people, quite , & such an odd crowd. We danced like angels in the sunshine, a waltz, Mozart ballet, South Slavian dance, & the Bauern Tanz, but the jolly old Indians & Negroes who came after us & merely wiggled their bodies about to an expressionless band received double the applause. The folks here just can't grasp the meaning of our dance, but anything simple & easy appeals to them greatly.

---

[2] Today I experienced something new.

The ridiculousness of the situation suddenly reached me while standing there in a yellow costume, with a great white collar, on a raised platform in the middle of an arena, surrounded on all sides by crowds & crowds of people. I wondered... just what my grandfather would have to say about this appalling escapade on the part of his venturesome granddaughter!

Last night we gave two performances, 6.30 & 9.30. We swallowed down a few sandwiches between the two, but felt desperately fatigué[3] at 12.30. Fortunately this doesn't happen often...

I have no desire to return [to New Zealand] immediately... Now the time has come for me to go home, I want to put it off, & I haven't been able to quite analyse why. I know this forthcoming tournée has lots of disadvantages, one being four performances no less on Sun & Saturdays in the hottest places in the world, but I would certainly see life, & make quite a little money into the bargain... I got a bunch of letters yesterday, & I realise more & more in what a different world I live... I find it even a little difficult to suddenly put myself in the place of these old school chums of mine. They haven't changed an atom, & I have a feeling which I despise as heartily as I despise this reluctance to return to my beloved N.Z. that I'm not going to find them interesting, & I'm going to slowly but surely turn into a snob.

13 September

Our new contract for 7–11 weeks tournée through Colombia, which I had been secretly rather dreading, has certainly been far from unpleasant up till now. Teatro Faenza is actually a Kino,[4] & we didn't exactly relish the idea of leaving the beautiful Teatro Colon, for an ordinary Kino. However our three weeks there have been three of the jolliest I have ever known...

Hilary attracts such attention. An admirer throws carnations onto the stage at each Bogota performance and stands unsuccessfully at the stage door, to ask Hilary if she will honour him with her company. We took little notice of him until he followed Hilary and me with our two companions, Jorge and Alberto, to a restaurant. Hilary's rejected suitor sat gazing at her from an adjacent table and then followed us back to our hotel. Shortly after returning to our room, we heard loud noises from the street below – Jorge and the carnation thrower were in fierce combat which would have done justice to the bull arena itself. Jorge was the victor

---

[3] Tired.
[4] Cinema.

and the other poor chap slunk away crying bitterly.

We shifted from Hotel Regina, where we were paying out almost all our salary, for an unpretentious pension, which we in short time discovered to be just a trifle too unpretentious & moved once more. This time we struck a gold mine...

We worked very hard, & as we found little time for fun outside the theatre we were forced to cut down our sleep allowance. We soon grew accustomed to it, & a day with Probe [5] all morning, a nap after lunch, a performance at six, another at nine, & a little party or a drive lasting until three or four or even five in the morning, was nothing unusual. In fact it happened night after night & we seemed to thrive on it. Every day we gave two performances & on Sunday four, & enjoyed it all heartily...

Bodie's idea of learning more Colombian dances proved an excellent one. The Bambuco where I dance the part of a boy, with Hilary as my partner, has been an outstanding success. The first night we were feeling just a little anxious. We had decided the people would be either disgusted or delighted, & they were the latter with a vengeance. As soon as the curtains were drawn the audience broke into terrific applause, & it continued all through the dance, so loud indeed that we could barely hear the orchestra... Because of Bambuco's undeniable success we have learnt Joropo, another attractive dance... with Magda gone, I slowly began getting more & more dances to do, & if I were to get ill today, it would not be such a small drawback as it was in Colon...

Our first Sunday with four performances was pretty hectic. We made wild dashes home for a meal & a tiny rest, & the rest of the day was spent in the theatre. Towards the end we danced like machine dolls, somehow all feeling had flown, but our new dances met with much appreciation...

On Monday 12 September the most terrible news was published in the Colombian newspapers. Everyone was in a funk until half an hour before the performance while in the act of making-up, the latest edition came out stating that 200 German planes were over England, War was proclaimed! [6] Stunned, appalled, we girls sat looking at each other a full five minutes, with all the horror of this new terrible situation sweeping over us. The first shock over, we began protesting, & giving all our personal ideas on the subject to anyone who would listen.

The consequence was that when the curtain rose only one girl was

---

[5] Rehearsal
[6] This proved to be a false alarm.

standing on the stage instead of four. We paid for it afterwards from the sharp tongues of Bodie & Strehn...

Our last performance [in Bogota] was a terrific success. The house was packed, people were standing in the corridors. We received many divine baskets of flowers & altogether were thoroughly spoilt. After the last dance the applause was deafening. Hats & coats were thrown on the stage & the crowds remained yelling & clapping, while we bobbed and smiled before them almost half an hour after the end... Oh! It is a nice warm feeling to know oneself really appreciated. Over appreciated perhaps, but that is still better. Alberto, Jorge & Otto & Ehrmann took us to Femina for supper after our great success...

November 1938

The journey by train [to Cali]... was exceedingly lovely. We passed banana & coffee plantations, & I could even pluck oranges from the trees through the carriage window. We passed tiny Indian hovels, & at every meagre little station Negroes... came past the windows selling delicious tropical fruits & oh! so cheaply. We descended very rapidly into the hot country & soon our clothes were sticking to us. We passed acres & acres of rambling downs, & mountains that looked as if they had permanent waves. We passed dead horses & mules almost invisible for the number of great black vultures eating the stinking flesh. At Ubique, a sticky town, we descended from the train, & all drove off in taxis up into the Andes...

On arriving in Cali the usual bouquets were presented, & fuss made... The sudden great change from the cold of Bogota to Cali's great heat came as rather a shock to the nervous system at first, but a comfortable hotel, four or five showers a day, exotic tropical food helped to accustom us to the change. The Theatre too was ideal...

Three nights we had to give performances at Palmeira, a tiny little village three-quarters of an hour by car... We had a veritable barn to dance in, & were openly shocked and indignant. Then we were furious, horrified that cucarachas [7] were so numerous one couldn't find a place to put one's foot, dismayed that the dressing room doors didn't shut, embarrassed that the lavatory was at the entrance door, where everyone saw you as they came in, & quite sick at the size of the stage! No, it really was too bad we thought, & grumbled merrily amongst each other. A hotel supper had been put together, & we sat on our costume cases hoeing [into]

---

[7] Cockroaches.

bread & cheese & hoping one hadn't swallowed a cucaracha by mistake.

The actual performance was a great success. I excelled myself by falling flat on my back again during the Bambuco, which brought howls of appreciation from the gallery. Old Murillo, [8] *who has begun performing with us every evening now, & who is to travel with the Group, received storms of applause for his Colombian music... Somehow all the defects of the cinema didn't appear half so bad when one had an appreciative audience... The second night was rather dull & lacked 'Stimmung'* [9] *as the Germans say. But the third & last night was terrifically exciting. I had been studying my new solo dance, 'El Fauno', with Marcel & Bodie, Mayer helped me with my costume & there it was eventually – finished. So in this tiny place I did it for the first time &... it was a decided hit. It is the dance that should appeal to any public, it's whimsical, daring, & altogether rather charming. I think Bodie is a genius at developing a dance – of course I consider my 'Faun' just too marvellous...*

We gave one more performance at the Bull Arena, which went off loads better, & then we had the great honour of giving a performance at the Teatro Municipal for all the school children. We had learnt a new dance called 'Terror'. I being 'Terror' strut round the stage like a soldier, while others make desperate efforts to ward me off, but they all fall down eventually & I walk over them. My costume is silver armour and suddenly just at the end whilst triumphantly standing on my victims my armour worked loose, opened & fell on the floor, & there I was in a black stocking garment. It was an anxious moment, but I mastered a wild impulse to laugh, & unclad, finished the dance. We all gave solos, but the most gorgeous thing was the appreciation of those kids, 6,000 there were & three sitting on each seat...

Medellin – 29 November

I have been spending the last 12 days on & off in bed, & never walked further than to the hotel door & back. Actually I've been a pathetic little figure lying here in the dreary room with the sun shining gaily outside my window. The trouble was that having danced my 'Faun' so often... I developed a very sore knee, the one which I come down onto from a high spring in the air & I scraped a little of the skin off. I didn't give two hoots about the scratch, & continued rolling round in the mud & filth of the stage, until one day it became very sore & I danced 'Terror'

---

[8] A Celebrated Colombian composer and pianist.

[9] Atmosphere.

that afternoon with much difficulty. The knee began swelling & I didn't dance at Noche.[10] *The doctor came the next day & ordered plenty [of] alcohol packs, & rest. His wishes were carried out until my knee appeared almost normal & the inflammation apparently gone. I got up & walked around all day...*

At 11 o'clock at night just as I was settling into my bed, the telephone rang. It was Bodie telling me in an agitated voice that Hanny had fainted, & that I simply must go along to the Circo [Bull Arena] & dance the Bambuco. I opened my mouth to protest, but thought better of it, threw on my clothes, rang for a taxi & in five minutes was at the Circo. Hilary my usual girl partner had to take Hanny's part as man with Hilja, whilst I had Poldi. She wasn't very sure of it, and having just popped out of bed, I felt exceedingly giddy. Hilary's trousers were far too large for her, & the sight of her giving them a surreptitious hitch every now and then was too much for Poldi & myself. We giggled helplessly all the way through the dance & the encore...

My knee didn't feel any better for having done the Bambuco & I felt it swelling again. The doctor came again next day, & was so deeply emerged in the relating of his life's story, that he quite forgot what he had come for – till I gently mentioned it, an hour later. The swelling went down again but a nasty hard lump persisted, looked very blue & didn't receive any of my pokes with much sympathy. I was rather worried about the whole thing & began telling Smithie[11] *my fears. He immediately got on his high horse & insisted that I should see several doctors about it. He took me to one who said 'Bueno I shall cut it immediately, or the poison may go right up your leg, & tomorrow you will lose the whole leg.' My mouth fell open & I stared at him, not in fright, but in amazement that any doctor could be so utterly crazy. I said I would have to consult my sister about it, & walked out.*

The next doctor calmly and confidently examined the knee & then told me to buy a certain putty paste, which I was to apply as packs every four hours. If the bump went down it was O.K. but if it brought it to a head, as he was inclined to think it would, he should be obliged to operate – but he looked horrified when I told him that the whole Ballet Vienesa was leaving the following morning for Barranquilla by river boat down the Magdalena. He promptly put a stop to my going with my knee in the infectious state it was... I felt horribly disappointed... because I had been

---

[10] Nine o'clock performance.
[11] Albert Smith, an American friend working for General Electric.

looking forward to this 3-day trip we were to make on the Magdalena through real jungle. I had a wild desire to see monkeys, crocodiles & tortoises.

They left on Saturday & now it's Tuesday. The morning they left I toddled along very bravely to the doctor's quite certain that I was about to undergo a nasty business. He gave me injections & then – we shan't go into nasty details, but he cut it neatly, & bandaged me up & sent me home... So once back on my bed, the deadness of the anaesthetic having departed & pain taken its place, I relapsed into silent sobbing.

One never really knows on such occasions, why one is sobbing, there are always so many reasons. I was left all alone in Medellin in wild Colombia with a cranky knee! No! I forgot, Bodie stayed on to keep an eye on me & to bring me to Barranquilla on Wednesday by plane...

My friends have been extremely good to me especially Smithie who brought me his wireless, his reading lamp, flowers, books & magazines galore. In fact, if it hadn't been for Smithie I would have gone by river & perhaps my whole leg would have been chopped off by now! Ray & Bernie the two rather slimy but kindly American brothers visit me every day. Also Gottschalt junior, nasty little man, Hans Weil & his terribly modern young wife, & Bodie of course.

I made three more visits to the doctor & every time he poured iodine into the hole, or did something particularly painful, Bodie would hang onto my hand & say, 'That's a brave little English girl, a real little English girl!' while I wriggled in desperate silence in my chair. She has a weird idea that all English people are brave, noble, honest & clean...

The flight to Barranquilla lasted two hours. The heat rushed up to meet us as we stepped from the plane, but fortunately Hilary, Hilja & Hanny sprang out from nowhere & relieved us of our numerous small packages... That evening we gave our première. The house was full, & the evening ran smoothly. I was required for one dance only, 'Mozart'. This was our first experience of dancing in real heat. We sweated profusely, & found it impossible to retain make up but on the other hand there was no desperate fight for air, no sudden catch in the chest. One could dance and go on dancing, throwing oneself exultantly into the air & still keep on going...

The journey to Cartagena we made by sea plane. We skimmed along the river about half a mile before taking off. It was beautifully done! The windows were large & with the wings being underneath we were able to see for miles. We passed great forests, jungle, long stretches of coast & swamps. In 35 minutes we came in sight of Cartagena...

The quaintness of the town struck us immediately but our impression of the hotels was not so good. The only respectable one, Hotel Americano, was full. Somebody mentioned there being a small hotel on the sea, I jumped at the idea & begged that we should see it. We were perfectly 'entzückt'[12] on sighting an attractive building with great balconies situated on the beach.

Deeper investigations revealed the drawbacks – despite the attractiveness of the situation a mere glance around was enough to assure us that it was none too clean, & primitive. Hilary & I decided that, despite all, we would rather live there 'midst romanticism & nature, than eke out a sweaty existence in the middle of that stifling town.

The others were not quite of the same opinion & returned to town, leaving Ehrmann as our bodyguard. We nibbled anxiously at our lunch, which we carried out onto the verandah in view of rolling breakers. The rest of the Group drove out in the afternoon & we bathed & revelled in the sun & fresh air...

We were to have given our première that evening, but all our costumes got stuck in the jungle, so it was postponed. We all went to an Open Air Cinema instead, which in itself was an exciting 'Erlebnis'.[13] Ehrmann left next morning in order to rescue our costumes...

Cartagena is still hotter than Barranquilla, probably the hottest place in South America. We perspired accordingly. I never felt more like Niagara Falls in all my life... At midnight three stealthy figures crept down to the water & refreshed themselves in the Caribbean...

I executed my 'Faun' for the first time in weeks, taking care to fall on the other knee. I was shockingly excited about it, & childishly delighted with the strength of the applause... Several mornings running I had an hour's dancing lesson for my new dance 'Adoracion del Sol'[14] (Gebet an die Sonne). I adored those private lessons with Bodie & Murillo. The music was his, (zusammen gestellt von verschiedene Indianishe Motiven[15])...

The officers [of a Colombian ship in port] took the Revista to a small Negro village Passakabia, on the coast. The road was atrocious but the evening was a dream. There had been a great bullfight that day, the greatest event of the year. The Torrero had been gored to death by the bull,

---

[12] Charmed.
[13] Experience.
[14] Adoration of the Sun.
[15] Adapted from several Inca themes.

causing even a little more excitement & enjoyment than the citizens had expected. We stopped the car in the main street & carefully picked our way on foot through buckets of mud. It had rained profusely, turning all the 'main streets' into cow yards. Eventually we reached the village square, where the great bullfight had been held. Everything was pitch black, no electric light, no moon – we had to find our way by the light of the stars & the torches held high in the hands of the dancers, dancing in the centre of the plaza to an African band.

Enthralled, we stood & watched these dancers, who as if in a trance, went on dancing & dancing. The movements originated from the hips down, the upper part remaining almost motionless. The women, scantily dressed in coloured rags and men's felt hats, held six lit candles above their heads, & glided through the mud, wet oozing through their toes. The men danced in circles round the women until they were pushed away by another, but not perturbed each continued his extraordinary wobbling from the hips, & in his turn pushed away another fellow & took a new girl. The dance seemed to mesmerise both dancers & onlookers alike. The expressions of the male dancers were intriguing. Some as if in a trance kept on dancing with a faraway dreamy look on their faces; others with elation & smug contentment, & grins stretching from ear to ear. The women on the other hand were expressionless, and continued to move round & round, the grease from their candles gilding white circles over their shoulders, their hair.

I felt lifted by this dance, & strangely & unaccountably elated. This dance meant religion to these people, & it could have appeared sordid & distasteful but I couldn't see it that way. On the contrary, I felt something inside me burning with a fire no sermon & no minister had ever produced. It was so ethereal, so magic. Those dark figures wriggling in ecstatic movements to the monotonous boom, boom, boom of the drum, & the low crooning & clapping of toothless old women who crouching in the middle of the circle, never lost the rhythm. Torchlight lit up their dark & sweaty faces, eerie but almost beautiful in their transformation.

I felt magnetised, & it was only after many entreaties on the part of the others that I was finally persuaded to go – broken out of a spell as it were. Everyone had been moved, I could see that. Nobody spoke a word all the way home, except for one instant, when some drunk held us up & threatened in a hoarse whisper to shoot us dead if we didn't hand over all the money we had. The driver merely drove off & a shot followed but he was far too drunk to hit anything. We arrived home at 7.30am, after one of the greatest & most impressive experiences in my life.

We were dragged out of bed very early next morning as an early start for Barranquilla had been planned. We had to hang around until 2 o'clock when Ehrmann finally managed to procure a trolley car for the 'Revista'.

We travelled for four hours through half-jungle, halting only occasionally at tiny villages. I spied some magnificently coloured birds, but of greatest interest were the vast swamped areas, & flooded villages. Peaceful little streets had turned into raging torrents, the water having risen above the window ledges of the deserted houses. All the inhabitants of the village were huddled together in tents & cattle shelters on raised land. Small naked children paddled fragile wooden canoes between the deserted houses, fishing for dead & bloated pigs, bedraggled cats, & hens.

We were well into darkness before the driver called a halt. Ehrmann descended with orders that we were to remain seated until he returned. Clouds of mosquitoes descended upon us. We turned the lights out, & sat in silence watching the fireflies & listening to the singing of cicadas & the croaking of frogs in the swamps. It was sticky & oppressive, & we were grubby & desperately hungry. After what seemed a lifetime Ehrmann returned, & told us to get out with all our hand articles & to walk very carefully because we had streams to cross.

We decided by light of candles & an occasional torch, that this was but another flooded village. In semi-darkness we proceeded to make our way across the streets, balancing precariously upon planks, & none too broad at that. Smelly little boys held our hands & waded through the water up to their waists. Fat old Murillo looked a trifle alarmed & we all took jolly good care to avoid walking on the same plank as he. We were just beginning to congratulate each other on having crossed safely when a loud grunt reached our ears, followed by a muffled shriek & – splash – Ehrmann startled by the sudden grunt of a pig lost his balance & fell headlong into the swamp. He appeared such a comical spectacle smeared from head to foot in black stinking dirt, & soaked to the skin, wearing such a disgusted countenance, that we burst out laughing – which was the final thrust at his hurt pride. He suddenly disappeared & we were left to the guidance of small boys till we reached the hotel.

… A terribly disappointing & unsatisfying meal was put before us… the usual depressing répas [16] *of rice, beans, papaya, bananas & tough meat (we didn't inquire of what breed). We still had two and a half hours to*

---

[16] Meal.

put in until the river ferry arrived at Kalamar at midnight. To wait in the hotel was unthinkable, the mosquitoes being atrocious. Walking was out of the question, every street being flooded, so at last we took a bedroom where Hilja, Hilary & I thought to sleep. The room was said to be mosquito proof, but it wasn't. We lay there whacking & banging, & cursing in agony & annoyance until midnight.

We slept on camp beds on the river boat deck, & between insects & a biting wind, with no coats nor blankets to cover us, we passed the rest of a very miserable evening. The sunrise was lovely & the Magdalena River was huge & swift, but the relief was great on spying the first roof of Barranquilla. The adventure wasn't much fun at the time, but we had many a laugh later. However, Kalamar was the cause of Greta's malaria which she developed three weeks later. I think Bodie was crazy to allow us to take such chances, but Cartagena hadn't been successful financially & we couldn't afford the more pleasant return journey by plane.

…We began performing again in the Teatro Apollo, the theatre with the large stage, but which held so many people that even a good audience seemed a mere nothing… I found Xmas shopping rather a problem in Barranquilla, but used up the last of my 'Garge'[17] on a little red umbrella purse for Hilary, chocolates & cigarettes for the girls, for Bodie & for Ehrmann.

…It was a very hot Xmas Day, & we had to work hard. Tommy called & took us to Mr & Mrs Laxtons' for Xmas dinner… We had only just finished the turkey however, & hadn't even smelt the plum pudding before we had to dash off to the theatre to prepare for the first of three performances that day. As anticipated, the audiences were poor, & our performance not too brilliant. All of us had no more than diez Candavos in our pockets, & the Meloparodista[18] & all those who relied entirely on the money they made from day to day were in rather a bad way. Xmas presents amongst them were rare & meagre, but they bore up pluckily & made light of the tedious afternoon. I admired them for it. Admired them for the gay & easy way in which they dispelled all worries & unhappiness because it was Christmas! Strehn, Relly, Wiener Cissy, Gotthelf, Spiegel, Herbert, Greta, Hanny, Bodie & Marcel – none could ever return to Austria. They would never again spend glorious Xmases in Vienna with their own people, in their own country which had turned against them.

---

[17] Wages.
[18] Entertainers who performed with the Vienna Ballet as part of the Revista Vienesa.

Hilary & I found Xmas Day on the whole rather amusing. It's not every day that one has the chance of spending Xmas in the tropics of South America on the stage!

...On New Year's Eve the whole 'Revista' turned up at the big dance hall, at the end of the pier. This was a charity ball at which we had promised to dance for the many hundreds of Jewish immigrants who arrive in Colombia every month, with not a Groschen in their pockets. The place had been decorated & numbers grew as the last day of 1938 came rapidly to an end... I did my 'Faun' which had of course to be extra specially good that evening... We did a waltz but without Poldi, as she was afraid that it might reach German ears in Vienna that she had danced in aid of the Jewish refugees. We also danced Bambuco, the old favourite, which had to be encored... Towards midnight everyone became very gay – paper hats, streamers & noisy instruments were distributed & the noise was terrific. The old year was dying... It had been a grand year, we all agreed, & who knows what great joy he would bring with him, this New Year, and what tragedies & sorrow!

...Hilary & I shifted from the Hotel Astoria to Hotel Royal, a German Hotel, where Bodie, Hanny, Hilja and Ehrmann were staying. Our engagement in the Barranquilla theatres was through. We were to mark time until Ehrmann had arranged something for us in Santa Marta, or Cuba, or Mexico or somewhere. Meanwhile we were slowly using up the tiny sum we had saved from our erratic salaries – so Hilary & I desired cheaper lodgings.

...Ehrmann had fallen very much in love with Hanny... Another German Jew, Block by name, also began paying her attention & Ehrmann didn't like it... Actually Hanny had a young Viennese fiancé awaiting her in USA... Eventually things became uncomfortably strained between Ehrmann and Hanny. As a result Hanny left the hotel & they never spoke to each other again.

...Hanny had a relapse soon after & grew hysterical & her nerves seemed all on edge. She gave way to tears easily & seemed quite 'ausser sich'. [19] *She held herself distant from all of us... Then came the day when Hanny announced her departure from the Group... It was as well I suppose...*

Poldi was sharing a room with Greta & they became friendly. Poldi had always been rather 'odd man out' & hadn't fitted in particularly. Now she chummed up with Greta & Herbert, & the Meloparodistas & we saw little of her at that workless time in Barranquilla. Unfortunately

---

[19] Beside herself

Herbert persuaded her that Frau Gerty should have paid her more salary & that she had been swindled. Poldi allowed Herbert to put through a complaint together with Greta demanding more money. A case was brought up against Bodie for broken promises...

Hilja, Hilary & I trooped along to the Court & confirmed that we were perfectly satisfied with the money we had been paid... They lost their case & we all felt sick about it. Bodie was terribly hurt. For a while she considered leaving Poldi behind, but later decided that Poldi was necessary for the survival of the Group. We were forced to take the unpleasant child into our midst & dance with her.

Barranquilla – January 1939

Two weeks had passed & the Revista Vienesa was without work. However, Ehrmann had soon arranged an engagement for Bucaramanga & possibly further towns to follow. The only method of approach to this town was by river boat, and I was determined not to miss this jungle trip.

...The river barge, an old cast-off from the Mississippi, was due to leave at 3 o'clock. Tommy saw us off & Hanny too. I felt very sad to leave the latter behind. She was a big part of the Revista. We were going to miss her.

Can you imagine anything more romantic than sleeping out on deck 'neath a bestarred sky & a tropical moon 'exotifying' the gruesome shapes of the jungle on either side? There were times of course when sudden swarms of mosquitoes descended & commenced devouring one without mercy & the heat during the middle of the day was insufferable. The food... was indescribable.

The Magdalena River was at some stages tremendously wide, that one could almost imagine a lake. Sometimes we drew up close to the shore enabling us a view of jungle life. Brightly feathered parrots called harshly at our approach, monkeys swung with amazing agility almost above our heads. We saw long green & brown lizards, & [heard] strange cries of unknown animals... Frequently on sand banks, what we at first glance took to be logs of wood, turned out to be crocodiles with tremendous mouths! Tortoises too, & electric snakes!! A passenger on board had snakes in boxes whose poison he had extracted. He allowed me to take one on my hand which rapidly began shooting up my arm & grew very active.[20]

---

[20] Bodenwieser, who at the time was horrified, remembered the incident well, and later in Australia she created a new solo for me called Snake Charmer, which became one of my most successful dances.

We reached Puerto Wilches on the afternoon of the third day. Ehrmann enquired about transport to Bucaramanga. It appeared nothing was travelling in that direction till morning... No-one appeared overjoyed – as Puerto Wilches consists only of one hotel, one street of decrepit houses & a jetty & a railway shed – otherwise there existed jungle, heaps of it, & a grey greasy old Magdalena River.

...We were up to an early breakfast, for the train left at 6.30am. The journey was thrilling but not long. The train started climbing towards midday, until we left all traces of jungle far behind. It was humid, so in search of a little fresh air I made my way shakily through all the carriages & stood on a narrow platform on the last carriage, clutching fiercely at an iron chain, staring with greedy eyes – loving it all – loving everything...

We descended at a station with an unpronounceable name... [and] tumbled into a ramshackle old bus if ever there was one. Loud agonised shrieks were produced from the engine as we set off. The luggage on the roof creaked & rattled dangerously, whilst the whole charabanc rocked & swayed at every corner. We had to stop often to pick up fallen luggage. Only a single board separated us from the engine, so that our legs trembled with the vibration. On alighting we all went on shaking as if with ague. It was a hellish journey, & we were relieved to find ourselves in Bucaramanga.

...A rather ugly episode caused some unhappiness... a cable came from Poldi's father, saying that her sister was seriously ill & Poldi was to leave immediately for home. Conditions having been strained since Barranquilla between Poldi & the Ballet, Bodie was inclined to believe that Poldi had requested her father to do this. Bodie made Poldi cable back inquiring if it were really urgent. Poldi did so with bad grace, & the reply came 'Urgent'. We were all rather upset about it, especially as a new contract had been made for Bucaramanga & Cúcuta. Bodie was still pondering the matter, when Ehrmann came to us with the startling news that Poldi had gone. We learned that she had caught the river boat back to Barranquilla where she would wait a few days for a German ship returning to Europe.

...The whole Revista was to travel by bus to Cúcuta but one of the Germans Hilary & I had met happened to be leaving the same day for the same place by car. He generously offered to take three of us with him... and so we rolled out of Bucaramanga, our tour dangerously near its end. Our journey promised to be something extra special. And it was. We soon started on a steep ascent, & we noticed the gradual change of vegetation from banana palms & cocoa to moss covered banks & the lichened boughs *of great trees hanging like Gothic arches over the highway – sometimes almost hidden in a thick mist. Large drops of water hung from the fronds of towering fern trees – the foliage reminded me of N.Z. – the dampness also. The road changed in character with every mile & sometimes it seemed we were crawling along the edge of a precipice. We had a strange picnic at 12,000 feet, on a small plateau overlooking ranges of harsh barren mountains – & behind these mountains one could see still another range, & yet another.*

From this point we began a rapid descent... For supper we reached Pamplona, the largest town at such a height (9,800 feet) in the country. The remainder of the journey consisted of makeshift roads cut wickedly through the heart of coffee plantations, & temporary lifts along the side of the swollen river... A glorious sunset heralded our arrival into the city of Cúcuta.

...Cúcuta was a fairly interesting town, but Hillox & I always felt it rather absurd that though the only remaining dancers were Hilja, Hil & self we were still announced in bold print as the Ballet Vienesa. 'And the funniest part about it,' we laughed, 'is that none of us are Viennese!'

Arranza had to be Hilja's partner in 'Bambuco', & Cissy took Poldi's part in 'Torbellino' & Bodie did 'Joropo'. Otherwise we managed our dances, the three of us, & I doubt if we had ever danced better.

...Here the inevitable break with the Meloparodistas came to pass. For a goodly time, the Melos had been kicking against the traces, complaining against their pay, arguing about the order of the programme... One day we heard they had packed up & left for Bogota by bus.

After two final appearances ...we too packed up & returning to Pamplona, gave one performance.

The ten months dancing throughout the length and breadth of Colombia, completely free from parental control, proved a liberating experience and a wonderful, if exhausting adventure for Hilary and myself. For others it was a very different story. The tour had succeeded in providing escape from the Nazis for many of our party. Now we each had to look to the future. As the rumbles of war continued in Europe, none of the Austrian members of the Revista Vienesa had any wish to return. Bodenwieser endured much heartache during these months of forced separation from home and loved ones, yet she kept up with the daily demands of teaching, rehearsing, performing and constant travel without complaint. As weeks became months and she still received no word as to the fate of her husband,

Dr Rosenthal, who had thought to escape the Nazis by remaining in Paris, she began to fear the worst. These fears were at last realised when she received a crumpled card from a German concentration camp. She recognised the scarcely decipherable handwriting as her husband's. This was the final word she would ever receive from him.

Frau Gerty was considering following me to New Zealand, as she sought a new country in which to settle and teach the New Dance. However, she still did not know if her sister and nephew would join her in Colombia and it was possible she might receive visas for the United States. She felt America would be more receptive to her artistry than what she called the 'unknown territories of the Antarctic'!

Although it had been clear for some time that our South American adventure was drawing to its inevitable close, the actual leave-taking was sad for me. Hilary's aunt had been sent by her family in Tsingtao to Bogota with strict instructions that she must not return to China without her niece.

As Hilary began enquiring about a steamer to China, I counted my pesos, wondering if I had sufficient to get me back to New Zealand. Things were made a little easier by the fact that Hilary and her aunt were travelling as far as Panama with me. Hilary and I then had to face the realisation that after living and dancing together for so long, we were about to be pulled asunder. She would board a ship destined for China and her family,[21] while I boarded the SS *Remuera* for New Zealand. The thought seemed quite unbearable. When would we meet again?

I felt so unhappy the first few days on board that I scarcely noticed how the passengers avoided me. A dancer boarding a ship alone in Panama obviously brooked no good. The lifestyle of such a person didn't bear thinking about! The exceptions were several young New Zealand farmers returning from their first overseas trip who helped lift my spirits with their friendly society – and by now I had learned how to handle the over-attentive.

I experienced mixed feelings as the SS *Remuera* docked at Lyttelton wharf. Uppermost was the sight of those familiar Port Hills, the cry of the gulls, the very smell of a land nearly forgotten.

---

[21] Hilary returned to China where soon after she became a solo artist in her own dance programme. This took her to many parts of the East under direction of the celebrated A. Strok of Pavlova fame.

Now, having just celebrated my nineteenth birthday on the high seas, I was returning a well-travelled professional dancer with an adventurous turn of mind, and showing a preference for all things foreign.

Mother was waiting for me in Dunedin and the thought of seeing my sister and her young family after so many years, as well as my brother and Edith, now ensconced in their Southland farm, helped ease the pain in my heart. My four years away from home had been crucial years, so that returning to the scenes of my childhood seemed unreal. I felt as disorientated as Rip Van Winkel must have, returning to his village after a sleep of 100 years. New Zealand was more beautiful than I had remembered, but smaller. Everything seemed smaller, quieter, and with so few people on the streets. I began to wonder if Frau Gerty was right, and whether New Zealand was ready to accept the New Dance.

In 1939, the country could not yet boast a ballet company, very little theatre, and had never been exposed to the Central European expressive dance which Bodenwieser and I were planning to introduce. To my very great joy, Bodenwieser wrote to tell of her final decision to come to New Zealand, with her musical director Marcel Lorber. However, upon hearing that six of her Viennese trained dancers were arriving in Australia in a Williamson and Tait Revue, Bodenwieser, Marcel and I agreed that we should move to Sydney and join them. Wellington saw a demonstration of the Bodenwieser technique and enjoyed several of her fascinating lectures before she departed. Major and Mother, finally having tied the knot as Major and Mrs Astley Campbell, were also finding it difficult to put down their roots – and so decided to join us in Australia.

Chapter Five

We lay and talked for a long time and after I had used every
argument against her marrying me, Shona suddenly seemed
quite indispensable to me and we came home by boat
under the most glorious sunset I have ever seen.

It was an emotional moment when the *Maunganui* docked at
Woolloomooloo and Frau Gerty embraced her Viennese
dancers. She had not expected to see them again. Sydney being
much larger and more cosmopolitan than Wellington presented a
happier picture to Bodenwieser, especially as it was home to several
of her dancers. For the first time since fleeing her beloved Wien she
began to feel a little hopeful. Her family and friends were lost to
her, but at least her art could continue. By immersing herself in
work, she could perhaps learn to overcome some of the pain and
anguish she had known.

The dancer I knew best in the new Bodenwieser Ballet was
Emmy Towsey (Taussig) who had prepared us for the South
American tour. I had taken classes in Vienna with Bettina Vernon
and Melitta Melzer and was still greatly in awe of an outstanding
member of the original Viennese Group, Evelyn Ippen. I had not
met Katya Georgieva, a Bulgarian by birth. In a very short time
Bodenwieser had us stretching our minds and bodies in a determined
effort to attain a standard of dance worthy of our teacher, and in
preparation for a dazzling entry onto the Australian stage.

August 1939 was not the most auspicious time for artists with
German passports and German accents to arrive in a loyal outpost
of the British Empire. The ominous approach of war must have
filled the hearts of my Austrian friends with new misgivings. The
early days of adjusting to what Bodenwieser dejectedly referred to
as 'this so beautiful desert' were difficult for all of them. Bodenwieser

and Emmy possessed a good command of English although their accents were strong, but the others struggled at first. I was greatly in demand as interpreter. The dancers were, thankfully, never subject to internment, but their movements during the war years were always checked. The first requirement during state tours made by the Bodenwieser Viennese Ballet was to report to the police station.

Until Bodenwieser was able to set up her own studio in 210 Pitt Street, she was loaned space by Vera Mathews in her School of Exercise. A kind and generous woman, Vera was one of the first in Sydney to appreciate Bodenwieser as a great artist. After some months of strenuous rehearsing our debut took place before a curious audience. The Conservatorium of Music, which resembled a medieval castle set alongside the Botanical Gardens, proved an ideal venue and for years to come remained our favourite Sydney theatre. Until then, with the exception of a few soloists, no modern expressive dance had been seen in Australia. To our relief and pleasure the Australian audience seemed enraptured by our performance, and it was not long before we built up a perceptive and discriminating following.

From this time on not even the outbreak of war could diminish the popularity of the Bodenwieser Ballet, or reduce the numbers of pupils who dragged themselves up the stairs to learn and experience the joys of the New Dance. Bodenwieser, who in the past never had to concern herself with the collection of fees, simply placed a cigarette tin on the piano top. Naturally, this method was not effective! The studio was unstable financially until Bodenwieser's assistants took over the task of tracking down fees.

Those years I danced in Australia with Bodenwieser were never subsidised. From the beginning she drew from her own meagre resources to meet production costs of the new ballets. The state tours were run on a shoestring. It was just as difficult for her dancers of course, but being some 20 to 30 years younger, they carried with them a youthful optimism for the future which Bodenwieser no longer allowed herself.

In April 1940, despite the escalation of war, we began our first National Tour. Tasmania was chosen as the ideal location to begin. Unfortunately, our parsimonious impresario bought us only third-class fares. We struck a particularly rough passage and because we were unable to face the stuffy cabins, situated right over the engines, some of us preferred to see out the night on deck. On opening night

I literally staggered through my parts with a sharp pain in my chest, racing back to a spartan stone dressing room at every opportunity to try and warm my shivering body. The doctor declared that I had contracted double pneumonia. It was a serious blow. I was rushed to Stowell Hospital where I remained for six weeks, unable to accompany the ballet on their tour of Australia. It was several months before I fully recuperated. When they returned the dancers entertained me with fascinating anecdotes from their tour, including the story of the black-faced coal miners who gazed amazed at this treat the Coal Board had offered up, while the dancers were forced to wear bedroom slippers to keep warm in the unheated theatre!

Before long the Bodenwieser Ballet was involved in supporting the war effort. We gave our services for dozens of causes: Airforce House, The Red Cross, The Red Army, The Free French Fighting Force, The Czechoslovakian Fighting Forces in France, and many more. The performance to assist the Czechoslovakian Force was a shared programme with the visiting Colonel de Basil Ballet Russes Company, whose lead dancers were the glamorous stars, Vera Nemtchinova, Tamara Toumanova, Serge Lifar, Nina Verchinina, Tatiana Riabouchinska, David Lichine, Olga Morosova, Yura Lazovsky, and Paul Petroff.

We were at this time as mistrustful of classical ballet as they certainly were of 'the moderns', but the very fact that this Russian Ballet was considered almost forbidden fruit made them seem more attractive to us. We couldn't resist watching them perform, dazzled by their technical virtuosity, but we felt rather guilty in doing so, believing, like most exponents of the New Dance, that classical ballet had nothing to say in the modern world. To our astonishment, some of the ballets presented by the Ballet Russes Company during their Sydney season were new, and very exciting. On our combined programme, which was stage-managed by Czech-born Edouard Borovansky, the de Basil Company presented excerpts from *Aurora's Wedding*, *Swan Lake*, *Blue Danube*, *The Three Ivans* and an exquisite solo from *The Snow Queen* by Nina Verchinina, while the Bodenwieser Ballet performed three popular numbers: *Sunset*, *Demon Machine* and *Slavonic Dance*.

Special permission allowed us to dance for troops in military hospitals on the Sabbath. Seldom did we receive more than expenses, but apart from the knowledge that we were in our small way playing a part in frustrating the Nazis, we were becoming recognised as artists of integrity and loyal citizens of the land. As the war intensified in the Pacific, money grew tighter and tighter. It was taken for granted that all services to the war effort were given free of charge and this made things very difficult for the group. Baby-sitting, crocheting, making string bags, and housework were some of the easier ways of keeping the wolf from the door. Some saved a few shillings by doubling up or even trebling in one room.

Before long Evelyn, Emmy, Bettina and I opened schools of modern expressive dance in the various suburbs where we lived. There was no shortage of pupils, and in time our financial position improved. By arrangement with Frau Gerty, I became her assistant for many of her classes. These took place in the Sydney studio but we also made weekly train journeys to instil grace into the girls of Woodford House Finishing School, the YMCA and longer trips to Abbotsleigh College on the North Shore. This was a wonderful opportunity for me to learn Bodenwieser's teaching method and technique first hand. Daily company classes, usually followed by rehearsal, teaching and performing made for very full days. I kept a bicycle behind the railway station and enjoyed the ten minute ride home. As we frequently danced in the evening, and were entertained at the end of the programme by our hosts or, failing that, a boyfriend, I often found myself wrapping a long skirt around the handle bars as I sped home in the 'wee hours'.

It seems remarkable that I was always able to find my way home at the end of the day, because my mother shifted house and district so often! It was impossible for her to purchase a house in Sydney during the war because New Zealand would not release sufficient currency. The houses we rented had leases for only six or twelve month periods, but at least we got to see the country. We moved from Lindfield to Killara, to Roseville, to Pymble, to Palm Beach and to Turramurra.

As restrictions eased my mother decided she would build her own house. She discovered a section on a Palm Beach headland some yards above the crashing surf, facing the lights of Barrenjoey lighthouse. This was where after years of nomadic living she would build her dream house. Major was dubious, I was enthralled, and the architect was very excited to be given this opportunity to show off his skill. The builder was less co-operative. 'This section is too steep,' he exclaimed. 'To get my material to the site I would have to build a railway first!' 'Then build it!' cried Mother. Building material was still in short supply, but luckily we found a highly recommended material known as Dampney's Cement. These were ten inch blocks consisting of ash, gravel and cement, and seemed to suit our needs admirably. It was only later, after Mother had sold 'Pegasus', and we heard that the toilet had slipped down the hill, that we questioned the long-term success of Dampney's Cement!

For the next few years I boarded with friends in town through the week, then swiftly headed for 'Pegasus'. As a bathing beach, Palm Beach was unsurpassed, and unlike many was green and shaded. Koalas nestled in the gums, while at night wombats snuffled in the undergrowth. The Palm Beach weekend situation suited me nicely, for it gave me more time to spend with a remarkable couple with whom I had formed a warm friendship. 'Golden Wind', the home of Lucas and Isobel Staehelin, became my second home. Works of art from Switzerland, the Pacific Islands and contemporary Australia adorned the walls of their attractive house. Under that roof, where the arts were taken seriously, my taste matured.

Lucas had left his native Switzerland to follow in the footsteps of Gauguin and he met Isobel while boarding with her family in Sydney. He loved the charm of the recorder flute and formed and trained a recorder ensemble. Every Thursday evening a group of seven or eight enthusiasts met and with bass, alto, tenor and soprano we were soon able to give a passable account of the sixteenth century music of Telemann, Orlando Gibbons, Josquin des Prez, Orlando Lasso, Palestrina, as well as some Schubert and Swiss folk songs. Before long we were playing in public concerts and in hospitals.

Isobel and I quickly became great friends. Lovers of art, music and theatre, the Staehelins responded to dance with equal enthusiasm. Isobel became a staunch Bodenwieser Ballet fan, attending all our concerts. She persuaded me to start dance classes for friends who were, like her, young mothers. My first godchild was Roslind Shona Staehelin, a little sister to Andrew.

I took holidays with them to the seaside but most memorably to Mt Wilson which lay beyond the more popular Blue Mountains north of Sydney. From 'Windyridge', an appealing Swiss-style villa, Lucas, Isobel and I took our flutes into the Australian bush, home to the common lyre birds. For several successive days we played a short Mozart aria many times over and by the end of the week we could hear in the distance the first four bars sung back to us. Before we left, the lyre bird (or perhaps several) rendered our Mozart aria almost to perfection. We also were fortunate to see a lyre bird courting dance.

Lucas suggested our ballet give a dance performance in their garden at 'Golden Wind' in aid of the Red Cross. Selecting the most appropriate dances in our repertoire, we danced in the floodlit garden, appearing and disappearing between the gum trees. Never had I performed my faun dance in so ideal a setting, feeling truly a woodland creature in that magic garden.

I spent nine years in Sydney dancing, teaching, touring, and assisting Mother and Major to shift from house to house, suburb to suburb. I taught children from five years of age in my own school of dance in the Killara and Lindfield Masonic Halls, and when there was a lull in the Bodenwieser Ballet's performance and touring engagements, I worked towards a dance recital of my own pupils. I enjoyed my first efforts in choreography, which were largely derivative of the dances I assisted Bodenwieser teach. I didn't question that I had a talent, but I believe working so closely to Bodenwieser's powerful creativity slowed down the discovery of my own.

My first longer ballet, *The Moving Finger* was inspired by the poem of Omar Khayyam and dealt with the passing of time. My second choreographic effort was based on Tennyson's *Lady of Shalott*. I was pleased to find emerging talent among my pupils. Some of the more ambitious moved on to classes with Bodenwieser in the city. Margaret Chapple[1] and Coralie Hinkley eventually became members of the Bodenwieser Ballet.

My greatest satisfaction came from continuing to work as a dancer under my astounding Viennese teacher. To be the material with which Gertrud Bodenwieser created her wonderful ballets was a great honour. All her dancers felt that they were destined to give physical reality to the work of a very great artist. The longer I knew Bodenwieser the surer I became of her artistic and intellectual strength. Although she clung to her dancers as her only ties to the past, we were all aware of the disparity in intellect. Eventually she did form friendships with people more like herself, yet being a very private person, she remained much alone.

As the youngest and least experienced dancer in her company when we first came to Australia, I was conscious of my limitations,

---

[1] Margaret Chapple became director of the Bodenwieser Dance Centre in Sydney until her death in 1996.

but with hard work and an absolute passion for dance, I began to make my mark. When the Viennese dancers married, had babies, or broke away to form their own companies, they were replaced by Australians, and I found myself at the top of the list. I liked that!

My life was not without romance. Circumstances brought to Australia a variety of young men who had escaped their beleaguered countries to fight under the British flag. I could boast of some weeks when I went out with a companion of a different nationality every night. Zygmont the Pole, Stephen the Hungarian, Hans the Austrian, Lucas the Swiss, Major Robert Dalsace a Free French Officer on leave from New Caledonia. Australian and New Zealand soldiers were also among my escorts, many en route to face guns, capture or death in Egypt and Crete. One of my friends, a naval officer, was seriously wounded in a sea battle on board the SS *Ajax*, while another vanished with his submarine in the waters of the Middle East. 'Missing, presumed dead' became a common explanation of the disappearance of many more. 'Eat, drink and be merry' was the attitude most young people adopted.

As the Pacific became the centre of Japanese aggression, thousands of American soldiers added to the quota of uniformed troops. Armed with gifts from silken parachutes to the first pure silk stockings we had seen, they were not short of female admirers. Not surprisingly, they were less than popular with the Australian forces, who for the first time were experiencing a shortage of dates when they came home on leave.

The husbands of Emmy and Evelyn were accepted into the home guard which gave them great satisfaction. Other German and Austrian refugee friends, believing they had escaped the concentration camps of Europe, now discovered they had simply exchanged these for the 'alien camps' of Australia. I did not find any who felt their lot to be unjust under this strange twist of fate.

My brother was demobbed from the British Air Force at the end of the war, and to Mother's joy he arrived unheralded at the 'Pegasus' front door. We had not seen Bonar for many years. He returned to us a pilot, not wounded in body, but certainly suffering in other ways. During the war years he had fought with the Finnish army against the Russians, had become cut off from the outside world, had escaped from a pestilent gaol, finally returning to England where he had joined the RAF. He served as a fighter pilot in the North African and Italian campaigns.

It took some time for Bonar to communicate and feel fully at ease with us. We worried about his depression, the aftermath of the dreadful things he had seen in warfare. The beauty of Palm Beach, the Hawkesbury River, Barrenjoey and the Pittwater must certainly have been balm to his soul, but so was the arrival into his life of a beautiful young woman. This was Margaret Chapple, my talented early pupil, who subsequently joined the Bodenwieser studio. Chappie, as we all knew her, became a friend of mine and frequently arrived at 'Pegasus' in the weekend, bearing great armfuls of Iceland poppies or bunches of sweet-smelling daphne for Mother. She proved the perfect medicine for my shattered brother and Mother and I watched developments eagerly.

Repatriation schemes, enabling returned soldiers to readjust and complete studies, gave Bonar the chance to attend the Sydney School of Art in 1945. His teacher, the highly regarded Lyndon Dadswell, recognised Bonar's talent and helped him regain confidence. Before long he was recommending Bonar as a sculptor for several large commissions in the city.

Suddenly we received an unexpected cable from Hilary in England, announcing that she was arriving in Sydney on a bride ship within a few weeks. This seemed a débâcle of the first order. Hilary had decided that with the end of hostilities, she was prepared to accept the offers of marriage Bonar had made to her in England. My brother was now faced with choosing between two women, both of whom were my dear friends. If he felt miserable, so did I.

By the time her mother arrived in Australia, Hilary had taken in the situation and decided to disappear for a while to allow Bonar time to make up his mind about whom he wished to marry. His first love won out, and big-hearted Chappie attended the wedding, even assisting the preparation for it. I found her attitude to the whole affair quite noble. She was incapable of the sort of resentment I am convinced I would have felt in such a situation.

The richest periods in my life seem to be followed by disaster. So it was in the loving Staehelin family. Isobel was expecting her third child and when her time came, was taken to hospital for the delivery.

26 December 1945

Pay last visit to Isobel. She is looking very beautiful – deep eyes. Took her shasta daisies with Xmas bush, and books.

Neither Isobel, nor her infant child ever returned. The true reason for her death was not revealed at the time, but we eventually learned that it was a medical error. Isobel had been administered a wrong blood-group during transfusion.

29 December

Chapple & Ken come to Palm Beach to break the news to me. Greatly depressed in mind and spirit. Pretty desperate. My poor family suffer for it.

This was my first encounter with death so close. I had never loved anyone so much nor as intensely as Isobel, and that she should die in this unexpected manner devastated me.

Grief-stricken and alone in my room at Palm Beach at the beginning of a new year, I missed Isobel terribly.

1 January 1946

Ils sont les jours tres miserables... Je suis meme presque mort. J'aime mieux et encore plus mon tres grande aimee. Jamais de la vie je serra comme j'etait.[2]

The moon rose and lit a path of light across the ocean. In my distress I became convinced that it would lead me to Isobel. If my mother had not restrained me at the cliff edge I believe I would have joined my friend that night.

As Isobel's closest friend, and frequent member of the household, it was natural that Lucas began to look to me more and more as a substitute. I was fond of Lucas and treasured the memories we shared, however I felt unable to become his wife. The situation became extremely awkward. Many people, including Isobel's mother, seemed to take it for granted that marriage would be the natural development, and for me the dilemma soon became intolerable. Isobel would have wished me to step into her place, I felt sure of that. Was it not my duty to do so and did I not owe her this?

The Sister present at Isobel's delivery made the remarkable decision to leave her calling and become housekeeper to Lucas, Andrew and little Roslind. Known as 'Mackie', she tried to fill the awful gap left by Isobel's death. It wasn't long before the children were calling her 'Mummie', and I suspect she hoped that it would soon become official.

---

[2] These are very miserable days. I am almost dead. I love more and more my great friend. I will never again be as I was.

The Revista Vienesa, Colombia 1938.
From left – Hilja Luukas, Poldi Peroutka, Shona Dunlop,
Hanny Kolm (standing), Hilary Napier.

Arriving in Cali

On the riverboat travelling down the Magdalena River.

Performing the Spanish Bolero at Barranquilla.

The Inconstant Prince at the Bogota Bull Arena.

Arriving at Medellin.
From left – Shona, Hanny,
Hilja, Hilary, Poldi, Bodie.

Local Bogotans

Hilary (left) and Shona with
friend, Bogota.

As the *Faun*, Wellington 1939.

Bodie (right) and Dory Stern at
Auckland Airport.

As Cain in *Cain and Abel*, Sydney 1940.

Making up for *Snake Charmer* at the Melbourne Town Hall.

Cinderella of Old Vienna. From left – Bettina Vernon, Bettina Brown, Emmy Taussig, Shona Dunlop, Evelyn Ippen.

Studio study for *Mask of Luzifer*.
From left – Evelyn Ippen, Emmy Taussig, Shona Dunlop.

Performing *O World* with Hilary (left) on the New Zealand tour, 1947.

I don't know whether Mackie knew more about the reasons for Isobel's death than she let on, but we all considered her sacrifice a truly noble one. It was a blow to her as it was for me when Lucas decided to return to Switzerland. The children were to be left in the care of relatives until their father was settled. A profusion of letters and telegrams from Switzerland over the next twelve months had me vacillating at times. Distance lends enchantment, but the passage of time also distances events and I no longer felt it my duty to take Isobel's place. Somehow I must have known fate had something different in store for me.

Bodenwieser began choreographing longer ballets rather than the exquisite cameo dances which were useful for charity performances and country tours. In the first of these, *Cain and Abel* (1941) I was given my most demanding and exciting role to date. I recall waiting in the wings of the Conservatorium inhaling large gulps of air in order to calm my nerves before the great leap heralding my entry. Cain was an eminently satisfying character to get inside of, and I felt considerable sympathy for him. He acted without thought but later tasted remorse, then terrible fear, as the voice of God began to hound him relentlessly: 'Cain, Cain, where is your brother Abel?' This filled me with such terror that I remember feeling that I must truly hide from God's wrath, and had to fight the urge to rush right out of the theatre.

Composer Marcel Lorber's uncanny feeling for dance was expressed nowhere more successfully than in *Cain and Abel*. He was able to identify completely with the kinetic, as well as the emotional requirements of dance, and the rapport was unfailing. The ballet's success owed a great deal to the Lorber score. Richard Parry and Dennis Glenny made the voice of God awesome, and audiences were impressed by the strikingly beautiful groupings, inspired by Bodenwieser's study of Renaissance paintings.

Bodenwieser made one of her rare appearances as Mother Eve in this ballet. Performing with her on stage was a special experience, and always raised the standard of our dancing. Evelyn, as a memorable Abel, danced her last significant role in the Bodenwieser Ballet. She and Bettina formed a partnership and eventually moved overseas.

Emmy and I frequently danced together after that. One of our most popular duos, *Russian Peasant Dance* with its high leaps could partly be responsible for my deteriorating knees of later years. The *Trilogy of Joan of Arc* (1945), the most ambitious of my solo dances, proved another test of endurance. The three scenes: Maiden, Soldier, Martyr and Saint, offered a wonderful variety of dynamics and expression. Frau Gerty created further solos for me, namely *The Cheat*, *Abandoned to Rhythm* and *Rosenkavalier Waltz*. All these numbers were in fact timeless, but in *The One and the Many* (1946) Bodenwieser drew her metaphor more directly from the effects of the present war upon society. She took the ubiquitous queue, formed by typists, business men, lovers, gang members, soldiers, mothers with child, etc. 'The Individual' enters, but does not join the queue, causing resentment from the others who, turning into a hostile mob, slowly encircle the non-conformist and force her to the ground. However she rises like a phoenix from the ashes, affirming Bodenwieser's belief in the triumph of the individual.

The last great Bodenwieser ballet I danced in Australia was the Eastern dance drama *O World* (1945), which was based upon the philosophy of Indian sage Krishnamurti, and used music by Tcherepnin. There were no men in the company at this time, so the role of the 'Glorious Prince' fell to me. I experienced the whole gamut of human emotions – the glory of victory, the ecstasy of love, the disillusionment to follow, scenes of great wealth and visions of inhumane poverty. This was another of Bodenwieser's prophetic masterpieces where she examined the paradoxes of warfare – the equally unacceptable conditions created for both victor and defeated. The victor enjoys the excesses which lead to shame, while the defeated endures the miseries of subjection. Touched by the situation around him, the Prince renounces his throne as the words of the prophet cry, 'Throw away O world thy vanity and follow me... to create happiness in others.' I could not have chosen a more satisfactory role in which to take my final bow. Emmy playing opposite me as 'The Chosen One' interpreted her role with great dramatic power. She so inspired me that I knew the last days of my dancing life were also my best.

There seems an almost uncanny parallel between The Glorious Prince and my own situation as I turned my back on a successful career at its height. Bodenwieser made a similar observation when writing to me later in China. 'Do you remember the words of the prophet in *O World*?' she wrote. 'For I know the way up the mountain, and I know the way of turmoil and grief.' I only wish that in climbing her mountain Bodenwieser had found it possible to free herself from *her* turmoil and grief.

The long-awaited tour of New Zealand took place in March and April 1947. This was a doubly happy occasion for me because Hilary and I (the only two Viennese-trained dancers left in the Company) were to appear as principals. The remaining dancers were by then all Australian. Crossing the Tasman on a troop carrier, we endured such atrocious conditions that the planned deck rehearsals never eventuated. While the ship plunged and heaved through mountainous seas, the director, the pianist and the ten seasick dancers scarcely managed to drag themselves as far as the dining room. The city of Wellington, crouched between the hills before a magnificent harbour, was a welcome sight. The tour extended from Auckland in the north to Invercargill in the south.

I was excited at the prospect of spending time with my sister Jocelyn, her husband and four children whom I had not seen in years, as well as my brother Wallace, Edith and their three. Upon arrival in Dunedin though, I was bitterly disappointed to discover Jocelyn in bed with the mumps. My long-awaited stay with the Ryburn family was no longer possible. However, in nearly every city we played there were cousins or aunts eager to offer us hospitality. The relatives were also anxious to meet Hilary, the newest member of the extended family.

It was a strange sensation to be returning to the land I had left as a child. I took considerable satisfaction in the knowledge that I returned head of a celebrated dance company, but I was equally proud to be able to show off the beauties of New Zealand to my impressed colleagues. Familiar landmarks in the South Island pulled at my heart. The sight of my birthplace at 121 Clyde Street, Dunedin brought back fond memories. The years fell away and I was once more the happy carefree child. Had I dreamed the travelling, dancing years, or was it the childhood years I had imagined? The first night we performed at His Majesty's Theatre in Dunedin my mind leapt back sixteen years, and I saw a young girl in a brown Archerfield School uniform standing on that very stage already tasting the power of performance and the attraction of applause.

I marvel at the way some unremarkable events can suddenly set off a whole chain reaction ending in momentous change. One of these proved to be my meeting with the Rev. John MacDonald MacTavish. After being discharged from the British Navy, Donald completed his Bachelor of Divinity at New College Edinburgh. He then wished to follow a boyhood dream to serve as a missionary to China, and decided he must farewell his family presently living in New Zealand, before venturing on the big journey. The SS *Shansi* was due to sail from Sydney in several weeks and Donald was taking services at city churches and speaking at meetings and making many friends.

Back in Melbourne the Bodenwieser Ballet was sharing a programme at the Tivoli Theatre with Chico Marx, when a letter arrived for me from good family friends, Dr and Mrs North. They invited me to dinner to meet the young Canadian minister on his way to China. I believed this must be the attractive young man I had met briefly two years before and never forgotten, and I was prepared to move heaven and earth to meet him again. The Melbourne box office had been good, and our impresario wished to extend our contract. Without fully understanding my own reasoning I would not agree and returned to Sydney with all speed.

I wore a red satin blouse complete with golden Chinese characters to the dinner. This turned out to be a better choice than I could have guessed. After playing the piano and singing some Russian folk songs, Donald turned his attention to my blouse. He picked out the characters he recognised – long life, happiness, fertility. His boyish charm and eager spirit had already disarmed me, but it was during the meal that the two of us shared a special secret. I alone noticed him drop a potato under the table, and his embarrassed glance across at me quickly changed to a grin when he spied a large tom cat appear from nowhere to gobble it up. Later Donald insisted on accompanying me home by metro to Turramurra. He told me about the Manchurian Mission he was heading for and asked me to test his Chinese characters. He took my pulse approvingly, declaring mine to be the lowest pulse of any girl he had known. Apparently this stood me in high favour!

From Donald's diary – 26 May 1948

In the evening I went to Dr North's, and there met, to my surprise, Shona Dunlop, whom I had seen last for a few minutes only, two years before. She was wearing a novel blouse on which were printed some Chinese characters. Dr North and I had great fun deciphering these. We also enjoyed a great singsong. It was so late by the time I saw Shona home that I stayed the night at Mrs Campbell's, being given Shona's room and reading for a while a book on China.

While he slept in my bed, I shoved clothes and boxes off the bed in the spare room and tried with little success to sleep. Donald would be leaving in a week or two. I realised I had to work fast. I heard him preach, play the piano, and saw him collect admiring friends wherever he went. I somewhat desperately asked him if he was interested in learning something about the Aborigines? He was, and yes, he believed he could spare the time to accompany me to the Aborigine settlement of La Perouse. We watched some desultory boomerang throwing, ate delicious John Dory fish at a seaside restaurant, then crossed over Botany Bay to Cronulla to discover Cook's first landing place in New South Wales, and inspect the graves of several of his crew.

Having given a measure of respect to Australian history, we sought out a private piece of bush. Donald climbed a gum tree to make a sailor's judgement on our position. 'Come down Zaccheus,' I cried. 'You will dine at my table. I have laid out sandwiches on the beach'. From then on our conversation became a sparring match, turning unmistakably to the prospect of marriage. Donald insisted he could not take me from a fulfilling and promising career into the obscurity and hardship of a missionary lifestyle in far-flung Manchuria. I assured him that it sounded like a wonderful challenge to me – that I was in sympathy with his mission, and that over and above all I loved him, and was prepared to give up everything that I had known to be with him and become his wife.

We crossed Botany Bay under a most glorious sunset which we took to be a benediction. Any qualms I may have held about this momentous step were swept aside by this manifestation of beauty, grandeur and yes, surely approval from above! We returned home eager to announce our engagement, and found a comical sight – Mother in bed with her umbrella up and rain pouring in through an open window. (This, the latest of her building exploits, had not gone according to plan. The promised completion date had arrived with windows still not installed. Unfazed, Mother occupied the house.) We shared our wonderful news with her. Emerging from beneath her umbrella Mother delightedly set about preparing a late meal for us. She served it on a trolley before an open fire, but I was so excited that I hardly ate a single morsel. So much to do and only three weeks before the SS *Shansi* would set sail for China. What had I done?

I AM ENGAGED

In morning with Shona to La Perouse... went inland and thought to cross the peninsula which seemed quite narrow, but walked a considerable distance in large arc, finally coming to the sea where sheer cliffs fell to the rocks 100ft below. We lay and talked for a long time and after I had used every argument against her marrying me, Shona suddenly seemed quite indispensable to me and we came home by boat under the most glorious sunset I have ever seen.

... Shona said she wanted to kiss me when we stood at the door, Saturday. And that she loved me when she saw me wearing my clerical collar. So the much maligned collar has done me a good turn at last...

The following weeks passed in frantic activity. My first and most difficult task was to write to Frau Gerty telling her as gently as possible about my forthcoming marriage, and requesting a release from the impending Bodenwieser Ballet tour of Queensland. I felt keenly as if I were absconding, yet realised that the time had arrived to withdraw from a now completely Australian Bodenwieser Ballet Company. Frau Gerty's reaction was a relief, and more generous than I could have hoped. 'I reluctantly release you from your contract Shoni,' she wrote, 'and wish you every happiness for a rich and wonderful life with your new husband.'

3 June (Donald's diary)

I've been lying awake for such a long time. I've thought of so many things, but mostly about Shona. Her lips, so soft and delectable, her eyes with their steady frank look, her long dark lashes, her mouth provokingly and winsomely petulant, her lithe young body like a panther, strong, vibrant and vital. And she is mine: Mine: MINE: Is this fierce possessive feeling wrong?

3 June (Donald's letter to brother Jim)

I met Shona 2 years ago in Sydney for 10 minutes but I never forgot her and when I met her again last Thursday – golly! Just a week ago, I knew that was the one!

She is the Prima Ballerina of the Bodenwieser Ballet. She speaks Austrian, German, French & Spanish. She was to have starred in the Command Performance when the King & Queen come to Australia next year. Instead she is marrying this old crock and ruining a wonderful career by leaving for China in three weeks' time. Boy! What a girl.

Donald and I had to have every sort of vaccination imaginable, and organise passports and other documents. We were invited to a Government House luncheon with the Wakehursts where we received a special document signed by Australian Prime Minister Ben Chiffley requesting safe transport for the said Rev. and Mrs J. D. MacTavish, kind treatment and consideration in whichever country they chose to travel. Time was spent frantically shopping for clothes (including wedding apparel), basic household equipment, medicines, and at the request of the Manchurian Mission large quantities of milk powder, Vim and Brasso. Preparing for an expected five-year stay in the vastness of Manchuria required careful consideration. Severe winters demanded fur coats, warm boots and clothing. Mother, Hilary, Chappie, and other friends worked tirelessly towards the wedding arrangements.

6 June (Donald's diary)
To Dr Taylor's for a very happy evening, with much singing and good fellowship. My love and admiration and respect of Shona grows with each passing day. I only hope she will not be disappointed in me. She said last night 'I am used to being the centre of attention, so it's good for me to be put in my place.'

8 June
Met Shona and we picked a nice engagement ring with stones called zircons (Indian), also a wedding ring. It's a cute ring with a blue stone in the centre and little white ones clustered in a circle around it looking something like a daisy. We didn't spend very much on them, not having too much to spend, which is perhaps a conclusive argument if not invalid.

Before leaving, Bodenwieser arranged a studio farewell for me, where for the first and only time I danced all my solo dances for Donald. He was also able to view excerpts from other works in a newly completed Australian Broadcasting Corporation film, *Spotlight On Australian Ballet*.

11 June (Donald's diary)

I watch Shona dance in a rehearsal at the Tivoli. She finds it exhausting. They do *The Demon Machine* & *Slavonic Dance*, the former depicting the power of the machine over man, an interesting study: but the problem is stated merely, and no solution is sought. At the end the machine has completely subjected the group. But this is not the whole truth. There are some who break away from its deadening & exhausting power, to live creative, personal, individualistic lives. Shona is one. I felt that I would have liked her to shake herself free of the Demon and dance so inspiringly that the Demon would shrink and cower and tremble.

The *Slavonic Dance* was gay, fierce abandon with a gentle, beguiling interlude. The *Water Lilies* which might more appropriately be called *Sea Anemones* was sheer poetry of motion, undulating, sinuous, sensitive.

21 June

... Read various books on 'How to be Happy Though Married', and no wiser at the end.

24 June

Wedding now 4 days off. It must be a horrible feeling if one wasn't sure it was the right girl. As it is – the time seems endless. It looks as though Shona will be the model wife as far as parochial duties go but will probably be unconventional otherwise. A kind of exciting unpredictableness...

Came the great day – June 28, 1948. The service, held in St Stephen's Presbyterian Church and conducted by Donald's friend, the Rev. Alan Tory, had some comic touches. Dancers, actors and musicians kept to one side of the church, ministers and missionaries to the other. My brother Bonar gave me away but decided to drive me around the block several times, awaiting the right moment for me to walk down the aisle. This moment was almost missed, as I was immediately surrounded by press reporters plaguing me with questions.

Fifty guests crammed into our house for the reception.

The living room looked delightful with wattle & iceland poppies, & Majie's green lawn looking inviting through the big plate glass window. How everyone fitted in is quite a miracle – but the atmosphere was a good one & it was rather indicative of my future to see the mixing of two such types as Bodie & Dory for instance with Cousin Don, or Aunty Bea...

My new husband and I then sallied forth into the night armed with a hamper of goodies and the remains of our pagoda wedding cake with its Chinese characters urging 'Benevolence, Fertility, Longevity in a life of Wedded Bliss!' In a euphoric state, with only a small flashlight to guide us, we made our way between tall gum trees to the cottage Chappie had lent us for the honeymoon. In the simple charming days that followed, we rowed, swam and read, discovering things about each other for the first time.

'Renowned Ballerina Marries Parson' and 'Engaged in Five Days, Married in Three Weeks and off to China!' wrote a delighted press. Donald showed enormous fortitude in face of such unexpected publicity. I discovered however, that in the many letters he wrote to family, friends and the Church of Scotland Missionary Society confessing he had married a professional dancer, he also added that my forbears had nearly all been 'men of the cloth' and stalwarts of both Scotland and the church!

My feelings for Donald were so overwhelming that I hardly had time to consider the seriousness of the step I was taking, or of the cause to which I was offering my life. China held enormous appeal for me, while the missionary side of things played a rather secondary role. My success in the world of dance and theatre had eclipsed my earlier childhood desire to 'take the Gospel to the poor heathen', but my home and upbringing had left me with a strong bias in favour of the Christian life. I found no difficulty falling in love with a man preparing to devote his life to teaching and preaching Christ.

The aim of the Chinese missions was to learn, share, and teach by example the Gospel of Christ. To my tentative inquiry Donald explained that the more uncompromising attitudes of the early torch-bearers had given way to a milder and more acceptable form of testimony. Impassioned preachers and hymn writers of the nineteenth century had inflamed thousands of young men and women to uproot themselves from their own culture and carry the message of salvation to a 'heathen' land. We were reminded of the sacrifices made by these remarkable early missionaries by the sight of the many tiny graves of their children. Any misgivings I had concerning the appropriateness of joining a group intent upon proselytising an ancient people who had followed the teachings of Confucius, of Taoism and Buddhism for centuries was gradually dispelled as I witnessed the amazing contribution the missionary had made to China, particularly in the field of medicine and education.

Saving souls for Christ had been a nineteenth century aim, but from now on it seemed the more practical development of Christian service had evolved and the signs were evident. Among the achievements were hospital medical training centres, schools, universities, leprosariums and orphanages.

Although it was a relief to learn that the SS *Shansi* had delayed departure an extra five days, all too soon our honeymoon was over and the day arrived when we began our journey to China. Friends and family had gathered, some tearfully, at the wharf to bid us Godspeed. I stood with Donald's arm about my waist, and in my shaking hand I clasped the streamers connecting me to my loved ones below. As the gap widened between us, I experienced a moment of severe panic, the reality of the situation hitting me for the first time. Had I made a dreadful mistake? What madness had brought me to this point? Was I really prepared to be incarcerated in a foreign land for five whole years without seeing family and friends? Did I even know this man at my side? Would I ever see my mother and loving friends again? Too late for regrets, I took my overcharged emotions to our cabin where a sympathetic husband encouraged me to allow them full reign. The pounding engines matched the rhythm of my own heart as we slowly moved out of Sydney Harbour into the open sea, and our unknown future.

Chapter Six

Christianity and Communism are incompatible...

The tensions of the past weeks soon dissolved during the blissful shipboard days that followed, and Donald and I began to relax – well, relax after our fashion. Afraid the lazy shipboard life would catch up on me, I began keep-fit classes on deck each morning which were usually brought to an abrupt close as daily deck ablutions began. I had some loyal keep-fitters in my group until the forbidding tropical heat brought us to a standstill. I taught Donald the recorder flute and he read to me from scholars Latourette and Weatherhead. He took several services on board while I sat proudly in the front row, experiencing a vicarious nervousness for my new husband. I began to appreciate the energy of the man when I found him organising quiz nights and debates as well. The subject of one was 'This house supports the New Look'.

In the dining room we had been allotted places at a very small table at the far end of the room with two very shy young men as companions. When it became obvious that neither Donald nor I looked or acted like the traditional T.M. (typical missionary), we were asked to join the officers at the captain's table. This gave us our first insight into the prevailing attitude held by many towards missionaries and we only reluctantly accepted this offer.

10 July 1948
Rev. & Mrs MacTavish inhabit one of the ship's best deck cabins, with two large windows on the port side. It is airy & comfortable, & the sun streams in of an afternoon. We are very happy – rather indulgent, but it's probably our last opportunity anyway!...

20 July
...We spent two days in [Brisbane]... I was strangely unconcerned upon spying posters & advertisements for the 'World Famous Bodenwieser Ballet' who opened there on Thursday night. It was my intention a few weeks ago to accompany them! I would never have believed I could regard such posters, knowing it no longer concerned me, with such indifference. I did however write letters for them to collect, Bodie & the girls.

On the night of the Equatorial Fancy Dress Ball Donald and I appeared as 'The Lady and the Lamp'. I wore a white negligee and shoved my lamp before me, albeit a very tall one encased in a large cardboard contraption (mistaken by some for a Xmas cracker). At supper time the captain fed Donald olives and peanuts through a small opening in his costume. To our surprise we even won a prize. After dancing the modish Hokey Tokey and Palais Glide, I succumbed to pressure later in the evening and danced a Viennese Waltz on the swaying deck under a black tropical sky.

14 July (Donald's diary)
Shona & I take turns reading a book by a Chinese writer. I end up with my head in Sho's lap and she reading in her sweet little voice, very 'mike-genic' until it became somewhat breezy when we retired to the cabin for a piece of wedding cake...
After supper we went a few times round the deck. The wind was increasing so we went right forward into the fore-peak and watched the ship ploughing through waves, the wind strong and wild. Then down and to bed. Australia farewell, China lies ahead.

27 July
Passing through Mindoro Straits, I take picture of Sho... We are still doing our exercises. I am now over my first soreness. Sho can lift her leg about twice as far as us men, & do every other movement better – especially bending backwards, when my backbone seems as flexible as a length of hollow steel piping.

Just off Thursday Island, our ship ran aground. One whole day we waited to see if we would ship water, then limped on to our destination. Early days were spent in vigorous games of table tennis and deck quoits, which became more desultory as we entered the tropics and the heat increased. One night Donald and I sat upon a box on the poop deck gazing romantically at the glorious sky and the phosphorescence which played upon the ship's wake. Only next morning we discovered our canoodling had taken place upon the coffin of an elderly Chinese man who had expired the night before. He had however achieved his aim, and his native land would be his final resting place.

Entering Manila harbour required great skill of our captain, for we were told 80 wrecks lay unrecovered in that watery grave. The masts and funnels that pierced the surface were reminders of the great battle of Corregidor. We explored the ancient city of Intramuras, and gazed with sadness at the bombed-out remains of such priceless historic places as Fort Santiago, and Saint Augustine's Church.

29 July

Donald & I jumped ashore to see a little of the city before dark. It is truly a shambles – the rumours had not exaggerated. I felt that old excitement last experienced this way in South America. As we made our way over muddy roads, under the burnt-out crusts of buildings, & looked with amazement upon the sordid little lean-tos, hastily erected by people in open squares or with great faith, established within the dubious shelter of precarious structures. The Filipinos are charming people. I tried my Spanish with some but theirs is really a kind of patois. They wear bright colours, & look clean & tidy. The children are enchanting.

Reaching the gateway of Hong Kong (Fragrant Harbour), our 'promised land', some days later was a moving occasion. I was excited by its throbbing life, and seductive mix of beauty and mystery. Before the gangplank was dropped however, we had a long infuriating delay. The police had been tipped off to investigate a second warrant officer who had tried smuggling in a large quantity of gold bar. We watched him being marched off the ship by two efficient police. After several hours hanging over the ship's rail in broiling heat, Donald, who had thought to dress for the occasion in his clericals, was close to collapsing. Then two gentlemen hailed us, assisted us ashore and soon we were gratefully sipping cool drinks in the comfortable apartment of the Nethersole Hospital with Dr and Mrs Ashton of the London Missionary Society. The apartment windows gave an expansive view of the harbour with its colourful array of ocean liners, Chinese junks, and sampans.

Our first visitors were Church of Scotland missionaries on their way out of China. Dr George Taylor and Frank Gavin made no bones about the seriousness of the situation in Manchuria which had already fallen to the Communists, and the new Communist Government's attitude to missionaries and foreigners. Although they spoke with sympathy and kindness it was clear they felt it very odd that while they were on their way out of Moukden, we were optimistically heading for the very same city.

What are we doing just arriving?! ...However they firmly believe, that the Mission must hold, & that it will do so.

Alas, their hopes and predictions were not to be.

Six lady missionaries on leave from their station near Canton also arrived unannounced to make our acquaintance and to vet the new recruits to China. Two of them had been students of my father at the University of Otago in the early 1930s.

We were now on the last stretch of our journey. While awaiting the sailing of the steamship *Hunan*, which was to take us up the coast to the port of Tientsin, we made several sorties from the city. Most memorable of these was the visit we made to the New Zealand Mission of Kongchuen near the bustling city of Canton (Guanzhou). This was our first experience of a mission at work.

We were only gradually becoming accustomed to the pressure of jostling crowds, the heat, endless colour and variety of the Chinese streets, and the smells – from the tantalising whiffs of burning joss sticks and incense, to the unspeakable odours of open drains or drying fish. So it was a relief to be driven at last to the attractive Mission Hospital set among paddy fields and tall groves of waving bamboo.

4 August

It is a delightful compound, bright with large hibiscus bushes, many trees, pawpaw, bamboo, lichee, banyan & dragon flame... Donald & I were delighted with our big room, with large windows, through which we could see the little country road winding to the village. This was a never-ending source of delight, for from early dawn, figures moved along it out into the fields – driving their water buffalos, balancing large panniers on bamboo sticks across their shoulders, filled with rice shoots for a fresh planting or a little child ... In pairs for very heavy weights, the rod was passed from the leading man to the one behind & often incredible weights hanging from it. These men usually jog trotted. Indeed they passed along in unceasing line with great speed.

Rev. Paddy Jansen, the senior missionary, had survived the bombing of the Mission Hospital during the Chinese-Japanese war, distinguishing himself as a courageous leader. Donald and I were made very welcome, and that night were feted with a genuine Chinese feast. Anxious to impress our hosts by our suitability, we insisted on using chopsticks, finished off with a belch in approved Chinese style, and then capped it off by singing *Jesus Loves Me* in Mandarin. We felt we had passed the test.

Paddy took us through the very interesting Silk & Fan Streets. Brightly coloured with richly embroidered Mandarin coats & shawls, & many coloured sticks of incense & sandalwoods. The families of merchants sat in the shop around bowls of rice & looked up unperturbed at the curious foreigner. I was attracted to fans which... I have discovered are indispensable in this land... We admired many beautiful pieces of jade & some curios of the Ming Dynasty.

We had flown to Canton but returned to Hong Kong by train in the company of Paddy and his new wife Nancy. During the journey Paddy drew me aside to offer a little advice to a novice. He told me of wives of missionaries joining their husbands on the mission field who had been unable to acculturate themselves to the lifestyle of the land, and because of this had forced their husbands to abandon the call and return home. He exhorted me to make every effort to avoid such a tragedy. 'Be vigilant,' he begged. 'Learn the language and customs of this land which you will grow to love. Share in every activity you are able, and rejoice in the Lord.' Had I not already embraced these sentiments, Paddy's advice would have put me in the right direction, but as it was his words excited me still further. Even as I searched in my seat for a bedbug, I knew I was going to love this land.

July being one of the hottest months in Hong Kong, Donald and I were relieved when friends invited us to the stone cottage encampment on the mountain top of Lantau, a small but mountainous island among the many that skirt Hong Kong. It was bliss to experience a delicate breeze, and the luxury of a sheet on the bed on cooler nights. Mists rolled across the peak at times adding still greater pleasure. Padres of various nationalities took services in the tiny chapel. The casual lifestyle of the mountain allowed for shorts and open collars for worshipper and preacher alike. Nancy Jansen and I enjoyed gathering wild flowers for a Sunday service, which was followed by a refreshing dip beneath a mountain waterfall. Older people arrived at the peak in rattan chairs born upon the shoulders of coolie bearers, but Donald and I chose to do it by foot and were proud to discover we had climbed 2000 feet in less than two hours.

Arriving back in Hong Kong I developed the first of what became searing stomach pains. At first I decided the pains must be due to the unaccustomed food, but as they increased I became suspicious. I had taken the recommended precautions against falling pregnant, but I knew they were not infallible. As the old SS *Hunan* ploughed its way up the Chinese coast, what appeared at first to be a bad bout of sea sickness left me in little doubt.

1 September

Neither D nor I feel 'very stylish' (as Evelyn would say). Manage breakfast, but have to rush out of lunch. Do not return to dining room till lunch next day. This is not an inspiring ship...

I do not recall the final lap of our sea journey with joy, but between bouts of nausea we also managed some hilarious moments. Donald was in need of a haircut. Any street barbers we had so far seen in the country had not impressed, so I decided to try out the hair clippers we had been advised to bring with us. It was not a good idea. Halfway up his head the clippers stuck fast. We collapsed in laughter when suddenly our captain arrived on deck and surveyed the sorry sight. 'I wasn't a cabin boy for nothing,' he remarked, and reaching for the clippers he finished off the job with precision and speed.

The threat of sea robbers was real on this route, so to prevent a take-over by robbers who often secreted themselves in the third class to the fore of the bridge, formidable spikes and much barbed wire were in evidence. Armed police manned the deck. Our only port of call was Inchon in Korea. The large cargo both unloaded and taken aboard kept us out in midstream for several days. Donald and I were delighted with this unexpected opportunity of seeing Korea and quickly made inquiries about getting to the capital Seoul. *Inchon best damn port in the Pacific*, we read as we landed from a small launch.

The US Army had already made an impact in the war-torn land. Bars and night clubs were flourishing at the port although the sight of gutted streets, ruined temples as well as the destruction of whole blocks in the capital revealed a land still licking its wounds after a fierce Japanese encounter.

4 September

The Korean women are a surprise. They wear long diaphanous organdie skirts, (ankle length) & v. short bodices. Even the farmers go trailing through the fields in the purest white for preference, tho' also strong bottle greens, indigo blues, maize yellow, aqua, & lolly pink, give conspicuous colour to the countryside. This latter is extremely lovely. Undulating hilly country with quite volcanic mountains commencing it seemed from the end of Seoul's main street. We raced past clusters of small thatch-roofed houses spilling a generous proportion of their inhabitants onto the street. These were made colourful by the large trays of red & yellow peppers drying in the sun.

The day we docked in Tientsin harbour, Donald and I could not hide our excitement. This was *real China*, the land we were destined to serve in the name of Christ, and our anticipated home for thirty years to come! We had neither doubts nor regrets, and maintained a strong belief in the purpose and direction our lives were taking. Rev. John Stewart, a member of our Moukden Mission, welcomed us as we alighted. I gaffed again as I hurried to meet him, a cigarette between my fingers. 'You would be wise to refrain from smoking,' he suggested before we entered the precincts of the China Inland Mission. I reproached myself that I had not spent more time studying the Missionaries' Handbook before joining their ranks!

A short distance by train brought us to our destination. Peking was surely one of the most fascinating cities in the world. Once there the rest of the world simply ceased to exist. Travelling by rickshaw through East Gate (Dung Se Pilo) along Tiananmen Square, then through a labyrinth of potholed alleys, we finally reached our long awaited destination, Hwa Wen Sweshau (Language School) on the Totiao Hutung. The Church of Scotland had assigned us one full year to study in this famous college before taking up our work at the Moukden Mission in Manchuria. As the great wooden gate slammed behind us and we passed through a courtyard and moongate to announce our arrival, I believe the enormity of the task ahead struck us fully for the first time. Would we really be able to handle this incredibly difficult Chinese language?

10 September

Here I sit in the sunlight which is pouring into our bedroom, in the College of Chinese Studies. We are really here! ...Donald, my husband, is playing the grammie while I write, & I am entranced to find he has such a fine collection of records – we suffered no breakages en route which pleased & surprised us. I experience a slight jolt each morning upon opening one eye in the grey morn... to see my old Van Gogh, Durer's 'Praying Hands', the 'Home Coming' (less favoured by my spouse) & my little 'Austrian Dancers' – familiar reminders of home, returning my gaze... In the adjoining room, which should with a little thought become a very passable sitting room, my Ballet poster enhances the wall, & the first instalment of D's books – oh! & our beautiful camphor chest, which gives forth an unmistakable & powerful scent. The College, & its adjoining Residential Wings, is laid in a lovely setting, with tennis & fives court, a lovely lawn, quantities of fine trees, & splendid splashes of colour from the flower beds. It is all the more surprising, as it is approached from a most odiferous drain infested lane...

The love I felt for my man had been paramount in all my decisions. Wherever he chose to live would be my choice also, and whatever work he took I wished to support. Becoming proficient in Mandarin was clearly our first objective. We steeled ourselves for that. We adapted to College life with little difficulty, making friends with the other students and settling into the daily routine of class.

Studying Chinese was a whole new experience. No European language we had studied seemed of the slightest assistance. Our teachers, both Chinese and American, were amazingly patient, but the almost complete lack of grammar proved baffling and distinguishing the tones called for acute hearing. We were fortunate, for although Mandarin has four tones, other Chinese dialects require as many as nine! The written language is the one unifying factor in that great land. The thousands of illiterate peasants and workers unable to communicate with their countrymen had kept China in a near feudal state for hundreds of years. We began to understand that to these diverse dialects could be attributed much of the ease with which foreign armies over the centuries have invaded China. But as we got to know the Chinese people better, we also learnt how their fortitude, independence, and mental and physical strength formed a barrier against complete conquest by a foreign power.

Admittedly foreign concessions did exist, and were tenaciously held in Shanghai and in Tsingtao. There were also the foreign settlements in British Hong Kong and Portuguese Macau, but even so China remained divided against itself. Dr Sun Yat-sen, the remarkable Christian leader of the Revolutionary movement which overthrew the Manchu Dynasty in 1911, was the man who first freed China from its festering sense of 'dyou lyan' (loss of face) as it languished beneath foreign control. Sun Yat-sen became the first President of the Republic of China, and leader of the socialist-oriented Kuomintang (National People's Party).

However Sun Yat-sen was unable to rid the Republic of marauding war lords and grinding poverty, nor did his dream of unification eventuate in the twenty years of his presidency. And despite his follower Chiang Kai-shek's best efforts, there was much corruption among the Nationalists who had by then become very right wing. This allowed Mao Tse-tung with his much smaller but well-disciplined Marxist followers to gain control. The Japanese also began plans for extending their empire, first into Manchuria, and later as far as Shanghai itself. For a brief time Chiang Kai-shek united with Mao Tse-tung in a successful defeat of the invaders. But the writing was on the wall before we even reached China. It was now a question of 'wait and see' until a complete Communist takeover. We still misguidedly clung to the hope that China would not become simply a puppet of the Russians, and that somewhere in that land we might still be permitted to serve the Chinese people.

Donald appreciated the Chinese calligraphy and soon began writing characters using pighair brushes with a skill I could never match. We had read that in order to master the Chinese language we required the following: bodies of brass, lungs of steel, eyes of an eagle, hearts of an apostle and memories of angels − to which I would add the lifespan of Methusela!

It was only after three months of oral language study that students at the college were faced with learning to read and write Chinese. We were told that a well-educated Chinese read and wrote 53,560 characters, but that we might just get by with a basic 3000. Donald had already made a start on Japanese characters in England as he thought that would give him a good head start on Asian phonetics. I on the other hand was just coming to grips with basic Chinese and learning with delight that the radical for 'home' consisted of the symbol of a pig under a roof, and that 'good' was represented by a mother and child. We began to realise what a very advanced method the College of Chinese Studies followed. No English was spoken during lessons, which were taught by the direct method. Allowances were also made to give specific vocabulary to those students preparing for scientific, business, or missionary vocation.

Donald and I enjoyed the lectures given in Chinese language, music, history, and perhaps most of all, the painting lesson conducted by delightful Prince Pu. Some nights we played the dictaphone, hoping the sounds would penetrate as we slept. Most satisfying however was in going straight from a class into the *hutungs* behind the College where we tried out the phrases we had been studying with friendly laughing children. They seemed delighted to exchange words with the funny 'foreign devils' with such 'da bidz' (large noses). 'You are small, I am big, but brother is bigger than his sister,' we mouthed.

Among the teachers were eminent Sinalogues Principal Dr Henry Fenn and Dr Tewkesbury (whom we nicknamed 'the purist' because he insisted on the purest Peking accent). These were the most senior, together with Dr Kennedy and the very popular Chinese Dean of the College, affectionately known to us all as 'Darling'. There was also the German historian Dr Ecce with his Chinese wife and young Chinese women teachers who would frequently hide their heads in their hands in despair at our feeble efforts, or when insensitive students asked embarrassing or personal questions.

The unfamiliar sounds reaching our ears late into the night or early dawn, of braying donkeys, tinkling rickshaw bells, and the multitudinous cries of street vendors, made us impatient to explore further the China outside our compound walls. To land straightaway in Peking upon arrival in China is perhaps a mistake. Like starting off a party with the cake. Its temples, pagodas and palaces were breathtaking. Thousands of cyclists and pedicabs, donkey and camel trains cluttered the streets. The vendors too, who hawked their wares from carts or carried enormous bundles on their backs, made such fascinating theatre! We were amazed by the marketplaces, where chirruping cicadas and many brightly plumed birds were kept in bamboo cages, and where we even found geese painted pink. Well-to-do families led their lives behind guarded courtyards with high walls and were rarely seen, but for most Pekingese the streets and alleys served as home.

The signs of great wealth and bitter poverty are seen in many a land, but in the 1940s China certainly displayed the most pronounced extremes. Both the enormous land area of China and the sheer size of its population made it hard to believe that the Communists could ever hope to succeed in controlling all of it. Communication, whether by train, truck, or by foot, was notoriously slow, particularly in the far Western provinces of Yunnan and Sikkiang. News of an invading army was seldom available to villagers before the invaders were charging the city gates. How little did we understand at that time the adoration of the masses for their new leader and the strength of the Maoist doctrine which brooked no counter action.

The weather began to cool during our three months in Peking, and hard on the arrival of fine dust coating the city from the Sinai Desert, came ferocious cold which had the people bundled up in great layers of cotton clothing. We saw death carts collecting from doorways the bodies of those who had died of exposure during the night. Despite the strong Chinese family structure where the elderly are traditionally supported by their kin, we found there were many who died through neglect and rejection.

Best of all I have to relate however, is this. Following the advice of American Dr Leadbetter, 'I am with child' & by next April, D & I shall have our own little child. It is very thrilling, though not exactly planned. However we've decided this is very probably the best time in our lives to have a child. The College offers every comfort, & we can always supply the extra foods & such necessary for me for the next months. I have since encountered two expectant mothers in the College also awaiting April with trepidation & joy.

Of pregnancy I knew very little but enough to know that expectant mothers should drink milk and take vitamin C. Without feeling a shadow of guilt, I decided to open some of the packets of milk powder requested from the Moukden Mission, and to augment the sometimes uninteresting college food with some of the dried fruit which we had brought with us. Donald tried to drag me onto the tennis court before breakfast, but I was beginning to take my condition seriously and decided an extra hour of sleep was preferable.

Between classes we tried to explore some of the historic and architectural marvels of the city. The Forbidden City, more opulent than anything I had seen, was encased behind a myriad of courtyards. Further in lay the Imperial City, where Emperors and Empresses spent pampered lives hidden behind towering walls and bodyguards. Behind those walls again lay the Tartar City, which in comparison teemed with life and noise and stench. Of the 3000 eunuchs (servants to the Dowager Empress Tzuhui) remaining from the Manchu Dynasty, the last few 100 were housed in an ancient temple to finish their days. Donald and I were taken to meet several pallid-looking individuals with falsetto voices who had undergone the castration demanded of those joining the service of the Empress.

Within our short stay we often cut down on sleep in order to see more of the wonderful city. The Summer Palace, Jade Fountain, the Altar of Heaven and Temple of Heaven, the Summer House on Cole Hill (an artificial hill, ordered by the Empress so that she might gaze upon her domain) we found equally fascinating. In our visit to the Confucian Temple we saw for the first time the 'Lily Feet' of foot-bound women who were refugees from the fighting north.

2 October 1948

Joe Wilkinson took us with him today to see numbers of homeless & helpless refugees cluttering up the Temple of Confucius. A more depressing revelation I have never met with before, not so starkly anyway. The families are separated from each other, in their little allotments on the stone floor, by the placing of stones in squares, & within those precious squares are stored their pitiful collection of personal belongings – a small pile of blankets & old clothes, a bowl or two – some chopsticks. The children are amazingly fatalistic – there is almost no crying, yet because they lack the normal energy & spirits of children they play only in a desultory fashion, with sticks in the earth or lie about listlessly... It was heart rending...

This is only one of many refugee camps in Peking, of those who have fled from the advancing Commos, or had land & property taken from them, but there are still more students who have been evacuated principally from Moukden & their problem is no less acute...

While visiting the Lama Temple and exploring a huge 250-year-old Buddha hewn from a single tree, my foot stumbled upon a small figure lying in the dust with other fallen broken idols. To Donald's amazement as we cycled home, I pulled from beneath my lambskin coat the little three bosomed figurine. 'Namse' (her name as I later learned from a Tibetan monk) has been most grateful to me for rescuing her from oblivion, and I feel sure helps to bring happiness and good fortune to all the houses I have since shared with her.

One day not long after this, a young Chinese woman arrived at my door. Her name was Goh Yeh Dai Aileen. Speaking excellent English she introduced herself as a modern dancer who had trained in London in the Laban Jooss dance method. She was currently seeking out indigenous Chinese folk dance. Her husband, a musician, researched Chinese music as they travelled together into outlying provinces of Chinese Turkistan, and Sinkiang. Aileen believed that many of these ancient dances, some – such as the Ice Breaking Dance – dating from the sixth century B.C., were disappearing in the sands of the Sinai Desert. Aileen and her husband were bent on bringing these valuable examples of China's heritage back to the people. They considered that teaching these dances to the students of Shanghai and Peking Universities was the best way to retain them for posterity.

I was fascinated by her research and we quickly began sharing our artistic lives. Before leaving Peking she had shown me several of these ancient Chinese dances, and in exchange Aileen delighted in the examples of Bodenwieser dance I shared with her. Years later I learned that Aileen became director of the Peking Ballet Academy where she was encouraged by the new Chinese leaders to produce ideological ballets supporting the ideals of Communism. During the Cultural Revolution Aileen, staff, and leading dancers of the company, considered intellectuals, were sent to the country to spend back-breaking hours working in the paddy fields. Four to five years given to such labour seized up their muscles and crippled their bodies, so that when they returned to the ballet school, none were able to take up dance again, and only a handful were able to continue teaching.

Our first visit to the Peking Opera left us deaf for days, for we had not yet acquired 'Chinese ears'. Chinese Opera is one of the most perfect forms of theatre in the world. We were quick to recognise it as an evolved and complex art form, governed by its own conventions and aesthetic dictates. Aesthetically it seemed a purer art form than our own. The orchestra, consisting of gongs and cymbals (Pi'tuang), flutes and the Chinese fiddle (Huchin), accompanied the singers. If one persevered I am sure this orchestral combination could be rewarding, but to our unaccustomed ears it sounded excruciating. The falsetto singing of the female impersonator in particular began to grate sorely. With rare exceptions women were not considered a match for men in the singing of female roles, and when women do play the female role, they must imitate the male exponents of the 'feminine art'. These impersonators of the female role also teeter and sway about the floor in imitation of a foot-bound woman, which we found both humorous and distressing. Acrobatics too played an important part in the opera.

The Chinese consider the detailed realism of the West atrophies the imagination. This made it easier to understand the reason for the bare stage as well as the lack of scenery, tabs, or curtain. The stark setting is in marked contrast to the lavish costumes and make-up. However as the drama begins to unfold, attendants run across the stage bearing banners upon which are painted the visuals the audience must imagine for themselves. For instance, red bricks denote a castle, while billowing clouds represent out-of-doors. Horses are indicated when the actor bears a riding crop, and Generals are recognised by flags attached to their backs. Even more stylised effects include a dying man crossing his eyes and falling into the arms of an attendant, then picking himself up from the ground and making all the motions of carrying off his own corpse!

On one occasion a magnificently gowned heroine raised her voluminous skirt before seating herself, while the owner of the costume adroitly aimed a cushion from the wings to land at the precise moment of need. As the play moved towards a declaration of passion, the noisy audience fell silent while the heroine, in preparation for a demanding top note, accepted a teapot from an attendant and lifted it to his lips. In hushed anticipation we watched him expectorate across the footlights, pause dramatically for a moment, then take his top note magnificently! Until then the audience had seemed almost oblivious to the drama before them as they chatted and laughed, breast-fed their babies and cracked sunflower seeds in their teeth for them, drank tea and hurled hot towels from one box to another, but at this haute pointe, all eyes turned to the stage. The audience responded to this splendid feat wildly...

We saw the grind of poverty, and the constant display of both love and cruelty to children and animals alike. We were fascinated by the many ceremonies and ancient rituals remaining from bygone days, as well as the Mao Tse-tung-inspired political rallies and military parades. Our life in Peking was so varied and so rich that

Donald and I felt we had scarcely lived until then.

By the end of October 1948 the victorious Communist Army was already in control of Manchuria. The students decided that despite the increasing rumours of the imminent fall of Peking, we should celebrate Halloween with a party. Donald and I were elected 'heads of entertainment'. Donald quickly learnt the Chinese for 'a pig's large intestine' which he brought forth in ringing tones at the meat market. The Hall Of Horrors he planned evidently required such material. We erected a tent in the big hall to hide the 'chamber of horrors' and encouraged our Chinese friends to 'walk the plank' blindfold. Their screams of terror and delight gave us great satisfaction. Pumpkin lanterns added to the atmosphere, helping us to forget briefly the scary developments taking place outside the College Compound walls.

The Dean of the College soon called us together to explain that with inflation rising in the city at the rate of two hundred per cent per day, cuts had to be made, beginning with our food. We must be prepared to make the sacrifices which the Chinese people were being forced to make throughout the north. When he suggested the first food item we could forgo would be butter, one young American missionary exclaimed, 'No, no, I simply could not do without butter!'

Donald offered his services to the Peking Union Church and was quickly snapped up as part-time organist and preacher. Services were also conducted in the College by students of various denominations which we attended. The rest of Sunday was taken up with Chinese Sunday School and a Bible Class for American and British Consular young people.

I never really discovered whether Donald was genuinely naive, or whether he took wicked enjoyment in watching people's reactions, but he often said to other missionaries, 'Did you know that my wife was a well-known dancer in Australia before we married?' His pride in me could be more than a little embarrassing. I was certainly conscious of the disapproval from some of the older missionaries, but there were others who believed an ex-dancer would bring only fresh air into the camp. I was grateful to them and appreciated their support and friendship.

Our first introduction to the Anglican Mission in Peking was via a New Zealand missionary living in the city. Marjorie Monaghan escorted us to the other end of the city by bicycle. As we sat down to eat at a long table with the Bishop and four tall red-haired missionary women, I was horrified to hear Donald say, 'But for the grace of God, Bishop, I might have been an Anglican myself.' To my relief an amused Bishop replied, 'And how did you avoid such a fate, young man?' Laughing, my impudent husband went on to explain that he had received his secondary schooling in an Anglican school in his home town of Winnipeg, but had somehow, despite the attraction, managed to remain a staunch Presbyterian. There was a lot of banter between the denominations, but we were impressed at how well they seemed to get on, showing a solidarity here not always found at home.

Our missionary predecessors had not been lazy. We learned in particular of the tremendous work they had achieved in medicine education, and of how they had opened up new opportunities for women, greatly improving their status. Credit must also go to them that the cruel practice of foot-binding had become a thing of the past.

In 1948 with two million Catholics and one million Protestants, China was fast beginning to develop an indigenous Chinese Church. A more responsible and self-reliant attitude towards their own expression of their faith and culture did not come too soon. More and more Chinese Christians had by now become highly skilled doctors, nurses and teachers, and were well able to maintain high standards in missionary-founded institutions. As we became more aware of such achievements, we were angered by the critical, even hostile, attitudes towards missionaries we sometimes encountered – which were the result of ignorance. If China became Communist the future of all Christian churches, schools and hospitals would be in jeopardy. Overseas financial support would also cease. It was generally believed however that in such an eventuality the Chinese would rise to the occasion, and realise the ideal of a self-governing, self-supporting Chinese Church. Perhaps there could be some comfort in the words of Job: 'There is hope for a tree if it is cut down that it will sprout again, and that the tender branches thereof will not cease.'

There were a few among us who optimistically believed that even under Communism foreigners would be permitted to remain and work in China. They held these views even after the occasion of the twenty-eighth anniversary of the founding of China's Communist Party, when Mao Tse-tung himself spoke these words:

Against all the 'running dogs' of imperialism, the landlord and the bureaucratic capitalists along with the Kuomintang reactionaries and the people who assisted them to commit murder, the People's Government will enforce the dictatorship of the people. We shall suppress them!

As for the people, we apply the democratic system granting them freedom of speech, assembly, organisation and other such rights. The right to vote is given only to the people. We do not grant the rights to the reactionary elements. For the people who are with us democracy, for the reactionaries dictatorship. For the combination of these two aspects of Government, we have what is called 'The People's Democratic Dictatorship'.

As Donald pointed out, such an ominous statement which juxtaposed diametrically opposed concepts was surely warning enough that a police state system was in place, and that both Communist and Western concepts of freedom could never be understood as one and the same. If this was insufficient to convince the optimists, perhaps this remark from foreign minister Chou En-lai might have changed their minds:

Christianity and Communism are incompatible... We hope that within three years there will be no missionaries nor any foreign funds in China.

Donald and I requested and received permission to visit the Great Wall of China, but fate did not allow it. Fighting in the area had increased and it was no longer thought wise to permit visits. We were disappointed, but decided to make a brief stay at the College's Western Hills Hostel. A short train journey brought us to a village where we were met by a man with two small donkeys in tow. I was seated in an hilarious, but surprisingly comfortable fashion upon my small steed, carrying my swelling bulk before me. Our guide walked alongside, balancing our bags on a stout stick across his shoulders. Donald read his Bible, his long legs scraping the ground beneath him. I had a sudden vision of the Holy Family travelling to Bethlehem – and it didn't appear the least bit blasphemous to this missionary! Our delight in the countryside and small village life around us was short-lived however, for the sounds of war became obvious. As the hours passed, the gunfire some eight miles distant increased, and sounded terrifyingly close.

While scrambling among the hills, we had come across a Buddhist Shrine carved into the hillside, and facing Peking whose towers and turrets we could vaguely make out in the distance. In that unusual setting with two other College couples who had joined us, and within the sound of falling rockets, we prayed for China and its many disinherited people who had been the victims of greedy war lords, marauding bandits and undisciplined armies for centuries. 'Peace!' we cried across the valley, 'Peace!' we sang. We had only been a few months in China, yet we felt caught up in the anguish of this great land. Stumbling back through the encroaching darkness to our hostel, tears ran down my face.

November 19 (Donald's diary)

A sunlit day and men digging trenches in the park – reminiscent of London '39. But this is surely a futile business. I understand they are also filling the city moat with water. It sounds as if they are gearing for a medieval war.

I endeavour to stop some bare-faced robbery by a soldier by appealing to an officer – without success...

The political situation remained difficult to assess. Questions began plaguing us such as: 'How much support did the K.M.T. really have overall? Were the Chinese more interested in Marxist doctrine than in actual land reform? Manchuria had fallen to the invading Ba Lu (Eighth Army) and it was reported that Tsinan, capital city of Shantung was already in Red hands. We heard of the great hardships Moukden was experiencing. Of how the inadequate food supplies went to the army, while the people starved, of how the Mission Hospital had had to close some wards because they could no longer feed the patients. The skeleton foreign staff stayed on because if they were to leave there would be no doctor left to operate in the whole of that stricken city. The Communists did not approve of foreigners. We were told of several doctors who had been condemned for 'cutting out people's hearts', or 'forcing people to give blood', and when any died in hospital the doctors were accused of murder. The chances of our ever reaching our final destination seemed very slim indeed.

Meantime, the problem of managing our own meagre finances was increasing. It was obvious that the Chinese National Currency (C.N.C.) was moving rapidly to a crisis. In Canton, where we had been just two months earlier, a short rickshaw ride had cost us 30,000 Taoi. Our train ticket cost us each 17,000,000, and tiffen (a main meal for five) 5,000,000 which was the equivalent of $12.50. When the new Gold Yuan currency was launched it too devalued quickly, up to a hundred per cent. American missionaries generally received more than twice the salary of other nationals, but the problem of dragging around suitcases of valueless notes wherever we went became a logistical nightmare for all of us.

We were back at our studies which the staff were determined should continue as normal, when word came from the American Consulate that an American aircraft carrier standing off the coast of Tientsin awaited all American citizens. Within 24 hours no American remained. The British Consulate was much slower coming to a decision. Reluctantly however, we thought it wise to start packing. Soon all British subjects were ordered to evacuate Peking without delay. The Church of Scotland sent instructions for us to pull out of Peking immediately, but to remain in Free China to see which way the cat would jump. Maybe it was thought Mao Tse-tung would not be able to hold the ground he had taken in Manchuria, and that Chiang Kai-shek could repulse the Communists and enable the mission to operate once more. We weren't filled with much hope, but having felt a strong call to come to China we could not give up easily.

Donald had a remarkable medical missionary aunt, Dr Isabelle MacTavish, who been a prisoner of the Japanese for three years. She was working at Foochow East Gate Hospital in the province of Fukien, and so to her we would go. Coz Belle, as we called her, was very fond of Donald whom she had known as a small boy when on furlough from the field. She had taught him his first Chinese words, and to sing *Jesus Loves Me* in Chinese. From these encounters Donald explained had come his first stirrings to bring Christ to China.

For the evacuation flight ahead we were asked to carry with us only essential luggage. Boxes of Vim and Brasso ordered for the mission were jettisoned, and a fair amount of dried fruit and powdered milk was handed to our Chinese friends. Many of Donald's beloved books had to be discarded. I even gave his black felt hat away and for years after I was reproached, for as Donald explained, it was his only funeral hat! After many sad farewells in the early hours of a bitterly cold morning, we and our baggage were piled into a truck and driven to the airport. I wore two coats, one on top of the other, but kept shivering.

Gunfire sounded just beyond the Western Wall as we passed through. I was frightened but also enormously sad to be quitting this beautiful city. And we were all worried about what might befall those who could not flee. Our two Manchurian mission colleagues Ella Gordon and Hester Stewart bravely accompanied us to the airport, before making their own last-minute escape some few hours later.

It was a little intimidating to discover that in order to squeeze in the maximum number of passengers all seats had been removed from the *St Paul*, one of two planes dedicated to rescuing missionaries from Chinese troublespots. Donald and I were bundled into the cockpit, and although blessed with a magnificent view of China as it unfolded below us, I developed the most dreadful cramp from being squeezed between hot pipes overhead and a hard floor beneath me.

'Hang on in there,' I begged my unborn child. 'All will be well in the end.' It was a long day, which ended not in Foochow as intended, but in Shanghai. Foochow airport could not accept planes arriving after dark, and it became clear that our plane could not make it in daylight hours. After an unmemorable night spent in the Shanghai Naval YMCA the flight was continued early the following morning.

November 22 (Donald's diary)

We watch the plains give way to the mountains, ridge on rugged ridge to 5000 ft in height, coming at last over the final ridge with the sun illuminating the ground, to Foochow on another plain, and Coz Belle at the landing field looking like a happy robin redbreast – tho' dressed in brown. She takes us in a jeep, very crowded with luggage piled high to the Hospital.

If the plane afforded little comfort to a pregnant mother, the jeep ride was positively gruelling. Earlier battle scars had left many potholes and bad corrugations. On top of this, we were bundled up in fur coats and woolly caps much to the surprise of people plucking oranges from the trees nearby.

By the time we were settled at the Foochow hospital, I questioned whether my baby could possibly have survived the traumas of the journey. For the next two months Donald and I were guests of Christ Hospital at East Gate, and our hosts Matron Izzard and Dr Isabelle

MacTavish. We continued to study Mandarin daily, although neither our teacher nor the Fukinese spoken around us made the task easy. We soon discovered that although educated Chinese from all regions spoke and understood Mandarin, their speech was far from the pure tones of our Peking teachers.

It was a great relief to have a kind and sympathetic Coz Belle to give me a full examination with numerous x-rays and injections, and to pronounce all well for both me and the babe. My baby's presence became daily more obvious. Since neither trousers nor skirts met round my middle any longer, and money was non-existent, I resorted to wearing shapeless cast-off missionary garments, usually of dark brown serge or some similar colour. However, as fashion did not appear to figure highly among the Europeans I met in Foochow, it did not worry me unduly.

The political situation was of far greater concern to us all. On 6 December 1948 Mao Tse-tung's troops began pouring into the city of Peking. Communication with the Manchurian Mission was no longer possible, but we did receive news of developments there via the Church of Scotland in Edinburgh. The Communist success in the North threatened the complete collapse of Chiang Kai-shek and his Kuomintang Army. Orders came for us to remain in the country as long as we felt safe in case those missionaries remaining in Moukden decided they could usefully continue to work under Communist rule – in which case we were to join them. This optimistic plan did not eventuate, and our Manchurian colleagues came to be virtual prisoners in the compound, and an embarrassment to their Chinese Christian friends. After numerous adventures, the remaining European missionaries in Moukden did eventually manage to escape. Others from the Ichang Church of Scotland Mission on the Yangtze were not so lucky – a number of them were imprisoned and threatened for many months before managing to leave the country.

The Hospital Chapel, and the American Board of Missions to Foochow were delighted to have a fresh eager preacher in their midst, so Donald felt useful despite this limbo state we found ourselves in. Any spare time we had we dragged our portable His Master's Voice gramophone into the hospital wards, hoping with early missionary zeal to brighten the lives of the sick and the dying. Nelson Eddy and Janette McDonald, Gershwin and Irving Berlin may have been surprised to hear their familiar strains coming from that grim building.

A most disturbing experience which returned to haunt me many times was the day we accompanied the prison welfare officer to a city prison. We entered a bare square courtyard surrounded on all sides by tiny cells. The guards ordered the prisoners to present themselves. Out shuffled the strangest assortment of human beings, aged from ten years to possibly eighty. Some of them looked like hardened criminals, but the blank, hopeless or desperate look of some of the younger men and boys tore at my heart. It seemed particularly inhumane to incarcerate such young boys – whose crime was probably no more than petty theft – together with vicious criminals. To the amazement of the inmates Donald took out a rope and demonstrated his spinning skill (learned as a boy scout in Canada). Having won their attention, he delivered a brief address, translated by the Chinese pastor. But the captive audience showed little sign of interest in a Christian God who permitted suffering in such atrocious conditions. Donald and I returned soberly to our lodging realising the complexities of our life ahead.

Our visit to a famous monastery high above the Min River was far more inspiring. Riding our bikes between foot and donkey traffic in Foochow's main street, skilfully avoiding the night soil buckets hanging from the coolies' shoulders, we eventually reached the open road. It was a long pull up the mountainside with frequent stops for breath at small wayside shrines before we reached the monastery. We were received by the monks with courtesy and slept that night upon a hard wooden platform, with a wooden pillow for our heads. We were woken at 5am by a young shaven-headed acolyte who, first placing a charcoal burner at our feet, handed us a steaming bowl of bean curd and then ushered us along many corridors to the temple. A long line of chanting saffron-robed monks moved between the columns of the great hall, some striking hollow wooden fish gongs and bells. The effect this whole scene made upon our senses was so mesmerising that, as had happened to me some years before watching Negroes dancing in South America, I fell into some sort of trance – or so Donald told me, after carrying me into the open air!

We knew that Confucianism, which is not strictly a religion, played a real role in the lives of the Chinese. It requires neither idol nor altar, but sets forth a high moral ideal. Taoism also had many adherents, but for some time now Donald had been particularly keen to become acquainted with China's principal religion, Buddhism. What did we find?

Pen & ink drawing of Shona by Bonar, Sydney.

Sea study with Hilary (left), Sydney 1947.

The Russian Duo. Shona (left) and Emmy Taussig, 1942. *M. Michaelis*

With Isobel Staehelin (right) in the Blue Mountains.

Mother and Shona, Sydney 1941.

Wedding Day, 1948

Ready to board the SS *Shansi* for China. From left – Major, Dick North,
Rev. Barrie, Donald, Margaret Chapple, Shona, Agnes North, Mrs Barrie,
Iain North. In front – Richard North, Mother, Hilary.

Donald and Shona
en route to China.

Teachers outside the
College of Chinese
Studies, Peking.

Missionaries to
China.

At the Confucian Temple, Peking.
Foot-bound woman and
Manchurian refugees

The Imperial City. Dr Tewkesbury with one of
the eunuch servants to the Empress.

Boarding the plane out of Peking, November 1948.

Standing outside first home in Formosa. Farmer sewing linseed in foreground.

Donald with the Abbotess of a Formosan Buddhist temple.

The basic principles in the Buddhist religion we found to be an intense belief in moral order in a universe which favours goodness and disapproves of vice. The nearest thing to God for the Buddhist is known as 'The Heavenly Veritable One' (Tien Lao Ye) who presides over the world of spirits and of men. The monastery where we spent the night gave an impression of orderliness, peace, and serenity. It seemed to us a theology of simplicity of belief and dignity of feeling. The Buddhist doctrine of transmigration (the accumulation of personal merit) would return one to earth to improve the conditions of the earlier life on earth. If, on the other hand, one's life had been unsatisfactory according to Buddhist doctrine, it was feared in the next life one might return as a pig or a snake!

The respect and gentle acceptance we received as guests of this temple gave us in turn a deep respect for the harmonious relationship the Buddhists seemed to have with the universe. Admittedly the remote area and beautiful landscape of the monastery did not oblige the monks to concern themselves too much with the poverty and misery of the overcrowded cities and villages in the valley below. But they did pray for the rebirth of the people to happier circumstances and a better way of life.

When we returned to Foochow, we noticed how much the temples varied. Some were drab and neglected, while others enticed passers-by with red and gold paint and glowering demon figures. Believing themselves to be under threat from the many Kwei (Gods), the worshippers clanged cymbals and beat drums with great humour in an ear-splitting manner. These demonstrations were intended to keep evil spirits from returning from the dead.

Comparing this gay display with the few sombre and often unlovely Christian churches we saw, made us wonder how any Chinese could be attracted to them. From the very beginning Donald and I felt the missionaries would be wise to adopt some of the colour and gaiety which we found so attractive among the Buddhist rituals and practices. In order to encourage people away from polytheistic Buddhism, both foreign and Chinese Christian workers tended to introduce a rather severe note. All the same, the Christian faith proved a popular choice for thousands of Chinese, and although the architecture of the churches left a lot to be desired, I can attest to the eloquence, warmth and beauty of many services I attended within.

The new theology in the West from which we had emerged, had scarcely touched the long-serving missionaries in this land. Old ways die hard, especially in China! Although deeply impressed by the courage, commitment, and great achievement of the missionaries, we – and others from the College – felt some of their attitudes were due for change. For one thing we felt we would best learn to understand and relate to the Chinese via the religion *they* practised. We had come to share our Christian faith but were not prepared to denounce or condemn another.

As Christmas approached our hosts led us across paddy fields to visit a renowned leprosarium. On the way we passed rows of coffins laid out in waiting houses for burial. By the Christmas tree in the leprosarium Donald and I were asked to play our recorders, and the patients reciprocated with carols. Even though their faces shone with warmth, the sound coming from people with such physical deformities was shattering. Using an interpreter, Donald managed a few words of comfort and assurance of God's everlasting love. Those eyes of the lepers which radiated a kind of desperate hope made me feel very humble, and as so often in this country, unworthy of my own enviable state. As we made our way homeward, a sudden volley of crackers exploded at our feet. My first reaction was one of annoyance, but one of our guides explained that in doing this, the lepers had only intended to frighten away any spirits of sickness which may have attached themselves to us.

Chapter Seven

The euphoria I experienced at that moment was like dancing 'Demon Machine', 'Cain and Abel' and the 'Russian Duo' all at once – truly a miracle enacted! Had we a bugle our baby's arrival would have been proclaimed across the Mission compound.

Our future looked uncertain, when out of the blue we received an invitation from the English Presbyterian Mission of Southern Formosa,[1] offering Donald the position of guest Professor of New Testament and Musical Instruction in the Theological College in Tainan. We accepted the offer, considering it to be an excellent way to mark time until we heard whether working under the Communists was a possibility.

New Year's Eve 1948
*   ...Coz Belle, Donald & I sit... by [the] fire. We play one half of our beautiful Verdi's Requiem Mass, which sounds amazingly good on our wee grammie. By the light of a kerosene lamp, & the glow from the fire, Donald reads us some of his very fine sermons, followed up by Coz Belle reading some excerpts of Tennyson, including 'Ring Out Wild Bells'. Outside it rained heavily, & the hour became midnight. It was a nice atmospheric little gathering for our first New Year in China. I thought vaguely of the extraordinary change in my life since New Year 1947.*

The island of Formosa (250 miles by 90), known to the first Portuguese explorers as 'The Island Beautiful' was a Dutch possession from 1624 until the people won their independence under the leadership of Cheng Cher-kung. It remained nominally under China through the Ming and Ching dynasties, until the Japanese takeover at the end of the nineteenth century.

---

[1] Taiwan

The Japanese built good roads, industries, hydro-electric schemes, hotels and railways, such as the Formosans had never seen. While Formosa became the shop window of the Japanese Empire, the islanders remained virtual slaves. When the island was returned to China at the end of the Second World War, the Formosans were initially very happy. They set about learning Mandarin (the Formosan dialect was different). However, as the mainland National Government under Chiang Kai-shek proved to be inefficient and corrupt, disillusionment set in. This led to agitation for Formosan independence. Shortly before our arrival an open revolt had been put down with great vehemence and all suspected leaders executed.

As I was now six months pregnant, I took the one hour flight across the Formosan Straits ahead of Donald who planned to accompany our seventeen pieces of luggage by Chinese junk on an appreciably longer journey. I greatly looked forward to the thought of our very own home at last. I badly needed to prepare a nest for the arrival of our child. My part of the journey was quite straight-forward, but Donald's sea voyage proved to be something of a nightmare.

23 January 1949

Coz B, Donald & I set off in jeep to river... 17 pieces [of] luggage come by slow method of hand cart. Take wee sampan down to Pagoda Anchorage. Awful filthy ship D. is supposed to take. Have to pay 2,000 G.Y. extra for cabin. D. returns as tub does not leave till next day anyway...

24 January.

Day I leave Foochow.

Discover D. must immediately return to his ship. Coz B sticks with me. Plane delayed from Shanghai. Visibility poor... Only 11 passengers for Formosa. [In] one hour we arrive. Bus breaks down. Take rickshaw to Mackay Hospital.

I was a guest of the Canadian Presbyterian Mission in Taipei. As the expected arrival time of Donald's boat came and went with no word of its whereabouts and the days passed, so my anxiety mounted. I spent six long days in a state of great anguish. I overheard several missionaries discussing the dangers of a sea voyage by junk across the Straits. 'Those old Chinese junks don't have life boats or even a life jacket and it has been a shocking typhoon,' I heard them say. What was I to think?

The Westerners I met in Taipei were sympathetic to me, and I tried passing the time by inspecting the city, which was still much marked by recent fighting. I found myself praying for Donald at every temple I came to: Shinto Shrine, Confucian Temple, Buddhist Temple and Christian Church. I tried to concentrate on playing our Chinese flute and studying Chinese. My hosts helped ease my days by recounting the colourful history of the island which was to become our home.

I took particular interest in the story of the East Coast Aboriginals (Gaushan Ren) or mountain people, and of their mass conversion to Christianity, their great love of the dance, and the mystery which still surrounded their origin. I hoped one day to meet them for myself.

27 January
I long for my Donald who may be now landed in Tainan, or else on the high seas, & I love him so. This separation is HELL!

28 January
Not feeling awfully well... Get really panicky because of no news re Donald. Ring up British Consul at Tam Swei. He advises ringing Foochow in [the] morning. Feel but slightly reassured!

29 January
Most beautiful day. Remain abed till lunch. Ne mange pas.[2] Sleep a lot. Lie out in [the] sun. Do Chinese. Take solitary walk about streets noting effects of Chinese New Year. Ganz interressant.[3] Cable from my hubbie 'Returned, sailing soon. Well. Donald.' Much comforted...

I felt weak with relief when first I heard the news but this quickly changed to a state of wild euphoria which I badly needed to express. Forgetting my condition for a moment, I broke into a series of cartwheels across the compound. This was not a common sight in missionary circles and a handful of passing nurses and patients appeared surprised. Years later our successor in Tainan asked me: 'Shona, there is a legend which still goes around among Taiwanese missionaries, that when more than six months pregnant a certain

---

[2] Don't eat.
[3] Quite interesting.

Mei Taitai performed cartwheels across the hospital compound. Is that true? Was that you?'

Unbelievably Donald stood before me, looking very white and thin and, having lost his voice, could only relate his adventures in a whisper. Most of our luggage had been stacked on the deck of the junk and for three days Donald had remained seated upon our boxes which he dared not leave. Some members of the crew had demanded an extra thousand yuan in payment, and when he refused to pay, they threatened retaliation by tossing every box overboard! A storm broke and mountainous seas made the captain decide to hove to for shelter behind a great rock. After three days, having run completely out of food, the boat returned to the mainland to restock. Donald was able to dry out and spend one comfortable night in a nearby convent. The following morning the boat continued its journey with no further mishaps, landing at the port of Keelung in North Formosa six days late.

It was an ecstatic reunion, and sincere were our prayers of thanks that night. We made the tiring, steamy, two hundred mile train journey south. Upon arrival in Tainan we left the modern station and bumped through the much-bombed streets in rickshaws. The Pride of India trees lining the roadway exploded in a blur of vivid reds. Arrangements had been made for our coming, and we hurried to the Tainan English Presbyterian Mission Compound to inspect our first home. We were not disappointed. It was a two storeyed cement building enclosed by verandahs running round both floors. They were scrim covered, but gaping with shrapnel holes and dubious protection from snakes, mosquitoes and other creepy crawlies. We were delighted to learn that the two upturned eaves rising like harpies from the tiled roof were designed to provide protection from evil spirits who would be swept back up into the sky.

One half of the house was inhabited by Leslie Singleton, aptly nicknamed 'Lanky' because he was exceptionally tall and because his home was in Lancashire. Lanky was a somewhat crusty gentleman, whose wife had not found a missionary's life to her liking, and returned home some years before. Although he enjoyed playing music with Donald, he had little time for women, particularly those of the dancing variety!

We took most of our meals with Lanky until we managed to gather together some basic furniture of our own. The Canadian Principal of the Tainan Theological College was Dr Montgomery who with his wife, affectionately known as 'The Bish and the Missus', had served forty years in the field. They were very good to us, sharing their hearts and their table, as indeed were other members of the Mission. Boris and Clare Anderson were our nearest neighbours and subsequently very good friends. Highly artistic and well qualified, Clare taught Greek, Boris Old and New Testament in the College, and each played the piano and flute with great skill. One day I found a book of poems written by Clare. Donald and I were drawn even closer to the Andersons upon learning that they expected their first child about one month after our own.

Several 'gwonyu' (unmarried women), engaged to teach at the Tainan Middle School were quick to befriend us and claim us as family. Dr Shoki and Winifred Hwang also became good friends. Formosan-born Shoki graduated from Tokyo Imperial University and made further studies at Westminster College, Cambridge. Later, as the first Chinese Principal of the Tainan Theological College, Shoki became an outspoken champion of the Formosans disenchanted by Chiang Kai-shek's Government in Taipei. Shoki's strong criticism of the Nationalists, whom he insisted were usurping all positions of power and leadership in Formosa and treating the Formosan-born as second class citizens, brought him into great disfavour and he was eventually exiled from his native land. He was only once permitted to return to visit his ailing parents.

Warmly as we had been received, we knew we were only guests of the English Presbyterians, and for our part they provided a temporary abode until future events opened the way for service elsewhere. Certainly we were tempted to accept their suggestion that we resign from the Church of Scotland and join them, but Donald remained loyal to the country which had trained and trusted him. There was also something very unsatisfactory about continuing to study a Chinese language not spoken about us, in the hope that we might proceed to our designated Manchurian Mission. The likelihood of this happening became more and more remote. Daily newspapers told of the virtual collapse of Mainland China, with the Kuomintang Government intending to make a last ditch stand on little Formosa.

Although we spent four to five hours daily studying Mandarin with our teachers, all of whom were evacuees from war-torn North China, I found it necessary to learn some basic Formosan in order to communicate with Lana our house girl and Shrchang our gardener.

Fortunately for Donald both the language and music classes he gave at the Boys' Middle School and his lectures at the Theological College were in English.

21 March 1949 (Donald's diary)

I go to Mrs Monty's for medicine for Sho. Classes at school in morning. I hear memory work, but 200 boys in a morning is certainly mass-production. Shift trunks from baby's room (to be) so Lana can clean it, as Sho realises how much there is to do before the wee 'un arrives – she having been told by the Chinese midwife who examined her today that the baby is now 'fixed' & could be here in 2 weeks... In evening Sho & I iron nappies....

23 March (Donald's diary)

Last night when Boris was up north Clare came in & I played records as the girls knitted & sewed. Bing's 'I'll gather lilacs' evoked the story from Sho that nothing did the Germans more harm in Vienna than the cutting down of the lilac trees in the park to use it as parade grounds. Sho is always coming out with fascinating remarks like, 'I think they have the best fish in the world in Riga.'

Donald's musical talents brought him face to face with Madame Chiang Kai-shek herself. The playing of Handel's *Messiah* at Christmas, introduced in Mainland China by the missionaries, had become a tradition, which continued with the arrival of the Generalissimo and his wife, who were both Christian, to Taipei. Isobel Taylor and Donald, the most skilled pianists on the island, accompanied a full Chinese choir on two pianos, while Lanky proved impressive as bass soloist. The performance took place in the Taipei Town Hall with the exiled leaders of the reduced Chinese National Government as honoured guests. Donald enjoyed these few trips away from Tainan. Once he and Lanky were invited to Hualian on the East Coast to adjudicate a music festival. Most of the seven choirs which took part were aboriginals from the mountain areas where peaks rose from 13,000 to 15,000 feet. Donald thought some of the singing quite good, and marked it accordingly. 'No, no!' cried Lanky. 'Tear those marks up. We never give marks. It would make bad feeling.' Later Donald learned that some of the choirs were former head hunters, and wryly commented, 'I could see how important it must be for an adjudicator to keep his head!'

I found the unabated heat particularly trying towards the end of my pregnancy. As there were no European doctors on the island in April 1949, we asked Coz Belle to come to Tainan to deliver the baby. Meantime I was experiencing some less than satisfactory reports from the local doctor to whom I went for blood and urine tests. In a makeshift surgery where ducks, hens and an assortment of small children roamed, the doctor told me on my first visit that I had dangerously high blood pressure, on the second visit dangerously low, and ordered me to bed on both occasions. I eagerly awaited the arrival of Donald's aunt from Foochow. When the time arrived for Coz Belle to fly over to us the airport was flooded and no flights forthcoming. Undaunted, Coz Belle walked the Foochow docks till she found a junk ready to sail the Straits and take her as passenger, if she was prepared to share the crew's cabin.

3 April (Donald's diary)

With Shoki & Boris on morning train to Takao. We witness an accident where a pregnant woman & child are killed by army truck which dashes off... We wait at the dock side till 5pm & see [the ship] come in. Soon I am in a sampan being rowed slowly across the windswept harbour. Coz Belle comes to the rail... we get back to the jetty in the gloaming with harbour lights twinkling & a new moon overhead.

After greeting Donald warmly, our intrepid aunt turned to the grinning crew, all of whom she had discovered came from the province of Hainan where she had worked so many years. 'Meet my boys,' she cried delightedly, 'I've converted the lot!' Coz Belle had laboured 35 years as medical missionary at Cheeloo Medical Hospital in the Hainan and then as superintendent of Cheng Te Hospital, before spending three grim years a prisoner of the Japanese. Even while she was with us the mail brought packets of the crossword puzzles and paperback thrillers to which she had become addicted as a POW.

For the next ten days till the baby arrived I swallowed many pints of quinine which I was told would hasten the birth. Coz Belle explained that she was expected back in Foochow Hospital to examine the medical students taking their finals, and her impatience for the great event made me nervous. I was very ignorant of the whole birth procedure. A sterilised packet sent from the hospital in Taipei containing basic instruments and medicines awaited the moment, but we knew Coz Belle had not delivered a baby for a number of years. As she sat at the end of the bed trying not to look anxious from the moment my waters broke, she transmitted a deal of her anxiety to me.

Greta, the one Western-trained nurse, was happily on hand and luckily for all of us the birth on April 13 was quite straightforward. Donald held me by the shoulders describing each stage of the birth in detail and encouraging me to that wonderful moment when the small wriggly morsel made her miraculous, noisy entrance into the world.

16 April (Letter to Mother)

The euphoria I experienced at that moment was like dancing 'Demon Machine', 'Cain and Abel' and the 'Russian Duo' all at once – truly a miracle enacted! Had we a bugle our baby's arrival would have been proclaimed across the Mission compound. As it was our spirited nurse Greta Gauld did almost as well, breaking out into singing the Doxology with gusto, a long time custom which she followed at every successful birth she attended.

Gifts began arriving, most of them traditional good luck red and gold envelopes containing money from Chinese friends. The gifts would have been greater had we managed a boy baby. To the Chinese the fact that our first born was a girl was considered most unfortunate. We asked our Mandarin teacher Harry Liang to select a propitious Chinese name for our baby. After a week he reappeared. 'After much meditation I have received the message for your baby's name. Her name shall be JungYing, which in translation means "Little English girl born in China".' Excellent, we beamed and upon investigating the characters, discovered Jung symbolised Jungwo (meaning Middle Kingdom or China) while Ying was one character of the word Yingwo (Heroic Land) which is the Chinese name for England.

Donald and I already wore our Chinese names proudly upon our lapels. Lede, meaning 'Worthy and Virtuous', seemed to suit him very well, although I was not quite so sure of Shiuna, meaning 'Graceful like a Willow', which had been chosen for me. As our surname Mei meant Plum Blossom we could happily respond to Parson and Mrs Worthy and Virtuous Plum Blossom! It was not easy to remain humble in China.

Upon seeing our little Terry Isobel for the first time Mrs Montgomery with her blunt Irish humour remarked, 'I do feel sorry for you, little girl, being at the mercy of your two foolish parents.' Among other things I think she had in mind the bamboo bassinet which Donald had ordered to his own measurement and which proved too high for me. I literally had to toss the baby into it.

Determined that our child should have as stimulating an environment as possible, Terry's room was made festive with coloured streamers, paper fairies and grinning dragons. Her wakeful hours were filled with the melodies of famous composers scratched out on the gramophone, and her reaction to Debussy, Mozart, Dvorak or Brahms was noted by her eager parents. We practised Chinese tones aloud as she lay sleeping, believing that all these impressions would produce a child of exceptional ability. Her tiny frame was also watched closely for signs of dancing talent.

We acquired several books on the subject of baby rearing. Truby King and Grantly Reid seemed too strict for us, and never seemed to relate to our tropical conditions. Gratefully we turned to Spock who always concluded his advice with 'Every child is different, just do for them whatever seems best.' So Terry was subjected to things strange and bizarre. As she had diarrhoea most of the time and gained weight only very slowly, we would hurry across the compound to the Andersons to weigh her both before and after each feed.

Then we made the horrifying discovery that Lana our cook/ housemaid/nurse was the victim of third degree trachoma, a highly infectious eye disease. Had we not insisted upon immediate treatment Lana would have been blind within a few years. There seemed to be dangers at every corner. Would we ever rear our baby? Our fear reached its zenith one day when Donald spied a deadly umbrella snake sliding up the leg of her cot. It was swiftly dispatched in valiant style.

Mindful of Truby King's insistence that all babies must be exposed to the sun, we placed our baby naked upon the lawn. In a very short time several dozen passing Chinese had gathered to gape at this poor little white child subject to some dreadful form of Western torture. On the other hand, upon leaving Formosa we found our little girl had no less than three different species of worm which we considered a form of Chinese torture!

Winifred Hwang produced a second son, Michael, one month after Terry was born. With the arrival of Jane Anderson two and a half months later, this brought the tally of missionary babies since the end of hostilities to three. Terry never wore more than a pair of diapers for the first years of her life, except on the day she and Michael Hwang were christened at the East Gate Presbyterian Church by the 'Bish'. Michael slept throughout, but Terry gazed about her with interest and in the great heat seemed to relish the drops of water falling upon her head. She received a pair of silver chopsticks to mark the occasion.

To ensure sufficient calcium for the mission's three nursing mothers, a milk goat was purchased, a welcome addition to the ubiquitous bean curd we had been having. The Formosan culinary conditions were simple in the extreme. Our stove, a cement structure of four grills with a smoke outlet overhead, used charcoal, a temperamental fuel requiring constant fanning. In the main we ate Chinese food, but there were times when a great longing for the taste of a scone or chocolate cake would send me into the kitchen in temperatures around a hundred degrees to try my hand.

The clash of cultures was most evident after Lana's departure (we did arrange for her subsequent treatment and checked on her progress). A new woman was brought in from the country to take her place. She had never worked for foreigners before and was quite terrified of us. I tried to explain how she should set the table for meals, and how we would like her to lay our foreign cutlery on the table. Overcome with terror and unable to remember any instructions, our new helper threw all the cutlery in one heap and fled the house, leaving behind her own bowl and chopsticks. Several weeks elapsed between maids, during which Donald and I struggled to cope with the cooking and laundry ourselves. I washed our two dozen diapers in a wooden tub of cold water on the ground. The heat was so great that by the time I had pegged out the twenty-fourth on the line, number one was already dry!

Going to the market was a daily, sometimes twice daily, affair. When we first arrived on the island 20,000 yuan was the usual amount required for one day's marketing, but with the arrival of Chiang Kai-shek and his ousted government, inflation became rampant. Depreciating currency had meant that poor Lana had staggered to market with a load of 60,000 paper yuan in her bag. It soon became obligatory to pay by catties of rice, which was the only stable commodity left on the island. Lana could buy better and cheaper, but I found the market irresistible. We would return weighed down by baskets of bean sprouts, bamboo shoots, eggplant, hot peppers, ginger, buffalo meat, pork and many fine sea foods and fruit, all tied up in banana leaves. We needed to buy little fruit as our compound was rich in pawpaw, banana, pomelo, dragon eyes, lychees, guavas, mangoes, rose apples and peanuts.

We waged a continuous war against bookworms, mildew, rodents, bats, cockroaches, snakes and dust. The dust brought by frequent typhoons was hardship, especially because it blew from surrounding fields which were heavily coated with human nightsoil. For this reason we were subject to worms of many varieties which weakened the body and were difficult to eradicate. The Formosans considered nightsoil a precious commodity. Our gardener Shrchang grew his own vegetable plot alongside our own. While we used bean curd to manure our poor soil, Shrchang preferred the Chinese method. His vegetables grew high, ours seemed stunted and gave little harvest, but we could not bring ourselves to adopt Shrchang's method.

Among the Mainland refugees who had fled from North China were some in desperate circumstances. They approached us anxious to sell their valuables in exchange for hard currency. Three exquisite Ming paintings were offered us which we would loved to have purchased but could not afford. The owners were very persistent however and as their hunger increased so the price of the paintings dropped. Finally to our great mortification we were able to scrape together but a fraction of the true worth of those beautiful works of art. Their previous owners hurried to the market to purchase several sacks of rice.

During this difficult time the missionaries decided that in order to reduce costs we should meet in each other's houses turn about, attired in our nightwear, to take our ablutions in a Japanese bath. Not relishing the idea of bathing last in line, I opted for taking my bath near the front of the queue. I was obliged to lower myself into a tub of near boiling water with a fire still burning below. I may have emerged clean, but I felt like a boiled lobster!

In September, I was roped in to share my talents with knowledge-hungry students. I had 63 pupils in my class for English, which made it difficult to remember them individually, despite their beautiful names – Laughing Life, Virtuous Pride, Jade Lotus Fountain, Keep Fertile, Political Beauty, Silvery Crescent Moon,

Golden Phoenix. Some of the English readers used in the school seemed woefully unsuitable. If the Chinese believed all foreigners mad, these books could only have added to the mystery. The English textbooks dealt with a life and setting completely alien to these Chinese students in a climate where temperatures rarely fell below a hundred degrees Fahrenheit. 'Brrr it's a cold night – ah, here is the Crown. It's a nice old place. I wonder if they can put me up for the night? I'll ring this bell.' Other unlikely phrases abounded such as, 'I rather pride myself on these old sporting prints.' Donald preferred to have his boys recite the words of Lincoln's Gettysburg speech with feeling and understanding. 'A plug for democracy,' he explained wryly.

Before long I was persuaded to introduce Western artistic dance to students of the Girls' Middle School. In order to give some background to my subject, and to capture interest, I decided to give my first talk in Mandarin. An interpreter stood by to translate my words phrase by phrase into Formosan for which I was grateful as it gave me more time to think. I finished by suggesting that all girls interested in learning this new dance come to the Assembly Hall at 3pm the following afternoon. Donald had agreed to accompany the class at the piano. I was flabbergasted to find more than a hundred eager young hopefuls standing to attention as I entered the hall. I have taught large classes in my time, but this number was a little intimidating.

One night three teachers from the school came knocking on my door. 'We hope you won't be angry with us,' they said. 'We too wish to learn to dance.'

Like other Asian students whom I taught at a later date, I discovered the Formosans to be graceful and expressive in head, arm and torso, but not at all eager to raise their legs. They had little understanding of dynamics or elevation. I decided to proceed with care and tried to keep my teaching as much as possible within the parameters of Asian dance concepts and experience. As they gained in confidence so they began experimenting with new ways of moving and new things to dance about.

Before leaving Tainan I had trained a small group of selected dancers to a high standard.

22 October

TERRY cuts her first TOOTH! Found by Daddy at luncheon! I give dancing lesson to Stella Chen. She is quite gifted.

23 October
DONALD PREACHES HIS FIRST CHINESE SERMON!
Reads it of course. V. successful... Canton fallen, so for present no home mail. Held up a while.

24 October
Terry breaks another TOOTH! Lower central incisors. She also sits up alone on rug in garden for LONG TIME before toppling over...

27 October
Lanky kills poisonous snake inside the house!!

28 November
I hate Taipei! Every time I come here I am depressed & miserable caused by a variety of reasons. The weather is always dull & rainy. Everyone is always too busy to take any notice of you. Terry or D or I are <u>*always*</u> *sick. My cold is wretched. Stuck [in] this dull old compound.*

The demands of my baby had for some time necessitated a rather restricted régime behind compound walls. I began to crave the opportunity to meet the people, and learn more of their culture, mores and rituals, and in particular to explore further the fascinating story of the Gaushan Ren.

The evangelisation of thousands of Formosan aboriginals to Christianity was entirely the work of one elderly woman, Cheong. The region was considered a hostile and dangerous environment where only the strongest and bravest missionary was sent. Prior to the Second World War, Cheong, one of the few converts in the mountainous West Coast, had been training at the Bible School in Taipei. At the outbreak of war all foreigners fled the island. The surprise awaiting the first missionaries to return was therefore incredible – no less than 5000 aboriginals awaited baptism!

Soon the story emerged of how Cheong and her followers managed to outwit the Japanese soldiers, who had been given strict instructions to ensure the mountain people worshipped only at the Shinto shrine. Hidden in a tatami basket Cheong was carried many miles from place to place on the backs of young men. They climbed over mountain ranges as high as 10,000 feet and through deep gorges in order to conduct prayer and Bible meetings. They evaded capture many times and such was the courage and faith of this woman, that thousands awaited admission to the Christian church.

One of Donald's students studying for the ministry was the son of a Haka minister serving his church on the East Coast of Formosa. Ken was a very friendly, outgoing young man who took a great interest in our Terry Isobel. As soon as Terry was weaned I accepted an invitation from Ken to visit his family at Neiphu village in the foothills. Terry was left in the sole care of Donald for the first time.

The first night as guest of this Haka family I shared with all three generations of the family a wooden platform-style bed with woven tatami for a mattress. With morning light the idea of a good shower became irresistible. I was ushered into a corner of the kitchen where two buckets of water stood waiting – one cold, one very hot. Had there been a third bucket I could have solved the problem! It is the custom for an honoured guest to eat with the 'prominent' members of the family, even if she is a woman. So my meals were taken in the company of Ken, his father and grandfather, waited on by the four younger sisters, while mother and grandmother remained well out of sight.

Ken produced bicycles, and we set off early towards the mountains. We approached a grey stone school building where I could have sworn I heard a familiar tune. How could that be? 'I'll be comin' round the mountain when I come!' could have been taught to these children by only one person, I thought. 'Yes,' explained the teacher, 'a tall Canadian Mei Boxu taught us this song during a recent preaching tour.' I was amused to discover signs of my husband's handiwork in this unlikely place.

After a further two hours of hard cycling we had left behind all sign of habitation, and magnificent scenery opened before us. Leaving our bicycles, we continued on foot, passing over some hair-raising swing bridges, across deep chasms and gorges and on through forest. A clearing revealed the first small aboriginal village. The houses were built of slate stone and thatch, with entrances so low you entered on hands and knees, and interiors so dim that until your eyes became accustomed you could see nothing. The hard-packed floor and several pieces of wooden furniture were blackened by smoke. Ken interpreted and received permission for me to watch the tribe dance. Returning from the forest each night, it was customary for the tribes to collect on the dancing place, to sing and dance out the history of their people.

Anthropologists have divided the Gaushan Ren (mountain people) into nine tribes. Each tribe speaks a different dialect, and as they possess no written language, dance and song become the single

144

means of preserving their history and passing it on to the next generation. For these Formosan aboriginals, like all tribal people I have since studied, dance is a form of spontaneous prayer. Whether their purpose is to cure sickness, or celebrate an important event – birth, death or marriage, or beg for a good harvest – they are courting the gods, seeking aid from, placating, praising them. Life without the supernatural would be untenable and the body is the sole offering.

Musical instruments were not in evidence the night we watched their rituals. The dance was accompanied solely by the clapping and singing of the dancers themselves. A large number had been converted to Christianity (those who had bowed to the Shinto shrine during the occupation, quickly demolished all signs of Japanese imperialism after its defeat). A small bamboo church stood apart in each village, but the congregation appeared equally at home singing hymns to a Christian god or dancing for a pagan one. Where once such a pagan/Christian mix would have been severely censured, contemporary thinking was much more tolerant. The Christian message could not be digested overnight. As the book of Ecclesiastes so wisely put it: 'There is a time and a purpose for everything under heaven'.

Not for the first time I wished I had studied anthropology. In physical appearance and in attire they resembled the Maori, more Polynesian in feature than Asian. As well I found the genial and social disposition of the Gaushan Ren similar to the Maori. After seeing some dances depicting the rowing of canoes I felt my hypothesis that both peoples may well have originated from a similar ocean region not unreasonable. Their hand-woven red, black and white costumes attested to the recent practice of head taking, when for every head a button was proudly attached to their costume. Although no longer practised, these greatly admired buttons were still worn with pride.

It had taken the self-imposed death of a Chinese – who was not a Christian – to achieve what the missionaries had not, the end of the barbarous custom. Gaw Hong was approached by the mayor of the village of Kagi on the plain below and entreated to go and live among the Gaushan Ren and discover how he might put an end to head-hunting. The Chinese of the plain were terrified of the Gaushan Ren and it was affecting the agriculture of the whole area. Gaw Hong made friends with the mountain people and as harvest time approached he guessed a raid on a Chinese village was imminent, in order to obtain a human head with which to placate the gods for the harvest.

Gaw Hong tried his best to convince the Gaushan Ren chief that they should cease the ancient custom, but the chief remained adamant that a head must be found. Realising that no amount of persuasion would change their minds, Gaw Hong told the chief: 'I know of a good head then,' he said, 'which you can take without the trouble of a raid. Come to the great camphor tree tonight when the moon is full. You will see a figure dressed in a red cloak. As you insist upon a human head to appease your gods, this will be he.'

The chief did as he suggested, and as a tall cloaked figure moved towards them from the camphor tree, he and his warriors attacked and killed him. Only when they gazed upon the face of the dead man did they recognise their benefactor and friend. Gaw Hong gave his life that head-hunting should cease.

My visit to the mountain people was a wonderful experience but I could not get back to my baby soon enough and was greatly relieved to find no harm had befallen her. Her daddy proudly produced a diary he had kept of every tiny event in Terry's waking hours. He recorded every nappy change, detailed the meal of each day, or bruise received, finishing off with an exciting observation of what he saw as the child's remarkable intelligence!

19 February 1950 (Donald's diary)

Hurry along to church to preach on 'The Importance of Little Things'. If I didn't know when I wrote the sermon, I sure do now. Coming home I gave Terry her milk and as she seemed sleepy put her to bed... At one o'clock Terry awake but good – and wet. Changed her. Looked around for a dry pair of panties. When I found them & before I could get them on her she was wet again...

20 February

Boy! Oh! Boy! Oh! Boy! This looking after babies is sure a job & a half!

21 February

My day hasn't started very well. While I was feeding Terry her milk the porridge burned. Then when I was racing upstairs with it & some milk, I tripped & cascaded milk all up & down the stairs...

Better time tonight... Terry & I had some fun & games together on the upstairs floor. Gosh! I love that little gal!

Donald soon felt confident enough to begin preaching in Mandarin which had replaced the Japanese language in the school syllabus. A growing number of church attenders were refugees from North China where Mandarin is the common tongue and they particularly appreciated Donald's preaching, politely overlooking any mistake. He did feel rather nervous after hearing of the unfortunate 'waigworen' (foreigner) who had unwittingly prayed throughout the service to 'the heavenly pig'. The word 'Ju' is the same for both Lord and for pig, the tone alone making the difference!

31 December 1949 (Donald's letter home)
[Terry] is nine months, with four teeth, and more popping through every other day, scudding about like a sail-boat with a broken rudder, crowing and yelling and generally bossing the house so that her poor parents are now wondering if *they* will survive!

We've settled into a routine and now the days whip by. Mandarin each day with teachers coming and going and varying in capabilities. Shona teaches English & Dancing in the Girls' School... I have a couple of English Bible Classes, preach in Mandarin once a month at a special service for Mainlanders, and teach Old Testament in the Theological College.

Eventually however, the Church of Scotland Missionary Society began to wonder, as we did ourselves, how much longer we should remain as guest workers of the English Presbyterians. By this time all overseas missionaries had withdrawn from Manchuria. We felt like migratory birds, alighted upon a small island between oceans awaiting a salutary wind to carry us to our destination.

18 February 1950 (Donald's diary)
If there is any field where we could be of real use without having to learn another language, we would be only too happy to go – anywhere in the world. The other alternative is that we all go to Australia... keep up our Mandarin & hold ourselves in readiness to return to China if [possible]... A factor which weighs heavily in favour of this course is that both Shona & I

are declared to have contracted trachoma. We are afraid to have Terry examined in case the doctor *gives* her some disease... However, I understand the treatment & cure are fairly simple and sure in the early stages...

Our next posting, it was suggested, could be India. For Donald the thought of facing yet another new language filled him with apprehension. He sent an unequivocal telegram to Edinburgh: 'Lingua phobia, Aussie bound'.

They must have taken the message seriously, because we shortly received a letter proposing instead a chaplaincy job in a South African Mission Institute where English only was required. We were due three months' furlough by this time, and the thought of seeing my home and family in Australia before setting out for a new land seemed very attractive. We eagerly began making preparations for departure.

Leaving friends and colleagues was more of an ordeal than we had expected. During the eighteen months living and working together, we had formed close bonds with Chinese and European alike. Chinese sounds and smells, Chinese food, and the entire Chinese culture seemed suddenly very precious. Leaving all this would indeed be a wrench.

Tainan College threw us a splendid farewell feast in the form of a Japanese sukiyaki. Six of my dance pupils performed two Brahms waltzes in a concert, we were presented with an exquisite Japanese scroll, and many light-hearted speeches were given, as well as prayers for a safe journey. Our hearts were very full.

A large turn-out of students lined up to farewell us at the railway station. 'Dzaijyan Mei Mushr, Mei Taitai, Yilu pingan!'[4] they called as they ran the length of the platform, tossing brightly wrapped flowers through the open carriage window. We may have had but a brief courtship with the East, yet our two Chinese years had been great learning years. We had experienced hardship but deep satisfaction from sharing our lives with the missionaries, some of whom had given long service in the field. Their remarkable faith, courage, and selfless concern for their Chinese Christian colleagues, as for the most illiterate peasant, impressed us greatly. Their example was a constant challenge which we felt unlikely to ever match.

---

[4] Goodbye Rev. and Mrs Plum Blossom, peace on the road!

31 March

Raining - Naturally!!

D ...goes down to Keelung early. Terry, MacMillans & I have early lunch & take train down later. Have to put on scene before boorish officials will allow me to go on board with T. They expected me to stand in drizzle with her on [the] docks!! I feed her, & get her to bed... D & I take no dinner for sea is pitchy the minute we leave [the] harbour – FAREWELL FORMOSA!

1 April

We three MacTavishes have entire run of ship as we are the ONLY PASSENGERS. Terry has bad cold & cough & is fretful – sleeps a lot.

Arriving in Hong Kong the city seemed a haven of luxury. Our impoverished tastebuds suddenly burst into life as we sampled such nearly forgotten delicacies as butter, milk, apples, mutton, cornflakes, chocolate and a miracle of choices from 'the shop window of the East'.

The time for cutting our links with the East came. We made our way gingerly up the gangplank of the SS *Taiping* on 11 April, praying that the boxes and crates swinging overhead would land safely into the hold.

12 April

Shona's Birthday

My husband cynically gives me a lovely book on China! 'Made in China', Cornelia Spencer. Lovely illustrations, & charming. We start reading together 'Cry the Beloved Country' as our new land is foreign to us. Food marvellous on board, making up for lean Formosan days. Passengers frightfully dull & middle-aged.

13 April

1st Birthday of Terry Isobel

Everyone congratulates our little lass who remains marvellously oblivious to it all...

20 April

John Donald's Birthday.
He is 38 today. Tells no one in case he must stand them all a drink!

The sixteen-day sea journey to Australia could not go fast enough. Our chief pleasure was in watching our thin, white daughter begin to put on weight, develop rosy cheeks and attack the wind and heaving deck with ever growing confidence. There were deck games when the seas allowed, and on Sundays Donald donned his parson's collar and took a service in the lounge. It seemed strange that we no longer needed to study Chinese characters, but reluctant to let go the language we had worked so hard at, we frequently spoke Chinese together.

Our warm welcome the day we berthed in Sydney Harbour helped dispel some of the strangeness we felt in returning to a land we had not expected to see for another three years. Life for the next three months in my mother's home at Palm Beach took on an unreal quality for me, while Donald moved around the churches of Sydney and New South Wales on more than a hundred deputations and radio assignments. I allowed myself to be spoiled by friends and family who were even more attentive when they learned that we were shortly to depart for our next mission field in South Africa. My sister Jocelyn and Donald's Aunt Maude flew across and joined Terry and me in the glorious surf of Palm Beach, and our health improved daily.

I felt very odd walking into the old dance studio. Bodenwieser embraced me in true Viennese fashion, and I was shown three of her most recent ballets, *Life of the Insects, Lucifer,* and *Le Malade Imaginaire.* The all-Australian Bodenwieser Ballet, including for the first time two male dancers, was about to begin a second tour of Australia. It was strange to think how my mother's impulse to visit Europe fifteen years before, had led to this Viennese school of modern dance setting up and developing in Australia.

The home leave slipped by very quickly and our departure on 23 October seemed in some ways more difficult this second time round. Quite blasé about ocean travel by this time, we felt, as we boarded the MV *Gothic* for Capetown, little of the excitement we had known on our China-bound vessel two years previously. Some of my lack of energy was due to the fact that I was again pregnant, but that was not the whole reason. Both Donald and I had fallen under China's spell. Chinese culture had taken root deep within us, and I for one felt averse to making a new beginning in a new land. I could see no connection between the ancient civilisation we had left behind and the seemingly still raw semi-literate continent of Africa. I felt uncertain whether I could embrace it.

Chapter Eight

Their policy towards the African is found in the word
'Apartheid' which I understand means 'separateness'...
I believe their ultimate aim is to separate the
Africans completely from the Whites...

The new appointment certainly sounded impressive, and Donald felt that to be called as chaplain to the Church of Scotland's Lovedale Missionary Institute, the oldest in all Africa, was honour indeed. Lovedale, named after Dr Love its founder, opened in 1841 and quickly set the standard in African education and Christian leadership. With the exception of three occasions when warfare broke out and Lovedale was turned into a barracks, it had served the African people for 109 years. Donald and I absorbed this and more information from a huge tome we had been sent by Dr Shepherd, the current principal, and were interested to discover that Lovedale had had only five principals since its foundation. Many African preachers and evangelists have been either trained or influenced by the work of the Lovedale Bible School. Set in forty acres of rolling country, studded liberally with cactus, aloe, and stunted mimosa bushes, Lovedale lay in a valley below the Amatola Mountains, in the Victoria East division of Cape Province, between Grahamstown and East London. It began to sound very appealing.

We were impressed to learn of the extent and variety of activities being carried out at Lovedale. Seven schools operated within its gates; High School, Training School, Practising School, Three Training Hospitals, (General, Orthopaedic, and Tuberculosis), and an Industrial School which taught the vocational students carpentry, brick laying, and farming. The Institute fostered the country's only Bantu press where over 3000 books in the vernacular were printed annually. The University College of Fort Hare, illustrious centre of higher African education, lay one mile distant.

Donald discovered that as chaplain he was responsible for both the boys' and girls' boarding dormitories. He was to oversee the religious training of more than one thousand men and women plus 150 members of staff. Quite a tall order I thought, but Donald remained blissfully unfazed and excited by the challenge. The students were chiefly of the Xhosa tribe and a smaller number were Fingo and Coloured students.

Our handbook stated '...This Institute is a Christian organisation and all members of its staff must be professing Christians and of missionary sympathy.' Competition to attend Lovedale was great, so it was not unusual to discover the professed Christian students wearing both a cross and a piece of string about their necks, to appease both Jesus and the witch doctors. We soon discovered that whether a student was a carpentry apprentice or studying for matriculation, they were genuinely proud to be part of such a distinguished seat of learning.

Our new land does not, and never could, come up to China for colour, noise, excitement, smell & general appearance – but it is on the other hand remarkably easy to live in. Everything seems so clean & regulated & orderly! Lovedale itself is a magnificent place. All its branches, activities & achievements of the last 100 years have been truly staggering and it could rank in beauty & achievement with many a European university. We arrived here just before the close of the school year, in time to attend the Prize-giving and for Donald to give his first Service, which was held in idyllic weather 'Under the Oaks', the Lovedale open-air church. The 1300 students then left for their various kraals all over the countryside.

The large unfurnished manse set in a wild garden appealed to us immediately. It was so roomy it even offered the possibility of a dance studio! Until we were able to furnish it ourselves we borrowed beds, chairs and tables from the hostels. The very first purchase by mutual agreement was a large refrigerator and otherwise we furnished slowly and sparsely.

3 December
We like our new home. I enjoy a very settled feeling altho' the home is so rambly & empty looking & the garden a wilderness.

The kitchen boasted a large coal stove and a wooden deal table. Apart from this we were faced with furnishing nine rooms. Needless to say we scarcely bothered with drapes and floor coverings while the front dining room remained altogether unfurnished, making it a delightful play area for the children on days when it was too hot to venture outside. The bathroom produced only a meagre supply of water. On the plus side the bow windows at the front of the house were imposing. Several spacious stoeps shaded by overhanging purple bougainvillaea offered precious cooling off areas in the evening, but the creeper proved to be a popular home for the common 'boomslang' (tree snake).

December 1950

Terry is now talking her little head off. She makes long sentences: She startled us by saying Daddy's collar was a 'lapel'. She bewitches us even at her naughtiest by saying dolefully 'Mummy cross, Daddy cross.' She loves the 'Can Can' by Offenbach. She knows lots of rhymes & songs already & will give us the last word of each line. Little Nut Tree & Hey Diddle Diddle are her prime favourites. She has put on weight, & looks really well. She shows off when visitors call.

31 Dec 1950

NEW YEAR'S EVE

Last New Year's Eve we certainly never pictured our present abode, but this goes for 1948 too at Foochow! Well I guess & hope this will be the scene of many more New Years for the MacTavishes.

Mrs Shepherd, the rather severe wife of the Principal, whom I later discovered to suffer from acute shyness, brought us two maids and a gardener. Our first morning in residence, Rose and Beauty settled themselves into the large hut in the back garden. As was the custom they went off into the veldt behind the house to cut armfuls of long dried grass to fill their mattress. Johnson the gardener arrived wearing gaudy dress, gold earrings and a large mirror attached to his chest. Alas, both he and the one who followed him were sacked within a few weeks as they spent most of the day smoking under a hedge. Donald and I had begun to despair as we watched the lawns dry up and crackle under foot like gravel, and the newly sprung carrots and tomato plants wilt, when we struck gold in the shape of old Albertus. From the outset Albertus's toothless smile was irresistible. Seldom moving or digging at more than a snail's pace, he nevertheless delighted us with his charm and gentleness.

Rose our cook, although a great favourite with Terry, turned rude and almost offensive with others. In her place came dear Adelaide, who stayed with us till the very end, a dear friend and second mother to the children.

Although one of the chief attractions about coming to Lovedale had been not having to learn another language (English was to be spoken with the students at all times), our work would take us to the African hospitals, the Bantu schools, and village clinics where sometimes very little English was understood. Therefore Donald and I made a start on mastering some basic Xhosa. The extraordinary Hottentot-derived clicks had the tongue doing frantic gymnastics and required a whole new approach. We did at least learn to master the Lord's Prayer which the students sang in beautiful harmony at morning assembly: 'Bawo wethu osezulwini, ma liphathwe nogubungwele egamo lakho. Ubukumkani ba khoma bufike. Intando yakhoma yenziwe emhlabeni, nje nokuba nathi sibozxalela aabo basonayo thina.'

We received frequent requests at the kitchen door for work, and our elementary Xhosa came in handy. 'Ufuna Ntoni?' (*What do you want?*) 'Ma'am, Ndi funa Umzembezi.' (*I want work.*) 'Uvukunjani kussasanji?' (*How are you today?*) 'Egamo lako? Uvela pina?' (*What is your name and where do you come from?*) The twin head boys Armament and Vacuum came often to our house. They were always in the forefront of college activities – church choir, scouts, student Christian movement, and most sporting events. We discovered later at what cost those boys received their education and Christian beliefs. In order to keep them at Lovedale their father had become a tinker. He went from home to home mending crockery, pots and pans. Whenever I saw him approaching I would rush into the kitchen and deliberately break a plate or cup for him to mend.

One day I heard the sound of bare feet rushing through the house and out the front door. Behind with equal speed burst a man wielding a stick and shouting angrily. I learned from an embarrassed Adelaide that our housemaid Beauty had fallen pregnant. She had no father, but her brother who automatically assumed a father's place, when told of the situation, determined to punish his sister. I sent our gardener to try and find Beauty, and bring her safely back, but he never found her and we did not see her again.

Church services were held outside, 'Under The Oaks' weather permitting. Otherwise the great hall became the gathering place for more than 1000 people. Visitors were always moved by the power and beauty of the singing at those services. The Africans' instinctive harmonising from even the youngest child was impressive. As I had carried a hatbox filled with hats all over China, none of which had been worn even once, I had determined not to repeat the same mistake in Africa. However at the first service I attended 'Under The Oaks' I was amazed to find all members of the African staff were wearing the most wonderful hats decorated with tulle and ribbon. Their disappointment with the chaplain's wife who appeared with no hat of any kind was very apparent! I lost marks from the very beginning. I persevered however, and remained hatless, but it took some time before I was forgiven.

Dr Cooper, the superintendent of the three Lovedale Hospitals, surprised us by refusing to accept responsibility for my approaching confinement. He insisted that he had no confidence in the small Alice Hospital and recommended that when my time came, I should be delivered at Mater Dei Hospital in East London. It seemed ridiculous and unnecessary to journey 160 miles in the heat of an African summer, but as Dr Cooper was the mission medico and we newcomers of only two months, we followed his advice.

As it happened I was admiring seals in the East London Aquarium when contractions began. Dugald Iain Dunlop MacTavish leapt into the world with all the vigour and enthusiasm which he was to retain for the rest of his life. I was so well endowed with milk, that I expressed enough to feed another two babies as well. No wonder I felt exhausted seven days later driving back to Lovedale in a temperature of 110 degrees! Terry was carried out by Adelaide to see her little brother who was wearing an absurd pink woollen beret. Terry was rather dubious at first, but it was not long before she began turning on any interested spectator crying vehemently, 'Don't you dare touch my little brother!'

It became customary for Dugald to take his morning and afternoon naps in his pram on the stoep outside Donald's study. One day Albertus killed a boomslang snake swinging from the overhanging trees. Boomslangs are pretty harmless despite their appearance, but puff adders had also been seen nearby, and so Dugald's siestas on the stoep came to an end. Some of the African fauna was a risk to children (we quickly got used to keeping an eye out for trapdoor spiders) but much fascinated us, and the entrancing chameleon which changed its colour to order was our favourite.

My duties as the chaplain's wife were to assist with the mobile library in the TB hospital, encouraging the patients to read uplifting books and discouraging the tawdry novels, as I believed befitted my calling! I visited outlying villages taking oranges and cod liver oil to the clinics. We weighed babies and checked for likely TB signs in the children. At Christmas time dress material was given to the mothers and when made up, prizes were awarded for the best.

Xmas 1951

Donald & Shona gave each other a piano which is now gracing our house – but as yet scarcely played – as life seems so busy even in the holidays. On Sunday D & I played carols on our flutes to the children at the hospital. Terry came too... I've had a couple of book reviews published in the S.A. Outlook – one on human problems in British Central Africa, and another on Land Usage in Rhodesia.

Donald's duties were numerous. He ran the Student Christian Movement, the regional scouts, and became Inspector of the country Bantu schools. He filled the position of Instructor of Divinity in all Lovedale schools, he conducted staff prayer meetings, and weekly shared preaching at Lovedale, Fort Hare, the Alice Church, Healdtown Methodist Mission, the hospital and others. As a member of the staff he also attended countless meetings, such as the disciplinary committee, the governing council etc. Each year along with other missionaries and Heads of Institutes he travelled long distances to Bantu Presbyterian Church senate meetings which kept him away some weeks at a time. There were some outstanding leaders, both black and white, who attended these senate meetings, giving Donald a welcome opportunity to develop relationships with the Africans whom he held in high regard.

The disciplinary committee was called together on one occasion in great haste to discuss a matter of some importance. Some boys and girls from the two dormitories had met one night in the eucalyptus grove for a night of love-making. They came close to being expelled for this affair, and were saved only by Donald's intervention. He pointed out that Lovedale rules were often in sharp conflict with the accepted African mores which understandably remained the predominant influence for the students, and that the school should not over-react.

The colour bar we encountered in South Africa seemed to us like a cancer at the heart of the nation. It was incredible that in a total population of 12 million, of which the whites constituted only one fifth, the black people had no vote. Among the many abhorrent laws being imposed by the Afrikaner National Government perhaps the worst was the enforcement of 'passes' on all Africans, Indians and Coloureds. If upon request they could not produce their pass they were immediately given prison sentences. The gaols were bursting with these victims.

December 1952 (Donald's letter home)

The days flow along with great smoothness and end of term is upon us before we realise it. And yet, with all this tranquility in the Institution we cannot but be aware of the turmoil outside the place...

The Blacks outnumber the Whites by five to one. The Whites are in power. They have taken the Blacks off the voters' roll & given them four White representatives in Parliament... When two million are represented by 150 and ten million by four, one can understand if the latter are dissatisfied...

I think it would be true to say, always allowing for exceptions on both sides, that the Afrikaner has a less liberal approach to the native question than the English-speaking Whites. The representatives of this less liberal group are the Government at the present time. Their policy towards the African is found in the word 'Apartheid' which I understand means 'separateness'. This policy is not really new but it has been pointed up by the present Government. I believe their ultimate aim is to separate the Africans completely from the Whites...

There have been a number of riots throughout the country & blood has been shed. Some feel that the Government has been inept in its handling of the riots. One cannot countenance law-breaking but at the same time one must sympathise with those who feel they are denied the ordinary democratic channels to change those laws.

The influence of the Christian missionaries may have seemed ambiguous at times, and sometimes dubbed as 'the soft edge of imperialism', but the influence they wielded and the contribution they made to the development of black leaders (most notably from

Lovedale, Fort Hare and the Theological Seminary) reads like an African role of honour. Nelson Mandela writes: 'I saw virtually all the achievements of Africans seemed to have come about through the missionary work of the Church'.[1] Mandela himself became a member of the Student Christian Movement at Fort Hare, attended services at Lovedale and taught Sunday School in neighbouring villages around Alice and Lovedale. He and Chief Albert Luthuli, both leaders at different times of the African National Congress, along with Bishop Desmond Tutu (who was one-time chaplain at Fort Hare) are some of the best-known of those who fought for African rights, yet adhered to the Christian principles of non-violence and reconciliation.

Among other radicals who fought the oppressive laws and acknowledged their indebtedness to religious educational establishments were Robert Sobukwe, James Moroka, Oliver Tambo, Steve Biko, Gatsha Buthelezi and Allan Boesak, as well as many modern-day leaders in greater Africa, including Robert Mugabe (Zimbabwe), Kenneth Kaunda (Zambia) and Julius Nyerere (Tanzania).

In spite of the heavy workload and coming to grips with the political and social difficulties, Donald still found time to enjoy his little family and loved to sing, read and play the piano for them. Proudly one day he brought Terry to me. 'Look,' he said, 'She can read the first verses of Genesis I. Isn't that great for a three year old?' Whether Terry actually read those verses is questionable, but it was true that her memory was so good that even a paragraph or two read aloud she could repeat word for word.

Once our household settled down, and life took on a measure of orderliness, I realised that I might be able to squeeze in some dance classes between the multifarious duties of the chaplain's wife. Classes I started for the African women students proved popular and a lot of fun. However, I was soon to discover that my role as dance teacher was not taken very seriously. Once the music began, my students lost all sense of decorum and my commands fell on deaf ears. They took up the beat and threw themselves into an orgy of movement, each as she felt compelled to do. I too was soon won over and moved onto the floor to share in the instinctive physical response to the

---

[1] *The Long Walk to Freedom*, 1994

rhythm. This discovery led me to an experiment which nearly got me into serious trouble with the Principal, but which also proved to be a valuable discovery for the future.

Donald had suggested I help out with a Sunday Bible Class but I found the students' response far less gratifying than for the dance class. My teaching brought no sparkle to their eyes, and I did not seem to be able to initiate discussion. In despair I suggested that one of the girls should demonstrate how she believed the contrite Mary Magdalene would have acted before Christ. Then I called upon a young man to demonstrate the strength of Samson. Suddenly the group sprang to life. They became physically caught up in a living response to what till then had been words only. The Bible seemed to take on a new significance for them, its stories and parables conceivable at last. A message arrived from Carona, the Principal's house. 'Would Mrs MacTavish kindly keep her class under control. The noise is unacceptable.'

This danced Bible Class, born out of frustration, was the germ of new thinking about religious dance. I later began exploring the possibilities of enlivening religious services, and for bringing greater relevance to the often outmoded forms of the traditional Scottish Church.

I was also persuaded to begin classes of expressive dance for European children in the nearby town of Alice. I found a suitable venue, a keen pianist, and about thirty girls aged from three to thirteen eager to dance. On two occasions when the temperature climbed to 110° F I was obliged to cancel the classes. We made history in the district when, at our dance concert in the Alice Town Hall, a previously unheard of event took place. We insisted that both African and European attend the same performance together. My little pupils prepared for their roles with great delight. It was a mixed programme: *A Nursery Tale*, a *Harvest Dance*, a *Russian Dance* and the major ballet for the evening, *Pandora's Box*. Terry made her debut as an imp, which suited her own character admirably. The record attendance raised a pleasing sum for the South African Anti-Tuberculosis Society. Dugald declared that he too would have liked to dance but only as a motor car!

The large, unfurnished dining room in the manse was covered with yards of 'Kaffir sheeting' (unbleached calico) and hand-painted for costumes by enthusiastic mothers. Some of these mothers were appearing at the manse for their evening class at the same time as various African headmasters were arriving at Donald's study in the adjoining room. On these occasions Mfundisi,[2] Inspector of Bantu Schools, would examine their reports and listen to their tales of woe. I wonder what kinds of reports the teachers in turn took back to their villages of strange bumps and bangs, and muffled laughter which they must have heard through the wall where my dance class was in progress!

A few weeks later the same room was transformed into a fairy glen, with logs of wood and autumn leaves scattered around for Terry's fourth birthday party. Invitations went out to every little boy and girl in Lovedale, Fort Hare and Alice. The only condition was that they must wear woodland costume. Terry was a buttercup fairy, Dugie a gnome, while their companions chose to be imps, beetles, butterflies, dragonflies and other woodland creatures. Their thanks were expressed to the Fairy Queen with a dance, a song, a poem, or a cartwheel.

When Dugald fell and cut his chin playing in the sandpit, he needed medical attention. Arriving at Lovedale Hospital, we found only a junior doctor fresh from his training. We would have preferred the Medical Superintendent Dr Cooper, and would have called for him immediately. However, as the junior doctor was black and we knew how much this reaction would hurt his feelings, we gave permission for the treatment to go ahead (six stitches without pain killer). This presented a dilemma for us as parents desiring the best treatment for our small son. Fortunately just as the operation was about to commence, Dr Cooper appeared and took over. At that time the rules allowed a black doctor to attend a white patient only in the case of no white doctor being available. So Dugald received his six stitches without any painkiller and his objections must have been heard for miles around.

The letters we wrote back to Australia and Canada of our life and work in Africa must have quickened the interest of our parents in both countries. Donald's father, a retired Winnipeg doctor, arrived in time to become an honorary 'nanny'. He and young Dugald formed a strong bond. Grandpa took a great interest in South African politics, accompanying Donald to rallies and meetings. He was very attracted to the African people and it was only owing to indifferent health that he turned down the offer of a position as medical superintendent at a nearby African clinic.

---

[2] Minister

Formosans on festive day

In streets of Tainan

Missionaries in Formosa.
From left – Boris and Clare Anderson, Dr and Jean Lansborough, Shona.

Gaushan Ren (Ami) tribal dance.

Dance students from Tainan Girls' Middle School.

The Tyal tribe of East Coast aboriginals.

On board ship for Cape Town.

Donald with Terry

The Manse at Lovedale

Donald preaching 'Under the Oaks' at Lovedale.

Dugald kisses a little friend in Alice.

Donald with Catriona
on baptism day, 1954.

Expectant mothers at Tugela Ferry, Natal.

Shona (with Terry) takes a Sunday School class in local village.

The Christmas
story enacted by
Lovedale school
children at the
hospital.

Dugald and friend

Terry and Dugald on the car
outside the Manse.

Esther doing the
washing with help
from Dugald.

Many visitors were brought to inspect Lovedale as an exceptional example of a Christian Education Centre in Africa. We missed the visit of King George V, the Queen and the Princesses Elizabeth and Margaret Rose by one year, but Donald was especially overjoyed by the visit of another illustrious visitor, Helen Keller with her companion Polly Thompson. Donald had idealised these two remarkable women since childhood. Miss Keller preached 'Under The Oaks' with shining face and eloquent eyes, while her strangulated sounds and hand language were interpreted by Polly Thompson. A reception was held at Carona, the principal's house, for the staff to meet the famous guests. Dr Shepherd selected those of the staff who had served longest at the Institute, starting with the managers of the Farm and Industrial schools, neither of whom had ever heard of Helen Keller. Donald was not considered sufficiently long-serving for the honour, despite having shared the same church service with her. I was furious about the decision, but Donald simply said, 'Why should I be more deserving than another?'

At the coronation of Elizabeth II in 1953 all students were ordered to parade before the main clock building to listen to the patriotic speeches of several dignitaries. Following a desultory singing of *God Save the Queen* (very unlike the stirring rendering they always gave to *Nkosi Sikilele Afrika*, their own national anthem), monogrammed handkerchiefs were presented to each student to mark the occasion. British royalty had never been more unpopular in Africa than at this time, during the Kenyan battle for independence. The students' rebellious mood was clearly demonstrated. Moving down the main avenue where the prefects were assigned to plant commemorative trees, each handkerchief was torn into shreds and scattered on the road. Some of the staff were very angry at this act of defiance. Donald and I discussed the affair and decided that had we been in their shoes we would have acted exactly the same way. The education the Africans desired so badly sometimes cost their pride.

Among visitors to the manse I recall two great friends of the African people – Anglican priest Father Trevor Huddleston and author Alan Paton. The courageous example of these men in championing the black cause was largely responsible for the stance Donald and I took, aligning ourselves with the protest movement. We joined like-minded people as eager members of an affiliated group called the Torchbearers which opposed apartheid in all its pernicious forms. All our close friends could be called 'Kaffir Buetie' (nigger lovers) but most outspoken of all were the bursar of Fort Hare and his valiant wife, Sir Fulque and Lady Swanzie Agnew. Subsequently their refusal to co-operate with the new segregation of the races – by allowing Africans to visit and to sleep in their home – led to their dismissal from the university. Some members of the Fort Hare staff, such as Professor D.D.T. Jabavu and Professor Z.K. Matthews served prison sentences for their non-confrontational support of the African struggle for freedom.

Grandpa had given us a secondhand Chevrolet, and we decided to visit some of the northern Church of Scotland Missions to meet missionary colleagues, and hopefully to see some of Africa's magnificent wildlife. With our car packed to the gunwales, we covered three thousand miles through the Transkei, Natal, Northern Transvaal, Swaziland, Basutoland, and the Orange Free State, before returning gratefully to 'our ain homeside'. We admired the missionaries who must have known great loneliness in some of those isolated mission posts. The isolation might also have been responsible for some eccentric characters we met. It made us realise how fortunate we were at Lovedale.

Tugela Ferry, in Natal, we judged to be one of the stickiest spots a European could endure... It was here that we saw the Zulu woman patient with her head well strapped up in a rather vain effort to sew back her ear-lobe which a sister had bitten off in a rage! That was mild, however, to the one Sister Kilgour told us of, who came in with part of her nose in her hand... I was admiring the flower-pot coiffures of a group of expectant mothers – with their long needle-scratchers handy. These elaborate hair-dos are nurtured with painful care, mud and string being important ingredients, and beads sometimes woven in with the strands. These coiffures have an almost religious significance & can never be removed without the permission of the husband & mother. On one rare occasion when the hair was cut to attend a wound, the doctor was staggered to find a wasp's nest! Personally, I'm surprised that was all!

In the Kruger National Park we marvelled at the grace and beauty of the lion, zebra, giraffe, and the numerous species of fleet-footed buck, gazed with less pleasure upon the fiendish behaviour of hyena and warthog, while the watery creatures such as hippo and crocodile held a strange fascination of their own. Of all the animals in the wild my favourite remains the elephant, even when one old bull with ears flapping decided to charge our car. Donald's backing prowess was never tested as on that occasion.

At the close of each day we booked into enclosed camps, grateful for the shelter of our little rondavel as wild animals began prowling a few feet away. The children surprised us by how well they adapted to a nomadic way of life, but there were times after a long day's travel, when faced with a large pail of kiddies' nappies, and overtired, demanding children, we wondered how we ever got the idea that this journey could be called a holiday.

We motored finally to Cape Town because Donald was to accompany Grandpa to Scotland, on a long-awaited visit to the land of his ancestors. As we waved off Donald and his dad from Cape Town, so we welcomed the arrival of Mother and Major from Sydney. It fell to me then to drive the newcomers plus the two children the five hundred miles back to Lovedale. I did not feel as confident about it as I pretended to be.

Once again in the heat of an African January our third child was born. Happily for me this birth took place in the small Alice Hospital. Catriona Margaret made a rather abrupt entry into the world with little fuss, assisted by a friendly woman doctor. Had the mosquitoes not found their way through the netting to feast upon her soft skin, this baby would have been the most beautiful ever born! From the very beginning Catriona showed great appreciation of the dance, and encored vociferously with both hands and feet as she watched rehearsals taking place in the Manse.

The first journey we made with our youngest was to the city of Durban where Donald, as Regional Secretary of the Bantu Student Christian Movement, was to conduct their first conference. We were accommodated in a two-roomed flat belonging to the matron of the African School in which it was held. The rather sparse daily menu of stamp mealies, dried beans and black bread was more than compensated for by the stimulating session discussions between members of the Bantu Church and the Dutch Reformed Church. In the face of the Government's generally inflexible policy of apartheid, Donald and I began to feel a stirring of hope for the message of Christ's redeeming love in South Africa.

Xmas 1953 (Donald's letter home)

As I predicted last year the United Party was unable to oust the Nationalists under the leadership of the much publicised

Dr Malan. What particularly struck me as a foreigner was how the non-European problem dominated every other issue.

'O! Why didn't we do what you did in Canada, U.S., Australia & New Zealand, and just kill most of them off so that they don't constitute a problem any more,' said one South African to me in a bantering way, but with enough truth in it to keep us humble.

The most heartening development of this year has been the formation of a new party, the Liberal Party, which subscribes to the following tenets:

1) The essential dignity of every human being irrespective of race, colour or creed, and the maintenance of his fundamental rights.

2) The right of every human being to develop to the fullest extent of which he is capable, consistent with the rights of others.

3) The maintenance of the rule of law.

4) That no person be debarred from participating in the government & other democratic processes of the country by reason only of race, colour or creed.

The Party pledges itself to employ only democratic & constitutional means to achieve the objectives and is opposed to all forms of totalitarianism such as communism & fascism. As Mrs Margaret Ballinger, the Party Leader, said to me at the end of a recent meeting on my complimenting her on the courageous stand she had taken, 'We can do no more: we can do no less.'

Well, there it is. Whether it has come too late; whether it will be banned, is for the future...

Our manse at Lovedale was the only other venue we knew of where all South African citizens, of whatever colour or calling, could gather to share problems, freely discuss all issues and form friendships. However, Government policy was to maintain 'separateness' between the races and laws were being passed daily to control where black people could live, what work they might do and whether or not their families might remain together. The Group Areas Act meant that whole districts were made 'white only' areas. With no thought for the suffering this new law created, entire villages and townships were uprooted and the people forcibly evicted. Most shamefully, the presence of an African in a white area was now tolerated only if his or her services were required for a white master.

Dr Hendrik Verwoerd, the Minister of Education, transferred control of African education to the much-hated Native Affairs Department. There they devised the Bantu Education Act, which further implemented the National Government's apartheid policy. Under the new regulations all instruction for Africans was to be given in the Afrikaans language, and they were to sit an African matriculation which would be inferior to the European qualification. The humiliation of the African student was almost complete. These laws effectively put an end to the efforts of the Lovedale and Fort Hare staff to educate African and European equally. It was a frightened attempt by the Government to turn the clock back, and it cast a shadow over Donald's position as chaplain at Lovedale. We were due home leave at the end of a five year term, but the Government's plans requiring the 120 year old Scottish Missionary Institute to comply with the Bantu Education Act put in doubt the long future we had hoped for at Lovedale. Were we jinxed? Kicked out of China – Africa too? We couldn't believe such a fate was ours.

Chapter Nine

Safe shall be my going...

Taking the opportunity of Mother and Major's visit, Donald and I decided to investigate other African Mission Stations, one of which might conceivably offer us a more stable future home and not be subject to the pernicious laws of South Africa.

We left our three children in the capable hands of their grandparents and two servants, and Donald and I set out hopefully upon a journey which we would wish we had never contemplated. With 'Squeak' Ralph, an enthusiastic companion, we pulled away to Dugald's pleas sounding in our ears: 'Daddy, Mummy, do bring back a baby monkey!' I did not recognise the heavy heart I felt at that time as a warning, nor stop to think what that unusual mood portended. We planned to drive as far as Kitwe, in the Copper Belt of Northern Rhodesia, inspecting various Mission Centres on the way. Things began well. We found shelter each night in far-flung outposts of 'missiondom'. Everywhere we were met with kindness by people who welcomed almost any sort of diversion in their isolated lives.

After the unremittingly bleak landscape of the Orange Free State, we struck the luxuriant red-soiled Northern Transvaal. Then, leaving Louis Trichardt to travel over many magnificent mountain ranges, we encountered arid country once more, enlivened here and there only by the fascinating bottle-shaped baobab tree. We became excited when at Beit Bridge we arrived at the 'great greasy Limpopo River all set about with fever trees'.

Continuing on to Bulawayo a faulty car spring brought us to an unscheduled stopover in Wankie, the largest coal-mining town of

Rhodesia. Then we found ourselves at the renowned Victoria Falls, 'The Smoke That Thunders' as the Africans call it.

We hired a little rondavel hut in the park where we fried sausages and stewed tea beneath the silvery radiance of a tropical moon. The affluent relaxed in the luxury of the Victoria Falls Hotel nearby, but we spared them no envy.

We were stirred by the power and magnitude of the Falls and enchanted by the double rainbow thrown upon the spray-spattered cliffs. We tottered along the edge of the rain forest which skirted the Falls, not protected by sou'westers and gumboots as instructed, but revelling in the soft drenching spray. Scrambling down to the boiling pot we marvelled at the waters of the Zambezi River, cascading 360 feet to an orgy of unchecked power in the depths of the gorge. A barefoot boy led the way along the river bank, where we smiled at the antics of monkeys and baboons, wishing that we might solve the problems of parenthood so easily! We wondered as we quenched our thirst, whether it was a hippo or croc which raised its head for a split second above the reeds. It was a place of magic and excitement.

We picnicked beneath the shade of a crinkly baobab tree just a few miles beyond the small town of Livingstone. Things might have turned out differently if Donald had not suggested I take the wheel. All the way to the capital, Lusaka, it was a dirt road with bitumen strips. It took all my concentration to keep the wheels of the car on those strips. Failure to do so meant that clouds of dust would obliterate the view ahead. Through the dust I could see a large truck approaching, and then quite suddenly a car attempting to pass the truck. The collision which followed was inevitable.

There was the sickening sound of crunching steel and a moment of breathless silence, before loud shrieks and wails exploded into the air. The other car was packed with Indians heading to a wedding. We learned later that the groom required a few stitches to his face, while the best man, the least fortunate, sustained a bad break to his leg. Although there were five adult passengers and five children in this car, they fared a good deal better than we. I was pinioned behind the steering wheel, my arm so entangled that in order to free me, the wheel had to be removed after what seemed like hours. Squeak Ralph was lying in a dead faint in the passenger seat beside me, his throat slit from ear to ear (from which he made an amazing recovery) while poor Donald, apparently concussed, muttered incoherently from the back, unable to get the doors open.

The first person on the scene offered to drive me to the nearest hospital at Choma. Because he feared I might black out in the seat beside him, he kept offering me swigs of whisky from his hip flask. Despite my groggy state and before my mouth closed up completely, I managed to down a nip or two. Choma Hospital kept us for the night, but next day the staff decided to put us on a train for Lusaka Hospital where amenities were said to be better. My right ulna was badly splintered and I was only able to take nourishment through a straw because of my dreadfully swollen face. Donald was so seriously concussed that he slept for four days without waking. Typically, upon regaining consciousness he underplayed his state of health. Bandaged and still very frail, he insisted he was well enough to preach in the Lusaka Church before we left.

Our return journey was an exhausting three-day train trip. Remembering Dugald's plea, we managed to acquire a shivery little galago (bushbaby) at a stop in the Kalahari Desert. We finally reached the manse and our welcoming family. 'Well,' said my mother brightly of the children, 'I've trained them at last!'

It was a moving reunion with our little family, and as I held each child close I was aware of how near we had come to making them orphans. The comforting thought that God had spared us for some special task ahead, was short-lived. Dr Cooper x-rayed my arm, only to discover the poor repair job done in Lusaka, and sent me in haste to an East London specialist. Our fears were confirmed, and I had to undergo a seven inch bone graft from my leg to my arm. While the Frere Hospital became my home for the next four weeks Donald made every effort to visit and on several wonderful occasions brought the children with him. I found it hard to believe that the seven inch piece of shin bone would grow back within seven months as I had been assured.

Back at Lovedale, I was taken on occasional outings across the veldt at the back of the house, with Donald pushing the wheelchair and Catriona sitting on my lap. A few weeks later Donald fell ill.

Xmas 1955 (Donald's letter home)

I am typing this on the lovely little portable Dad sent me as a Xmas present last year, but which has only just been repaired after being badly smashed in our car accident. It flew off the shelf and hit me in the back and I thought until recently that my back had come off best but now I'm beginning to wonder. About 5 weeks ago I developed a sharp pain in my back with all the symptoms of sciatica but with a slight temperature. Soon I had to take to bed and life became endurable only by constantly taking codeine. After two weeks and no improvement the Lovedale doctors decided that I should come down to the Frere Hospital in East London, and here I have been since, taking all manner of tests... all of which have proved negative, but the pain just as persistent as ever. The only constructive thing I've done here apart from some theological reading is to conduct ward services each Sunday from my bed, and appointing myself Ward Chaplain, have experienced a real enrichment, hobbling about among the men praying with them and seeking to bring the healing peace of Christ into their pain-wracked lives.

'When I get out of here,' Donald told me, 'I will be able to minister to the sick with fresh understanding. I have learned so much.' Now it was my turn to wheedle a car lift to East London whenever possible. My heart grew heavy when I found his condition deteriorating with each visit.

As each doctor failed to claim a diagnosis in their specialised fields, we decided to move Donald back to the little Alice Hospital where he could be near his family and friends. We had planned to spend our upcoming furlough visiting Scotland and tickets had already been purchased. I began alone the task of packing our goods and making decisions about which furniture to sell.

The weather became incredibly hot as we approached Christmas. I decided it was imperative to get both Donald and the children to the cooler air of the Hogsback Mountains. I did not believe that this would prove the miraculous cure we had all been praying for, as Donald's condition was deteriorating fast. He began bringing up his food and early on the morning of the third day, lapsed into a coma. Fortunately our friends the Lloyds were holidaying nearby and Geraint immediately agreed to drive us back to Alice Hospital. I strove to make Donald as comfortable as possible as he lay against me in the back seat.

The matron of the hospital took one look at the patient and phoned the St Joseph's Hospital at Port Elizabeth some 150 miles south. Our good friend Jack Munro offered transport, and so began the most dreadful journey I have ever made. We laid Donald's inert body upon the back seat of the car while I crouched on the floor beside him, and Jack put his foot down to get us there in record time. With the temperature well above the hundred, I constantly applied a cool cloth to Donald's forehead from a thermos. There was just one moment when his eyes fluttered open, and he squeezed my hand. I felt greatly heartened, but this was the last sign he gave me.

Almost immediately upon arrival, he was rushed into the operating theatre as the doctor had detected a tumour pressing on his brain. I sat numbed in the waiting room, which was dominated by a large wooden crucifix. Two nuns approached me, trying to bring me comfort. 'Come,' they said, 'kiss the feet of the blessed Lord. He will answer every prayer.' I thanked them but declined, fell on my knees and prayed more fervently than ever I had done in my life. How could things have come to this? Even as I prayed I knew it was too late. The anguish I was to know in full measure had already begun.

After what seemed hours of waiting, I was taken to the ward to see Donald returned from surgery. They need not have troubled to operate, for he did not survive. The nurses who had been called to the emergency chatted around his poor bandaged head. 'I never thought he would go so quick,' said one. 'Nor I,' agreed the other. Suddenly I could stand no more. 'Goodbye my love,' I whispered as I bent over the already strange figure. 'I shan't be long following you.'

There had been many errors in assessing Donald's illness. I was surprised to learn from the autopsy that he had died from cancer of the bone. If the journey made only 24 hours earlier from Alice to Port Elizabeth was a nightmare, the return journey on 19 January 1955 was equally horrendous. Even in my state of shock questions began hammering at my brain. How do I tell the children? How do I now earn a living? To which country do we now flee?

Donald was cremated in Port Elizabeth, but a very beautiful memorial service was held for him 'Under The Oaks' at Lovedale, where his voice had rung out so many times, offering words of love, peace, justice and hope. On this occasion his close friend Rev. James Jolobe, one of Africa's most distinguished ministers and poets, gave the eulogy. The Lovedale African Choir never sang more beautifully. The love and sympathy of many friends who spoke so movingly of Donald's contribution to Lovedale, of his powerful preaching, but above all of his warm and friendly spirit, brought much comfort to my broken heart. A tangible tribute to the recent chaplain of Lovedale was made by his students shortly after we had left. Donald would have been greatly pleased to know that of their own volition they gathered coloured stones from the surrounding veldt and erected a bird bath to his memory 'Under The Oaks'.

The small bronze plaque read: 'John MacDonald MacTavish, chaplain to Lovedale 1950-1955'. A similar plaque was laid in the chapel of the Bible School by the Tyumie River where Donald's ashes lie. The inscription adds John 3 verse 16: 'For God so loved the world, that he gave his only begotten son, that whosoever believeth in him should not perish, but have everlasting life.' Donald's whole life had been testimony to those words.

When I finally found the courage to enter Donald's study I found his recent sermon open upon the desk. It was entitled, 'The Divine Protection' and my eyes fell upon his final lines quoted from Rupert Brooke:

> *War knows no power. Safe shall be my going,*
> *Secretly armed against all death's endeavour;*
> *Safe though all safety's lost; safe where men fall;*
> *And if these poor limbs die, safest of all.* [1]

It felt as if Donald had expressly left the lines there for me to find.

In something of a dream, I proceeded with the packing and selling up of furniture, and the sad farewelling of our devoted African staff (particularly Adelaide) and many friends. Mother and Major who had been visiting East London at the time of Donald's death hurried back to us with gifts for the children. The tickets we had booked for Scotland were exchanged for fares to New Zealand. I spent three weeks in Cape Town with the children, awaiting our ship's departure as guests of kind friends. I found this hold-up after such activity difficult, and in a fit of bravado I decided to test my recuperating leg by climbing Table Mountain. After several days waiting for the 'tablecloth' to clear, a perfect day eventually arrived. As I reached the top I became tearful with joy. Climbing heights has always been a wonderful catharsis for me, and this climb succeeded in bringing Donald very close. The overwhelming grief at a life unfulfilled which had engulfed me upon Donald's sudden death, was partially relieved as I realised that although Donald's earthly mission was over I had the power – perhaps through dance – to continue it.

The *Dominion Monarch* took us first to Sydney where my parents disembarked, then on to Wellington. Mother was eager to return to

---

[1] *1914* Sonnet II, 'Safety'

the last of her Sydney homes at East Pymble, which had been rented during her time in Africa. I had relished the idea of four weeks of inactivity on the ocean, but after only a few days at sea, Dugald broke out in spots. The doctor diagnosed chicken pox, and dispatched not only my son, but also both perfectly healthy girls to the sick bay in the bowels of the ship. I continued shedding pounds as I raced up and down companionways and long passages between decks to tend the children and keep them occupied for the next three weeks.

I was excited to make out Bonar and Hilary awaiting us as we docked at Sydney Harbour, but frustrated that the children were still not permitted ashore. We were forced to introduce them to their cousins and entertain them as best we could in the ship's hospital. There followed another two days of travel across the Tasman Sea. My elder brother Wallace made the long journey from Invercargill to meet us when we docked in Wellington. That same night we all crossed Cook Strait on the inter-island ferry. Wallace took us to a hotel in Christchurch for an enormous breakfast, where the children found the array of silver and starched white linen quite bewildering. We then headed south by car to Dunedin.

As we drove up the Knox College drive my sister Jocelyn and her children came rushing out of the lodge to welcome us. It was an emotional moment when Jocelyn met my three little waifs for the first time. As her husband Hubert Ryburn was the Master of Knox Theological College, there appeared to be no problem in housing us, at least temporarily. I felt almost disembodied finding myself back in my childhood town, the same person, yet oh so different! Our South African friends had sewn a so-called winter wardrobe for Terry, Dugald and Catriona. Winter, that is, by South African standards. In that great, largely unheated, lodge we froze, and as we had left owing Lovedale quite a sum of money, I was in no position to go shopping. Old school friends leapt to the rescue and began knitting warm jerseys and socks.

When the three children were safely tucked up in their beds, I took solitary walks trying to come to terms with the great change in my life, and expressing the grief which I dared not show the children, or even my sister. Like Job however, our problems were not yet over. Within days the two girls went down with Dugald's chicken pox, and I was soon bedridden with a painful and prolonged attack of quinsy. My poor sister climbed the lodge stairs bearing trays and medicine without complaint. A new life lay before me but in my

172

miserable state I would quite happily have had it end there and then. I knew that Donald's and my children were our legacy – the result of our great love, and for them I would learn to live again. I would dance and laugh with the children as he had so loved to do. I would hang the print of the Black Christ walking on the water on their bedroom wall, that they might grow without prejudice, loving all men and women equally as their father had done. I had a big job ahead of me, and no time to waste. Dunedin would be my home again as this dancing missionary began teaching the art of dance once more.

Chapter Ten

You won't die too, will you Mummy?

I was too full of self pity to realise at first how much the uprooting of their lives and the strangeness of the world around them was affecting the children. The two girls, just turned two and seven years of age, appeared most disturbed by the changes, and soon even I became aware of their suffering.

Terry was nervous and began showing every sign of insecurity – frightened of other children, disliking all food and resorting to the comfort of books, which she began reading avidly. I made the mistake of suggesting she take dried snake skins from Africa to show the teacher at Opoho School. She also took along a box of Chinese curios – tiny dolls, paper cut-outs, chopsticks, pigskin brushes, dried ink sticks and embroidered Chinese slippers. Unfortunately this did not endear her to her Kiwi classmates who decided she was strange. They began calling her names.

Catriona – still very much at the baby stage – became extremely shy, showing her unhappiness by hiding under the bed if people called at the house. When spoken to, she would cover her face with an arm, trying to be invisible. I worried about both of them terribly.

Dugald on the other hand seemed far less fazed by the change of circumstances in his life. The large Knox College garden offered great scope for his adventurous spirit and it wasn't long before he had tested every tree, and explored every nook and cranny of the rambling building. Then Wallace and Edith, taking pity on my poor sister Jocelyn, invited Dugald to stay with them on their Southland farm. He was rapt by all the farm activities and the abundance of animals, though less enthusiastic about his first introduction to school. His two big cousins teased him because of his South African accent, but otherwise seemed to tolerate him with good humour.

The children's South African accents and quaint expressions (they still called me 'Mummy Man'!) soon changed to the broadest Kiwi. If they can adapt to everything new as well as they have done in speech, I shall have no worries, I thought.

Meanwhile, problems of a practical nature needed my attention. Somehow we must find a permanent roof over our heads, all together in one place. The children in their prayers each night assured God that they knew their Daddy now in heaven would take good care of us – and so it seemed. This is how it happened.

An elderly aunt died suddenly, leaving a sizeable estate to be divided between her numerous nieces and nephews. For me her death seemed perfectly timed. Enough money became available to meet our immediate needs. I was able to buy a neat little cottage in Maori Hill, and for the first time in eight months we were one family again, under one roof.

Then a letter arrived announcing that Mother and Majie had decided to sell their Sydney house and join us in Dunedin. It was with mixed joy that I received the news. I knew they would add to my responsibilities, especially as they grew older, but I would be glad of Mother's company and her help in bringing up the children. Coincidentally, the house next door to us fell vacant, and soon Mother and Majie had moved in. A hole in the hedge grew larger as the kids went back and forth, visiting.

The first hurdle had been overcome but the second hurdle remained. This was the pressing problem of how to stretch a meagre income to meet the daily cost of living. The answer was obvious – I would do what I had dreamed of years ago in Vienna – open my own studio of modern and creative dance. It quickly proved a success, and not only paid the bills, but provided me with a creative outlet and that special joy which teaching dance to children had always given me.

Jocelyn's unremitting support made all the difference. Just as she had taken our woebegone family into her heart and home upon our return, so she supported and helped us as we struggled to make our own life. Despite her own duties as hostess of Knox College and National President of the Plunket Society, she took charge of Catriona several afternoons a week while I was teaching. Indeed, she made life possible for us.

The children attended the Maori Hill primary school nearby. Later Terry, at the age of twelve, was granted a scholarship to Columba Presbyterian College, as was Catriona five years later. Costs for attending this school did not amount to much more than the uniform, and some extramural subjects. I was also more than happy to be employed teaching dance at the same College which had shown us such kindness.

Bringing up my strong-willed son however, proved not to be all 'beer and skittles' as my grandfather would say. Dugald's behaviour at Maori Hill school began to worry me. He had some tough little friends, including three other fatherless boys. One day I opened the back door to find four grinning lads. 'Show us your muscles Mum,' pleaded my son. Anxious to oblige, I flexed my dancer's muscles to their great delight. To be strong and aggressive had become the ideal for Dugald and his friends.

One day our local Mr Plod arrived at the house to complain that Dugald had been seen dangerously climbing the scaffolding of a house under construction. I tried to discourage his antics but it was to no avail. The day I had been dreading came. Angry with Dug over some misdemeanour, I tried to punish him, but he escaped up the street with me at his heels. I could not catch him, and gave up in despair. He was out of control and I felt utterly powerless.

Baffled by what I saw as a change in his character, I determined to investigate the cause. It didn't take long. Dugald, I found, was being regularly thrashed and humiliated by a teacher when his work was not up to standard – and he had become defiant and resentful. Fortunately I was able to arrange for him to switch schools to nearby John McGlashan College – and Dugald began to change for the better immediately. He became a keen scout, and greatly benefitted from the discipline and the outlet for his creative energy. Scout camps soon became the most eagerly awaited events in his life.

The exciting years I had spent in so many countries, first as a dancer and then with Donald, had hardly prepared me for the gentle pace – and yes, somewhat boring lifestyle I now faced in New Zealand. In place of daily language study, broken occasionally by journeys to watch Buddhist, Christian or African festivities, I now faced a day of domestic chores. No longer did I wake to the sound of stirring music, or beating drum, the sound of marching feet, or distant gunfire. No revolution in sight! Life in New Zealand by comparison seemed very circumspect, and the lack of drama more unnerving than peaceful.

However, as my student numbers increased and dance classes multiplied, I became very busy, with little time to mope. I seldom reached home before six-thirty at night. After school the children would often go next door to their grandparents, Trina (who became known as 'Nurse MacTavish') making afternoon teas, Dugald chopping kindling and filling the coal scuttle. The moment I returned however, three hungry children would meet me clamouring for food and attention. A quick sherry helped restore me sufficiently before I set about preparing the meal, hearing their homework, then bath and bed.

There was one very bad day. The weather was atrocious, the children were fractious and I trod on the cat's tail for the second time, sending it screeching out of the house. Feeling the need for space and quiet, I too banged the front door and disappeared into the bush. Climbing Mount Flagstaff was a wonderful cure. I returned home after several hours to find three perfectly behaved children offering to set the table, wash the dishes, and go obediently to bed.

> *Four corners to my bed*
> *Four angels round my head*
> *One to watch, two to pray*
> *and Daddy to keep all fear away.*

I assured the children that their daddy was looking after us, and guiding our lives. But the day Terry turned to me and whispered, 'You won't die too, will you Mummy?' I realised how fearful and insecure she still felt. I could at least assure her I had no intention of that. There was now order in our lives and for the first time I began taking an interest in things outside the house and studio.

Once we acquired a Mini, which we christened 'Lovedalia', Saturday afternoons became a day for family adventure, exploring the bush, the mountains, or one of Dunedin's marvellous beaches. In school holidays we had longer adventures, often spent at 'Seven Sisters', my brother's holiday crib at Lake Hayes in Central Otago.

But I also began to use school holidays as an opportunity to farm the three children off to various wonderful friends and relatives. Terry joined the warm-hearted Russells at Arrowtown, where she buried herself in books, and Dugald threw himself into farming life with Wal and Edith at 'The Gree'. Trina wasn't far away, with the doting Hendersons on their farm at Winton. From these holidays with their 'extended family' I hoped the children would grow more independent and self-reliant. And I was especially pleased to see Dugald find some male role models to emulate.

Apart from being a welcome addition to my income, the classes I held at Columba College were very therapeutic for me. Among many gifted young girls were those with special creative talent, who in their turn fed me with fresh ideas.

By the close of my first teaching year at the College we were tackling themes with real depth. *The Exile*, a ballet in three acts – the first of my angst-ridden ballets – was partly conceived out of my own feelings of loneliness and uncertainty as to whether I would be able to adjust to this new life ahead. Although I had returned to my native land, and everyone was trying to be kind, I felt as much an exile as my Jewish friends had felt arriving in Australia.

Antony Elton, our talented but eccentric pianist, wrote the scores for both *The Exile* and the following *My Skin Is Black My Skin Is White* – a ballet based on my experience of apartheid in South Africa.

This work was directly inspired by a visit to our Lovedale home by the author Alan Paton. I quoted from his book *Cry The Beloved Country*: 'I have one great fear in my heart, that one day when they turn to loving, they will find we are turned to hating.'

Soon I was asked to choreograph for theatre and opera in the city. The first of these were for two operas – Purcell's *Indian Queen* and *Dido and Aeneas* in collaboration with Professor Peter Platt and Patric Carey at the University of Otago. Following these came Gluck's *Orpheus*, Eliot's *Murder in the Cathedral* and the Southern Comedy Players' frothy musical *Salad Days*. For these early engagements I auditioned dancers in the city, but later the classes at Columba College and the studio began to bear fruit. I was soon able to draw from a number of talented students to form the Dunedin Dance Theatre. This small company began playing quite an active role in the community. For some years we appeared annually with the Dunedin Opera Company. *Fledermaus* (1963), *La Traviata* (1964), *Amahl and the Night Visitor, Hansel and Gretel, Carmen* and – most exciting of all – the Walpurgis night scene in Gounod's *Faust*. One of my fauns in *Faust* was a young Patrick Power. Not a singer at the time, he traces the beginnings of his career to the day he danced in *Faust* and heard Gounod's wonderful melodies for the first time.

Working with the Opera Company was exciting, but it was with Dunedin Dance Theatre that my creative juices really began to flow once more. We devised and performed annual dance recitals of our own, which were often taken on provincial and national tours.

Musical accompaniment has always been integral to my teaching. I have been blessed with some remarkable and inspirational pianists over the years. Ken Weir, Ian Fraser, Vivienne McLean, Jean McIntyre and Roger Dunbar among others, all added ambience to my classes. Most memorable of all was Sir William Southgate. We had a great rapport, and shared a crazy sense of humour. The young Bill revealed himself already a sensitive artist. His improvisational skills especially inspired both dancers and teacher to great heights. When he became excited he would rise from the piano and do a handstand or cartwheel, scattering dancers before him.

Bill's first composition for us was *The Other Side of the Wall*. Originally inspired by the Berlin Wall, this was a dance of the haves and the have-nots of society and the racial, religious, economic and political divisions which separate them. Our most successful collaboration came in 1970 with *Pania of the Reef*, the first New Zealand ballet of a Maori legend. It was first mounted with a small string orchestra playing music based on pre-European Maori laments. The première took place in the Logan Park Public Art Gallery to a haunting Maori chant sung by Elizabeth Murchie.

Some years later Television New Zealand decided to restage *Pania*. Bill managed to rescore the original for a full New Zealand Symphony Orchestra to an unbelievably short deadline. I rehearsed *Pania* for three weeks with members of the New Zealand Ballet in Wellington. Both Jon Trimmer dancing Karitoki the Maori chief and Linda Anning playing Pania gave outstanding performances. Some members of the company were tasting a new expressive style of moving for the first time. They pronounced themselves quite delighted to be able to dance barefoot and to be allowed their hair swinging free. Although strictly classically trained, the corps picked up the lyrical qualities of my choreography amazingly well. The Maori warriors, with moko painted on face and bottom, made a strong contrast.

I have always enjoyed choreographing strong vital movements just as I preferred dancing in powerful roles myself. But Viennese lyricism and soft flowing movements were also an intrinsic part of my training. This, joined to my dawning feminist consciousness, heightened my interest in developing the more passive roles of the women who wait, who heal, who grieve. *Hunger* (1965) to Dvorak's melting lento movement of String Quartet in F, was created for the children of Biafra. The dance portrays the anguish of mothers who must watch their children starve, and the way in which each individual accepts life's tragedies.

For Amnesty International in homage to prisoners of conscience, I choreographed another conscience piece some years later called *Bars*. Mozart Fellow Christopher Cree Brown (the son of my little playmate Johnstone, whom I'd once hoped to marry) wrote an outstanding sound score for this ballet, using some rhythms taken from authentic African music. For the riot in prison scene Chris had come up with some explosive sound. I asked him how he had achieved such an unusual effect. His reply came back: 'Oh, just me peeing in a bucket and amplified a hundred times.' We also had original Shaun Burdon slide projections of bars and skulls thrown onto the backdrop for dramatic effect. The ballet dwelt not only on the prisoners, but equally on the women and children – those who wait for their return.

After participating in African worship with all its fervency, colour, sound and spontaneous movement, I had found the New Zealand services very low-key and uninspiring. Church rituals here took place only rarely. Christmas, Easter, and periodic communion services appeared to be the sole occasions when the congregation could become at all involved in the experience. I felt the time had come for the dance to play a visible role in worship – as once it had done – to assist the church back to a celebration of the fullness of life.

In 1961 a Harvest Festival service at Maori Hill Presbyterian Church became a catalyst for a completely new direction in my life. The church on that occasion looked more like a grocer's shop than a place of worship. The congregation sat in front of an intimidating collection of processed foods. Bags of flour, packets of cornflakes, tinned fruit, and baked beans were balanced precariously beneath the organ pipes, a great wooden cross towering all! Were we giving thanks to God, or saluting human consumerism? I put this question to our minister after the service.

'What would you do instead?' asked the Rev. Tom Corkill.

'I would have young girls dancing down the aisle to the chancel, bearing sheaves of wheat, freshly baked bread, and pitchers of new wine in gratitude and praise – a return to the ancient tradition of bringing the first fruits of our crop to lay before the Lord.'

'All right, you're on!' said Tom and for the next Harvest Festival I had to live up to my word. This was the first of many dance services we initiated in churches of various denominations throughout the country, and I soon became known as a pioneer of religious dance.

Church buildings are seldom suitable for dance. A chancel after all is not a stage. Space is often a problem, but my dancers became adroit at coping with baptism fonts, lecterns, pulpits, and communion table and rails. Such obstructions for dance became a challenge for us, and sometimes even improved the choreography. We soon became masters of improvisation. Our first experiment at Knox Presbyterian Church in Dunedin was with *Dances of the Spirit* a selection of Negro spirituals. One of these, *Nobody Knows the Trouble I've Seen*, was accompanied by contralto Patricia Payne. I wondered how my father and grandfather, both of whom had preached from that very pulpit, would have reacted to such a display of female exuberance. In a later version I was lucky enough to have a dancing minister in Len Pierce, who as Moses, literally danced his congregation out of the church.

In 1971 St Paul's Anglican Cathedral in Dunedin was about to consecrate their newly acquired chancel. The Dean was keen to add dance to the liturgies planned for this special service, and delighted in my suggestion of a ballet I wished to choreograph. *The Prodigal Daughter* was a gender switch from the well-known parable of The Prodigal Son, reset to match the growing trend of daughters leaving home – and I wonder now if *The Prodigal Daughter* may not have been the first feminist ballet seen in New Zealand?

One day the minister of Wakari Union Church suggested I help him with a group of leather-clad bikies who had surprised him by arriving at his church on thundering motorbikes. He asked me if I thought dance introduced into the service might help retain their interest? I suggested my ballet *Liberation,* which covered subjects likely to be relevant to the lives of the gang, could be a good start. It dealt with protesters (who oppose the establishment), flower people (who preach love not war), drug addicts (who resort to escapism), the hungry (who demand freedom from starvation) and the glorification of war.

This dance was a contemporary Christian message, offered to an initially critical and suspicious audience. We felt unsure of the reaction we would receive, but the gang's interest was obvious from the start. Infected by the passion and the energy of the dancers all the bikies later joined them in spontaneous dance down the aisles. Dance classes I held for interested members of 'Hells Angels' and 'Coffin Cheaters' followed. It was with difficulty I got them to shed their leather clothing and great boots. Although speech for the majority was not easy, they discovered communication through movement a language more natural, and one which suited them better.

Eventually our combined efforts took shape. My bikie group danced in a service where they were saying things about love, trust, and prayer which they really believed and in a manner of their own devising.

I did not divide my dances into sacred or secular. The dances we performed in theatres, or at conferences, in hospitals, prisons or in the street, were so often concerned with social or philosophical issues that they fitted either category.

I learned a great deal from this bikie experience. I was no longer able to feel that worship was complete if utterly divorced from the life around us. I recalled the words of J.G. Davies whom I had heard speak some years earlier: 'We no longer enter into a second realm to encounter a deity, but preferably to celebrate experiences of the NOW. The Holy is best met through the Secular'. I followed on pioneering dance in worship, or liturgical dance, in many countries to follow. Suddenly churches seemed ready and eager to explore once more, as they had in the fourteenth century, the mix of the mind, the spirit and the body.

Chapter Eleven

A revolution. A revolution in the Chinese Church!

I was excited when in 1964 I received an invitation to become dance advisor for a conference called 'Communicating the Gospel Through the Arts and Mass Media'. To my especial delight I found it was to be held at Tao Fong Shan in the New Territories of Hong Kong. I had never imagined I would return to that magical city where Donald and I had first set out on our missionary journey.

Before the conference began, I made a visit to my friends Dr Mooi and Jean Moore on the nearby drug addict island of Shek Kwu Chau. They were the only foreigners among 150 men voluntarily seeking rehabilitation from opium addiction. I was again impressed by the courage and compassion of missionaries. Courageous they certainly had to be, because even the one night I spent with them in their small house on a cliff edge, the patients rioted and were attacking each other with iron bars. Jean explained to me that such outbursts were common and the result of severe drug withdrawal. Mooi ordered us to lock all doors and windows, make a large pot of tea, play Beethoven, and pray! He then returned to the dormitory to try and quell the angry men. Jean and the ayah, the only two women on the island, had lived through worse terrors they told me. They seemed much calmer than I. 'What do we do if they turn on us?' I inquired. 'Just jump in the sea,' she replied, 'and swim to the island of Cheun Chau, it's not more than a mile away!' Around 2am Mooi returned looking exhausted but pleased, having patched up the wounded and pacified the ring leaders. We all gratefully crept to our beds.

I arrived back at Tau Fong Shan in time for the opening ceremony of the conference. I was delighted to discover that this seminar was led primarily by the indigenous church leaders of East Asia, some of whom I already knew. The Study Centre – featuring a Buddhist temple and a huge Christian cross – was situated on a high mountain overlooking a most beautiful bay.

For the first time the dance was to receive equal consideration with its sister arts, drama, painting, architecture and music. I was delighted to be able to demonstrate my lecture live, with twelve young Chinese girls whom I had selected from Yinghwa Girls' School. Once my Harvest Dance began to look presentable, we all descended to the Shatin Village below and purchased bolts of white and blue material, fruit and flowers for the dance, which they danced for the delegates with grace and charm.

Although dance has never been associated with Christian worship in the East, things were changing, and even dance now was being looked at afresh. (There has always been a rather conservative element in the Asian churches, a carry-over from the early missionary influence.) I showed slides and film of my work also, but the live interpretation of the message proved the most meaningful.

At the end of the conference, a friend and I organised a brief visit to see the temples of Angkor Wat and Angor Thom. These amazing ruins of the ancient Kingdom of the Khmers, half-buried in the jungles of Northern Thailand, revealed to us a civilisation as astounding as those of Rome or Greece. The conflict between rampant jungle and the ruins themselves appeared like a passionate love affair. We were overawed by the five hundred temples we saw, the size and complexity of which defied description. We were fascinated too, by the magnificent carvings and sculptures so clearly influenced by both Hindu and Buddhist art. The bats winged and squeaked overhead, the palm trees spread large fingers against a darkening sky, as we watched exquisite Royal Cambodian dancers bend and sway around the colonnades of the temple. It was magical. How lucky we were. Only months later Pol Pot and his soldiers began destroying much of it.

The success of my religious style dancework to date had led me to believe there could be no theme too grandiose for the dance, and so upon my return to New Zealand I launched into a work which drew heavily upon the various cultures I had experienced.

Encounter examines the various ways in which people have felt and expressed spiritual need. We moved from animism, to sun worship, to subjection under the yoke of a prophet, and finally to an encounter with the 'living Christ'. Following its first performance at a Youth Ecumenical Conference in Hamilton, I was invited to recreate the ballet for the 1966 Australian Church and Life Movement. I was most happy to be loaned nine excellent dancers from the Bodenwieser Dance Centre and to perform it in the Sydney Town Hall. The reception was so warm that the Australian Broadcasting Corporation made a film of *Encounter*, which was shown in Australia and then to an appreciative audience in the religious section of the Cannes Film Festival.

Encounter was to explore the waters of still further shores. Through Dr John Fleming, an old Manchurian missionary colleague, I was engaged on a three month tour bringing religious dance to the Christian colleges and universities of South East Asia. Singapore came first. I began holding workshops with youth workers and Bible leaders from many denominations, on the theme of 'Dance as Communication'. I also auditioned ballet dancers chiefly drawn from the Goh Singapore Ballet Academy, including one slender young man, Goh Choo San, whom I chose for the main role of the Prophet in *Encounter*. Choo San was later to become one of America's leading choreographers.

The first performance of *Encounter* was held in Singapore Anglican Cathedral on a specially built twenty foot stage. As it was Easter, Television Singapura decided to make *Encounter* a special feature for transmission. My Chinese dancers worked hard and I was impressed by their adaptability and skill.

Because the Chinese so respect their teachers I was farewelled with the customary large and delicious Chinese meal a few hours after the final film take, then I packed the still steaming costumes for a quick exit. *Dzaigyan yilu pingan, kwai hwei lai.*[1]

It was only a few hours later I was unpacking the same damp costumes in Taiwan (formerly Formosa) for another group of dancers. Within the hour I was giving my first class.

Returning to the Tainan Theological College, where Donald and I had been so happy, was a sobering experience. Our Chinese-style house with the turned-up eaves had been replaced by a modern

---

[1] Farewell, peace on the way, return again soon.

one, and much else in the compound had changed. The weather in February was freezing. I took classes in the new communication building, and the dances were filmed as they were learnt. I felt like a ghost as I wandered along well-remembered places encountering faces, which with the passage of time seemed both familiar and unfamiliar. I wrote home to Terry:

I met a man today who told me that he had been Donald's student, & how well he remembered his singing lessons, his rope-spinning & his teaching on Amos...

... I took a photo of the church you were baptised in, seeing the home you were born in is pulled down...

My students in Tainan were neither as sophisticated nor as dance conscious as my Singapore dancers had been, but with some volunteers from the city ballet school I was able to achieve a very presentable interpretation of *Three Images of the Lord's Prayer*. The dance consisted of a Gothic plain song, an ancient Hebrew melody, and a West Indian calypso. This dance was presented to a packed and eager congregation in the main Presbyterian city church. At the conclusion the college principal, Dr Song, rushed into the changing room. 'A revolution,' he cried excitedly. 'A revolution in the Chinese Church!' By this I concluded we had done well.

Arranging to be away from home for three months hadn't been too difficult. Trina and Dugald boarded for the duration at their respective schools, and Terry, who was now in her second year at University, remained at home and also took over several of my dance classes. We exchanged many letters and everything appeared to be running smoothly, although I worried about any hint of unhappiness in a letter, constantly advising them to check on each other, eat well and visit their grandmother! I was somewhat disturbed to hear that Terry's boyfriend had returned to Dunedin and was spending long hours at home with Terry. It was the seventies, times were definitely changing, but I worried about my daughter who had been born in this very place not so long ago.

Believe me darling, I've lived quite a time, as Tainan keeps reminding me, and I do know the pitfalls in life... Keep the standards I'm sure you set for yourself some time back. Standards are things one never regrets, impulsive or unwise actions one often does. Because you are Donald's daughter, I felt no qualms about leaving you to cope for yourself. I wonder why I feel a few now? Your growing up has sadly missed out on much of the sound Christian faith which I believe you would have gained had Donald lived. Mine such a poor reflection of his unwavering faith & purity of mind.

In response I got a good ticking off from my eighteen year old daughter who assured me her own set of standards were very much intact – although I wasn't sure what *that* meant! Her brother likewise was enjoying quite a social life.

I was not pleased to hear of your bad behaviour at the Ball, Dugald. I did not think you would ever take so much drink – you were unaware of your own behaviour. Sounds poor to me, and very rude to your partner. Dad would not have been amused. Why do you think I would be? Haven't you any standards of your own?

This parenting from a distance was trickier than I had anticipated. However, present concerns must take precedence. I flew to Bangkok – hardly enough time to shake off Taiwanese dust before facing another people, a different language, a new culture. At least the heat was the same! My Thai students tried to follow my strange dance with grace and patience. Their own dance which is exquisite to watch, is also very stylised and follows a prescribed formula. My students at Chiangmai Theological College were already being exposed to a good deal of Western teaching, so, upon my insistence that dance could do more than just tell a story, they began to show a growing interest. 'Statement Through Dance' was held in the open air theatre one night before a rather stunned audience.

I had some experiences which stunned me, too. The most memorable was joining a Thai Buddhist family who wished to free a departed spirit whom they explained was unhappy and would not leave her ancestral home for Nirvana.

'Please help us to bring her happiness,' they cried. 'Dance with us that she may go free,' and they thrust flowers in my hair and hands, and draped a cloth about my shoulders.

I tried to copy the dancers as best I could – three steps and a lift of a bent leg behind, raising first one arm high, then another. A Thai orchestra accompanied. Suddenly a sword dancer leapt into the space and remarkably picked up seventeen swords to place in different parts of his body without losing a step. There was a sudden shrieking sound from the crowd, then: 'The spirit has ascended to

Nirvana. Thank you.' With sweat still pouring down my face I left, feeling virtuous and strangely elated.

On the way home, we passed a highly decorated twenty foot bier, part of a cremation ceremony being given for a well-loved abbot. Saffron-robed monks filed past the bier to pay their respects, and to receive a new piece of saffron cloth. Suddenly fire crackers rent the air and the bier exploded into flame. A cry went up: 'A snake!' and the crowd scattered. From the loud speaker a voice came, 'Even the serpents come to pay their respect to our great leader'. No sooner were these words spoken than a loud thunder clap followed by flashes of lightning burst overhead. 'And the elements also come to acknowledge our beloved leader.' Meanwhile the bier had become an inferno, with just two bamboo poles still holding a piece of cloth, symbol of Buddhism, aloft. What a colourful ceremony, I thought. Buddhism is a part of these people's daily lives, in a way contemporary Christianity can hardly match.

My tour of South East Asia ended in the Philippines. In Dumaguete City on the island of Negros, I was amazed to discover the beautiful, flourishing Silliman University. Founded by an American missionary in 1910, Silliman must be one of the most alluring campuses to be found in the whole of the East. Situated on a stretch of tropical beach, and backed by towering mountains, it also claims to be one of the leading universities in the land. I was entranced from the moment I stepped on terra firma, and equally delighted with the friendly staff of many nationalities who immediately launched me into a succession of Christian Arts Festival activities.

January 31
What a great time I've been having. Nothing will come up to Silliman University I'm sure. Just everything – the dancers, the place, my hosts & the work I did were terrific, all of them.

The Filipinos are a talented, delightful people. They impressed me so much that when invited to return to the university to take up a twelve month position as Professor of Sacred Dance, I accepted without hesitation. I did, however, make it clear that I would prefer to be known as Professor of Sacred *and Secular* Dance, as I was unable to divorce one from the other.

By now I had discovered that for Chinese, Thai, or Malay, my workshops seemed at first something of a mystery. Not so for the

Filipino – which should not be surprising, as they have been exposed to 350 years of fiery Spanish dance, followed by 50 years of American jive. These influences have given them a wide range of body movement and expression, which made my teaching a joy.

With the dance troupe from the School of Music and Fine Arts, I stepped outside the traditional church themes, and taught my ballet *The Other Side of the Wall* which I considered very appropriate for a country which showed such disparity between the rich and the poor. The following two weeks I rehearsed almost from daylight, with a brief siesta and a dip in the sea after lunch, before returning to work into the cool of the evening.

I left Silliman University reluctantly, although happy in the thought I should be returning full-time.

My next port of call was St Andrew Episcopalian Seminary in Manila. My students were Igorots from the mountain regions of the far north of Luzon, studying for the ministry.

This has been a big day – with 3 hours giving a class & rehearsing 'Encounter' this morning – then [a] 2 hour workshop here in the Seminary with 120 students & nurses from the nearby hospital. They screamed with mirth at everything – so we had good fun, but didn't achieve an awful lot... This evening back to the Studio of Dance Arts for [a] further 2 hour rehearsal. I get taken & fetched in a late model Chev by a chauffeur. This is such a bad place they say it is unsafe to even take a taxi alone at night. Some women won't even walk alone on the streets by day!

One day in order to show their gratitude for the dances I brought them, these young Igorot men offered to show me their dance. They threw off their garments with lightning speed and to my delight replaced them with only a woven red and black G string! The sole addition was a headband decorated with feathers from the calou bird. Several nurses of the same tribe joined in the Courting Dance, accompanied by ganza players. I found these dances very wild and exciting.

There may seem to be a wide gulf between animist customs and the rituals of tribal people, and the tenets of the Christian faith, yet we shared many of the same values. The Peace Pact for example, practised by Igorot warring parties at the close of battle, is an extraordinarily meaningful act, and surely close to the Christian teaching of reconciliation and love. The Peace Pact truly is a 'burying of the hatchet'.

The two chiefs face each other, and thrust their spears into the ground. Their two loin cloths are removed, attached to the spears, and joined together. Squatting on the ground to discuss boundary lines, the pact is completed, and a wine cup passed round and shared to symbolise peace.

Where once the people placed figures of idols in the rice fields to assure a good harvest, they now as Christians place small wooden crosses. I believe ritual is vital to the human soul, and that it is disastrous to forbid physical expressions of either pain or joy. From pre-Christian times the dance was a means of influencing the invisible powers and establishing contact with them. For over 3000 years the Filipino from the mountains of Luzon danced and sang for every important occasion in their lives, from birth to death.

I was most interested in passing on the dance forms and expressive qualities of the many cultures I had studied. Each time I returned from visits overseas my students learned the dance of Thai, Chinese, Balinese or Filipino. It meant also dramatising their mythologies, and following some of the religious practices and rituals of the people. Through the study of a people's dance, we found we came to a greater understanding of their customs and behavioural mores.

Once again it was hard to return to the routine of life in New Zealand and I began making plans for my year at Silliman University. This time my house and studio were taken over by dance teacher Ann Woodhouse. Terry was at Teachers' College in Christchurch and Dugald was studying at Lincoln University. I took Catriona out of her final school year with me, and together we entered into the life of Silliman University.

Trina, faced with her first experience of poverty and injustice, was soon playing the role of nurse and social worker. I wrote home:

Trina says she walked past the open door of the city hospital yesterday and watched an operation calmly exposed for all the world to see...

She has started collecting sick children off the streets and bringing them home to be treated. She spent 7 pesos on a home medicine chest...

She treated the sores of beggars, visited the sick in hospitals, and began teaching creative classes in the city schools. Most remarkable of the achievements of this seventeen year old was the role she played in the provincial gaol.

The conditions were appalling. Dozens of young men were locked up together in large cages with no activity allowed. Trina began her crusade by collecting books and magazines to start a prison library.

What a girl she is. Intrepid, to say the least. Nothing scares her. She's been doing a great round for magazines for her prisoners. After lunch when everyone is supposed to rest, off she goes. If you can post a basketball to us, she'd jump over the moon. This is apparently what her prisoners want most of all.

Trina saved enough money to buy the basketball herself, and begged wood and tools from the Industrial School for inmates to do carpentry. We were amazed to see the standard of work some of the men produced.

Upon finding two women each with a small child who had been held without trial for over a year in that prison, Trina brought the case to the local magistrate. Both women were accused of having murdered their husbands. After investigation, the magistrate admitted that these two women had indeed been wrongly detained. Apologies were belatedly made, and they were freed.

The prisoners seemed to prey on Trina's mind. On Christmas Day she woke the sleeping dancers from their hostels, and hurried them along to the prison chapel to give a special performance for the prisoners. I was not surprised to be told that Trina was known by the inmates as 'The Angel', and I was very proud of her. Trina was able to attend any lectures at Silliman that she chose: French, Anthropology, all dance classes, as well as daily classes in Visayan, the local language. Exciting as all these experiences were, they also took their toll. Quite suddenly one day Trina announced that she could not see.

She retired to her bed and slept for several days. The doctors seemed unable to find a medical reason for this strange affliction, but whenever she became stressed the blindness recurred. It was put down to a kind of culture shock or culture 'fatigue' and she was urged to take things more easily.

Trina and I went to town just a minute from the university gates to get her measured for a dress. By the time we got back she collapsed on her bed. Tomorrow I'll have blood tests taken, 'cos she is not well and sleeps

191

every spare moment. I think it could be a hangover from the tremendously full and exciting week in Cebu. Last night was another 100 mile per hour typhoon...

For me the varied commitments at Silliman were a fascinating challenge. Some liturgical dance was already known at this school, so I was not obliged to waste time explaining its value. We straightaway began working on a piece which I have found the most rewarding to explore in many cultures. *The Rock* is based upon T.S. Eliot's *Choruses from the Rock*, the theme being that we build in vain unless we build together in the Lord. Depending on where I stage this dance, the building scene is adapted. Some cultures build with bricks and mortar, others with bamboo, abaca, and nipa palm. Some use wheelbarrows and earth-moving machines, while others carry loads in baskets upon their heads or upon a pole balanced on their shoulders. For this reason each creation becomes a new and exciting experience. In the Philippines our production proved to be an ecumenical *tour de force*, bringing Catholic priests and seminarians together with Protestants in the Silliman Chapel.

Trina and I shared a nipa and wood faculty house with two American professors. Our little windowless house was gay with red poinsettia and yellow cassia trees. We began to feel this was both a culture and a way of life we never wished to leave. One of the reasons for this was the Filipinos' way of looking at life as a gift, and we loved the ease with which they adapted to all circumstances.

Their tight-knit family society produces people with great durability and strength. However there was one exception. Against their usually gentle, self-controlled nature we discovered the Filipinos could also resort to a terrifying state commonly known as 'Wayang Hija' (meaning absence of shame). Their repressed side asserts itself, and they 'run amok'. Perhaps this was due to the co-existence of two thought and behaviour patterns which are inconsistent with each other – one being the introduced Christian Western ideas and attitudes; the other, behaviours handed down from their ancestors.

The one and only time I faced hostility at Silliman was the occasion of our dance performance during the Festival of Christian Arts. An anti-Western, anti-religious student activist group, for whom dance and ballet were, according to their leaflets, 'decadent meanderings in the land of the never-never' picketed our show. They collected outside the Silliman gym with bull horns, rocks and posters, threatening those brave enough to enter. The dancers carried out their full programme which included *Liberation*, a ballet almost entirely devoted to the concerns of our time: hunger, drug addiction, profiteering in high places, and, irony of ironies, government violence against protest marches (the Kent State University incident was topical). The protestors outside must have felt very perplexed, for they fell silent and stones stopped raining on the roof. As the last dance ended, without even acknowledging the warm applause, we hustled the dancers out the stage door for a quick getaway, while the activists took over the stage with rousing communist song.

Despite the frightening turn of events, we felt we had proved conclusively how powerful a medium dance can be. I experienced some nervousness following the incident and decided this was the time to start planning the tours I wished to make to research the dance, music and customs of the minority groups of the Philippines, who inhabit many of its 110 islands. Before getting very far with these plans, I was surprised and not a little flattered to be invited to become choreographer for a Cebu City production of the rock opera *Jesus Christ Superstar*.

It was a novel experience for me sleeping in the infirmary of the College of Immaculata Conception, and rehearsing with 150 enthusiastic cast members both day and night. There were inevitably occasional differences of opinion between the producer, musical director and myself regarding costuming and other artistic issues. A few theological concepts also had to be thrashed out. This was, after all, a revolutionary presentation and a complete break with all religious and quasi-religious productions the Filipinos had previously known.

If the final production was not a fully Rice-Webber conception, it was still considered a 'believable' interpretation for a Catholic audience brought up in the strict traditions of the past. The combo band, the trailing microphone, the flashing strobe light – all the gimmicks of modern theatre were used. But for me it was the beauty of those young people who sang and danced with such sincerity which made the three seasons of this production so memorable. The handsome young Jesus in the final Silliman performance touched us all by stepping down from the stage and embracing his tiny widowed mother proudly seated in the front row.

Terry and Dugald joined us for their Christmas holidays, arriving at Mactan airport just in time for the première. It was an exciting time for us all. The implications of this celebrated rock opera were far reaching. Upon our return to Dumaguete we were delighted to hear snatches of *Superstar* being sung wherever we went – on campus, in concert, or from pedicab drivers in the streets and barrios. It really seemed that *Superstar* had awoken Filipinos to the idea that the story of Jesus was not one of suffering alone, but also one for rejoicing.

Three separate research tours for me to examine the minority tribal groups of the Philippines were made possible through the assistance of the University Research Centre and the Ford Foundation. My interest in making these tours was the hypothesis I had reached, that all primitive dance stems primarily from religious aspiration and from our conscious dependence upon a greater power. Through witnessing dances of fertility, marriage, courtship, against sickness, or for a good harvest, I formed a definite impression of an animist god present in all.

I was usually accompanied on these trips by a daughter, a friend or a social worker. We studied tribes from the north of Luzon, and as far south as the isles of the Sulu Sea. We began by visiting the pygmy Negritos beyond Mabinay on Negros Island.

23 October 1971

Priscilla Scott, Alan, Trina & I set off by jeep two and a half hours up into mountains. From Mabinay we walk with 2 Negrito guides for one and a half hours to reach Research Centre. A short rest, then on foot through jungle growth, and swollen rivers (with caribou!) – over hill & dale, to reach a little church on the mountain top where a revival meeting is in progress. I preach, Trina speaks (in Visayan). Heavy rain, so we all spend night in the church. Very hard boards. Many ants. Great experience.

24 October

Rain clears at dawn. Forest peers through our shutterless windows. A sort of breakfast. Trina teaches the children action songs.

Taken to visit Negrito house. Old man over 100 years in a g-string, his daughter alongside 2 years old!!

Trina gives him Vicks for his T.B.

Watch them grind corn on a stone wheel.

Walk back. 30 kilometres. Jeep returns us weary home.

It was disappointing to find the Negritos had so little original dance remaining. More exciting for me were the remote Mandayas.

They are a kind of nomadic people... the forest companies constantly push the tribal people further and further away... they feel very insecure.

These people have the fastest walk I have ever seen – not a jog, a real long stride – even across the sharp stones in bare feet, rather as if they were on ice skates!

They are very shy, and wilder-looking than any I have seen so far. Their teeth are filed and they press special herbs into them... also red with betel nut. The women are often sewn into their tribal dress which is not removed until it falls off them.

I tasted my first durian fruit – by holding my nose tight with left fingers found the flavour most pleasing. They say this is a sign I will 'come back'. Now – hours later – that revolting smell of the fruit lingers still on my hands – Trina is not impressed!

Mindanao was the next destination. We arrived on the final day of the thirty day fast of Ramayana. That would have been colourful enough, but it also happened to be the time of the crucial Lu-uk election. We could not have arrived at a more extraordinary time. From the window we watched a man run amok, and begin shooting wildly, peppering the building opposite with bullets. We learned that this is not uncommon when a zealous Moro is released from several weeks of abstinence. In the fracas which followed this unfortunate man managed to put a bullet into his own backside!

Thinking all danger past, we ventured out of the hotel hoping to see something of this beautiful little island, surrounded by palm-fringed beaches and clusters of boat houses built on stilts over the water. As we turned back into the main street, shots rang out again scattering people before us. Our jeep pulled up sharp, and we joined the fleeing crowds. We cowered beneath a restaurant table, and only when all seemed quiet, did we make our way back to the hotel, keeping our heads low and avoiding several sprawled figures on the ground.

We still felt uneasy tonight eating our meal in a barricaded restaurant where people were allowed in & out only through a tiny opening in the door by a nervous-looking proprietor...

The next day we had gathered enough courage to visit the mosque where the entire population came as a last act of worship before feasting began. The frenetic physical ritual of standing, kneeling and bowing accompanied by sound from a thousand throats made for a moving religious drama.

By far the most rewarding experience for us was in nearby Jolo where we made contact with the Badjau or Sea Gypsies, who agreed to dance for us. As we approached their stilt houses, the Badjau, half-naked and dark-skinned, many with hair streaked blond from sun and salt water, came whooping down their ladders dragging kulintang and wooden clackers with them. Long silver finger nails they adopted seemed absurd in that wild setting. Muslim influence was obvious in their dance, but their strong animist beliefs were still adhered to, particularly in such dances as the Sabat (Salvation) – a dance so secretive that foreigners had never been allowed to see it. Through friends however, I was given a detailed account of the Sabat which I found most useful for my research.

The Sabat dance is considered supernatural, in which dancers call upon the spirits to either assist them in childbirth, to heal sickness, or to assure an easy death and a joyous trip to heaven. A white urn is placed on the ground and covered by a white cloth. After much hypnotic dancing to the spirits, the cloth is removed, and it is thought the spirits now enter the bodies of the entranced dancers. They make strange utterances, and continue dancing until they fall unconscious to the ground.

Dugald was obliged to live with the Badjau for several days, as he waited hopefully for a storm to cease in the Sulu Sea. Every night a crowd would collect to view the stranger and insist he dance for them. His Maori haka may have lacked subtlety, but clearly passion was not missing. Each evening his leg broke through the floorboards to the sea lapping below, and each morning the floorboards were renewed, and he was begged to dance the haka yet again. Because the Badjau diet is primarily slugs and seaweed however, Dugald became very ill, and returned to us in a pretty sorry state.

To complete my studies, I travelled alone to the mountainous northern region of Luzon where I was again delighted by the ceremonial dance of the hardy, one-time head-hunting Igorot and Ifugao tribes. The Banawe rice terraces which these intrepid people hewed from inhospitable land forty thousand years ago, are today recognised as the 'Eighth Wonder of the World'. Much of their dance is to placate or propitiate the gods. Among their many rituals, I found the death dance the most interesting. The Igorot consider a natural death is a cause for rejoicing, not mourning. They tie the deceased person to a chair, and dance around them for three days. The Igorot crouch as they dance, their feet pounding and stamping, a complex rhythm beat out by gong and drum. In the case of a violent death no honour is given, but a wild dance is performed with hisses and shouts, as they exhort the dead to rise and avenge their death.

Emma Paras, a social worker who had befriended me, took me to her native village to meet her Chinese Ifugao family. Still further north in that tiny village of Hapid (meaning Happy) a few miles from Lamont, I took great delight in the sharing of a wild fiesta. As I tried to follow the dance steps, my bare feet attacked the earth with glee, and I began to feel those wonderful rhythms calling on everything that was basic in me.

The girls murmur something about 'Ballet' – disappear and return with a well worn record of Beethoven's Ninth Symphony – asking me politely if I would please dance to this! I was overwhelmed and rather touched. It was obvious I had to dance something, but fortunately the Beethoven disc wouldn't give forth on their wee machine – so I chose from among a pile of ancient 45s 'The Last Waltz' & surrounded by delighted spectators of all ages I bashed my way through it, battling with clotheslines & [the] confined area. Then I dragged in others & soon had them doing chassé & Hupfe, vor und ruck – Schwung, Schwung, seitwarts chassé und Bein heben![2]

It was a marvellous means of communication – speech itself unnecessary after this.

As I crept under a mosquito net on the floor that night with the scent of pomelo, mango, papaya and coffee blossom in my nostrils, I wondered how surprised the next anthropologist to visit Lamont would be. It will take them some time to work out which of the many migrations to the Philippines could be responsible for introducing the Viennese Waltz into the otherwise pure Igorot forms!

Reverend Gilbert Rice and his wife Esther had already impressed me through their writings. They too considered that as music and dance were integral to animist culture their use as a medium of communication for the Gospel should be sympathetically studied. I

---

[2] Step & hop, forwards and back – swing, swing, side-step and lift the leg high!

learned that the Rices had only just managed to rescue much aboriginal folk music from oblivion, and use many of the tunes for hymns. Dance too threatens to disappear. I'm afraid missionaries must take much blame for the reduction of so much tribal dance.

I found my way with some difficulty to where the Rices lived and worked with the Kalihan people of Nueva Visaya.

Emma & I up 3am, but bus has puncture so don't get started till 5am. We encounter two landslips and I am the only woman to lend a hand hurling rocks down the precipice – but then I wanted my breakfast very badly! One student in seat ahead of us was returning to Silliman. 'Aha,' he said, 'You are THE Mrs MacTavish!'

We enjoy the hair-raising mountain road though often terrified of the washout and the closeness of my wheel to the yawning cliff edge! Awful 'Comfort Rooms'.

We avoid the 'Dog Meat Restaurant' & buy cream crackers and coke instead...

Emma & I must part, she to return to Manila... Looks like I'll have to spend the night in Sante Fe, till I spy the Mayor. He is kindness itself, & arranges for me to hire a flowery jeepney (12 pesos) & sends a policeman along to keep me safe!

Climb 8 kilometres to the small untidy barrio of Imugan, Mission Station of Deibert and Esther Rice. Meet the two sons and collection of 'family', including cute 2yr old Filipino daughter, a dying T.B. patient, 2 convalescents & a badly burnt girl with attending mother, a cadet minister and sundry lovely students. Much prayer, study, hymn singing. Glorious bathroom & W.C., surprisingly – plus HOT WATER – in this remote area!

Sunday Morning

8.30-11.30am – Church! Following the three hour service, people gather on the lawn outside house to rehearse for me. Esther's pet monkey (now 5 years) suddenly attacks a 2 yr old child, cutting and clawing at it severely on face & leg. Esther patches the child up and gives tetanus injection.

The fiesta just gets underway when a man is attacked by the same monkey, & when Esther goes to his assistance receives bites and scratches also. I jump in and ram a stick down the monkey's throat when I see a chance. More first aid.

No matter how much the Rices wished to retain the ancient dance and music of the Kalihan, I felt doubtful of their success. I left Imugan with one clear picture in mind: the sight of four little girls with gyrating bodies, dancing with pleasure, not to the powerful rhythms of their ancestors, but to the popular hit 'Pearly Shells' coming from a juke-box in the sari-sari store! Children of their time.

Because the island of Mindanao offered so much scope for my research, I made three trips there. The Bagoba people living in a tiny mountainous barrio of Sirib were extremely excited by our arrival and showed us unexpected hospitality. Trina and I were offered a section of the floor in the house of the elderly Christian Datu and his wife. We arose to a fine breakfast of pomelo, rice and chicken. I then began my inquiries about their dance, while Trina collected children about her, handing out the small gifts we had brought and teaching them songs and dances. A fiesta was ordered by the Datu for that evening. We taped music, took photos and learnt rudimentary steps of a wedding dance called Salustan. We even made a feeble attempt ourselves to play the great ganza orchestra which swung from the roof of the meeting house. The entire village was there, and the excitement was catching. We felt we must make an early departure next morning in order to allow the men to return to their ploughing and the women to finish off the washing they had left by the river. In a sudden downpour, we headed back down the mountain using a large banana leaf to protect us from the rain.

To learn something of the Aetas, we were given a rough jeep ride to hunt down Carlito Buntas, self-styled Rajah of his people. One time dancer with the famous Bayanihan Dance Company, Buntas now lives in a barrio north of Tagum. Considered a bandit by some, Buntas is also revered by others for trying to rescue the Aetas from the encroaching lowlanders' attempts to take over their land. By special request he was allowed out of the provincial gaol for several hours in order to bring us to his home, and meet his pregnant wife and four children. Donning his grandfather's blood streaked costume and with the accompaniment of nose flute, guitar and song, Buntas danced for us. I taped the following dances: War Dance, Witch Dance, Harvest Dance, and the Mashed Potato. Some of these were skilfully accompanied by a wild-looking Aeta on a rusty petrol drum and two coca cola bottles.

Largely due to the work of the Maryknoll Catholic Fathers the

Christianised tribes in this region showed far less suspicion of strangers than their animist cousins. My companions, German Dorothea, Arciel (Filipino social worker) and I, were lucky enough to spend some time deep in the Maragusan Valley with a most unusual Catholic priest and his Mansaka (people of the mountain) flock. Because the majority of this tribe had received only love and respect from the missionaries, their interest in us and our quest was eager from the start. Although they had accepted the Gospel, they were encouraged to remain faithful to most of the tribal expressions of their ancestors.

Father Walter Maxey, who retired outside to share his night with the rats and cockroaches, was like the legendary Father Huddleston of Africa.

He vacated his 6ft by 6ft bedroom & wooden platform for the ladies and seemed quite excited by the unusual occasion. Conditions of his home & outside 'comfort rooms' are on a par with an old miner's hut – though hygiene conditions I would guess even worse! Water is carried from the spring 20 mins away.

He amazed me no less when I spoke of my admiration in particular, for the way he shared his dwelling and all that it contained with the entire congregation. But he corrected me: 'No,' he said, 'There is one thing I cannot share, and that's my toothbrush!' Father had sent word that a dance contest was to take place, so a large crowd gathered, many in tribal wear. The Mass over, spears and shields were removed from the church walls for the impassioned war dance which followed. We were then privileged to witness a variety of dances, from young to old. Some were courting dances, or to heal sickness, while others were intended to chase away evil spirits.

The famous 'dancer from overseas' was to be the judge, but chose instead to allot prizes to everyone. These came in the shape of chewing tobacco, sweets, gum, raisins, Chinese wine and bread. The walls of that church rang with laughter. Before leaving we were soundly embraced by the chief, and dozens of toothless old women as well as some truly beautiful young ones. Father Maxey explained to me that the beautiful Mansaka bead necklace the chief presented me with, also served as a kind of wedding ring. Should I ever decide to return to reclaim my husband, my sole task would be to join his other wives and weed the carmote (sweet potato) fields. I have not yet succumbed, but there have been occasions in my life since, when this thought seemed quite appealing.

Because of the inter-racial fighting between the Muslim recessionists and Christian Filipino in the southern region of the Island of Mindanao, my research in that region had had to be postponed several times. By the time Trina, Terry and I were permitted to make the journey, conditions were believed to be fairly stable again. In actual fact I think we were very lucky to get back alive. Muslim and Government forces were still at each other's throats, and ten thousand were dead. The resurgence had not ended, and our bus journey from Iligan to Marawi could so easily have met with ambush and death. It was with relief we crawled from beneath the bus seat to a warm welcome at Mindanao Christian College. The situation was certainly dangerous for those indomitable missionaries who chose to sit it out. Only a few weeks after our visit, the director of the College was kidnapped by Muslim extremists, and kept hostage many months.

The Moros constitute the largest minority in the Philippines, and having become increasingly politically aware, they seek independence for their Maranao tribe. We were consequently very pleased to hear of the activities of the Muslim-Christian Brotherhood which was making a courageous effort to bring the two warring parties together. My daughters and I stayed in the student hostel of the Mindanao State University. Their Darangan Cultural Troupe favoured us with a marvellous, very sophisticated display of their dance and music. The regal quality of both costume and movement depicted the long and splendid history of what is known as the Maguindanao Sultanate. Terry in particular was fascinated by the grace of the malong which is worn by all Muslim women, and has a language of its own. On the shores of Lake Lanao, (known as the largest open air toilet in the world!) within sight of the great mosque, she learned the many ways the malong can be worn, and for what occasion.

Back in Dumaguete my life resumed a more normal pace. My three children returned to their studies in New Zealand, leaving me to face my final weeks in the Philippines with something like dread. The thought of leaving this fascinating land I had come to love seemed quite unbearable. Surely life could never be as exciting again. One final unforgettable experience for me was at a Silliman Easter dawn service. We gathered at 5am, groping our way in the half-light between coconut trees to the sea. There, choral groups gathered to sing of the triumph of the resurrection. And then, as the sun rose above the edge of the sea, five golden-robed dancers appeared, dancing my *Il Dulce Jubilo* which seemed to dispel the sorrow of the night, bringing promise of renewed hope and glory. The new day had begun.

I was to return to Silliman University ten years later in 1981 to mount *Requiem for the Living*, a ballet protesting against the prospect of nuclear war. This piece, set to Penderecki's *Threnody* for the victims of Hiroshima, had been successfully performed already in churches and theatres in New Zealand. The timing for *Requiem for the Living* in Dumaguete proved very apt. From the reception which followed after, attended by faculty, guests and the dancers themselves, came a decision to make a formal complaint to President Marcos concerning the nuclear reactor the Government planned to build on the island of Negros. I don't know if the cancelling of this Government scheme came as a direct result of our ballet, but it most certainly inspired and stimulated a university to take action and declare their objection to machines for making war in their own land.

Chapter Twelve

I come to church to hear of hell fire and damnation,
not to be tempted by women's legs!

The Soviet customs officer searched the contents of my luggage with practised fingers. Suddenly he drew out several reels of recorded tape – a fresh interest on his face. Colleagues were summoned and a noisy debate followed. I resigned myself to a lengthy delay and searched in my mind desperately for a plausible explanation. None of the officials spoke either French, English, or German. They stood glowering at me till I felt my expulsion to Siberia to be imminent. Suddenly a happy idea struck me. 'Ballet,' I mouthed, 'Musica Ballet' holding up the offending tapes, and executing a small pirouette. It was like magic. Faces about me relaxed as they smilingly returned the tapes and closed the cases. I was ushered out of the air terminal and into a waiting car with ceremony. So it was true, I discovered, the patriotic fervour with which the Russian people view their celebrated ballet companies.

It was 1970. The children mostly grown up and able to fend for themselves, the studio thriving, I had been suffering from a bad case of itchy feet. As a long time dance critic for the *Otago Daily Times*, I persuaded them to accept articles I planned to write upon the state of dance in various lands and took off on a world trip.

At the end of each packed day, I would dash off my thoughts and impressions to New Zealand, before facing the next country on my list. First on the tour was Canada, home of so many MacTavishes I had never met. Donald's brother Jim and wife Jane introduced me to snow-shoeing and curling in temperatures of 30 degrees below freezing between viewings of the Winnipeg Ballet. Chicago and

New York proved as stimulating as I had heard, I made friends with Agnes de Mille, and in San Francisco I sat in on a class with the amazing Anna Halprin. Wandering alone around Brooklyn at night, and becoming lost in the subway scared me more than anything I had experienced in Asia or Africa.

Swinging London was a thrilling place to be in 1970. I visited both junior and senior ballet classes of the Royal Ballet, and watched them in performance at the Royal Opera House where I was especially impressed by Ashton ballets, *Monotones* and *The Dream*. I was amazed to see nine to eleven year old immaculately turned out little boys, subjected to a very strict intensive training session. For the casual observer this stretching of the body and goading of the limbs into unnatural positions seemed not unlike some medieval form of torture! For a scholarship child who possibly comes from a fairly squalid London street to find himself sleeping in a dormitory where Lord Nelson once planned his campaigns, or doing his homework in a room where Henry VIII was said to have first seen the light of day, must surely be a difficult adjustment. Despite the magnificent park surroundings and strong sense of history at White Lodge Ballet School, I could only feel pity for those vulnerable young boys.

I investigated the experimental Martha Graham-influenced London School of Contemporary Dance at The Place and saw the once-classical-turned-modern Ballet Rambert where the remarkable 82 year old founder Marie Rambert still held the reins. This sprightly lady amazed us all by turning a couple of cartwheels backstage after the show to the delight of her adoring dancers. Already in 1972 I was able to write of this little company:

At last we find a thoroughly satisfying fusion of the old and the new, which we dare hope may always remain with Ballet Rambert, to challenge the mind, stimulate the emotions, and delight the eye.

It was not easy to turn from the absorbing sights and events of London to work with the small dedicated Radius Drama Group from Finchley. But in a short time I presented a religious dance programme and lecture at Southwark Cathedral, followed by the first liturgical dance to be seen as part of a service in the hallowed chapel of St Andrews in Scotland.

And then to the suspicious customs official in Moscow. When it was learned that the prime reason for my visit was to write of the inner workings of the Soviet ballet schools, doors opened up for me everywhere. My accommodation had been booked second class, but now I received first class treatment wherever I went – private bathroom (albeit no plugs and sandpaper instead of toilet paper!), extra food coupons and excursion tickets. I was provided with a university professor of literature and English languages as a guide and it was decided no moment of my time in Russia should be wasted. My first choice was to spend one day inside the celebrated Kirov Ballet School. Here I jotted down my impressions.

(1) Small classes not exceeding 10 students
(2) Raked studio floors
(3) Very strict teachers (Pushkin, teacher of Nureyev)
(4) The proud and serious bearing of even the youngest student
(5) The obvious outstanding talent among graduating students
(6) An unscheduled peep into a room of young children at rifle practice!

I watched a company class conducted by the directors, Natalia Doudinskaya and Konstantin Sergeyev, which I thought a miracle of discipline and application. Praise was scant. 'Are you ill?' demands Doudinskaya of a patient row of fairies. 'How can you work this way?' The Swan Princess fares little better at the hands of Sergeyev. 'What to do with them?' he fumes. 'The simplest fouette I ask of them, and it looks like a boxing match!' These same dancers gave the most faultless performance of *Swan Lake* that evening I have ever seen (and I've seen many). To my query 'Do you perform only the well known classics?' Sergeyev replied, 'Classical ballet is the heritage of a dancer's years, each new generation speaks differently again through those classics. We don't make a museum of our classics. Why should we be forced into new but inferior works?'

There was one new ballet I heard of which was occasionally shown in Russia, but was hardly popular. Named *Bedbug* it is an ideological exposure of evil in our time. It became clear to me that the Russians will always prefer *Swanhilda* to bedbugs, and fairies to the kitchen sink, and from this visit I could now understand why they claim the classics as rightfully theirs.

My last night in Russia I experienced a ballet of another kind. Walking the snowy streets I marvelled at the tireless industry of armies of Russian women shovelling the falling snow from the streets, which was replaced as fast as it was scraped away. Two unflinching figures stood guard at Lenin's tomb, alongside the magnificent spires and towers of the Byzantine Prokovsky Cathedral. In softly falling snow, I walked the length of Red Square, while students and soldiers marching ten abreast sang in wonderful harmony as only Russians can. For a moment, standing in that floodlit square, I felt I had stumbled upon a scene from the Nutcracker Ballet.

I was wearing a fashionably short fur-edged leather coat and a fur hat, and was perhaps a little conspicuous, an unaccompanied woman striding across Red Square at midnight. Suddenly several overly-friendly young soldiers moved alongside me. I could not understand the Russian words whispered in my ears, although the general gist was not hard to guess. Becoming bolder they peered up into my face, then broke into delighted laughter. 'Milaya Matriushka!'[1] they cried, as they stroked my shoulders. I could only smile at the swift transformation into harmless lads, and so, laughingly we linked arms and they accompanied me along the snowy streets to the entrance of Hotel Metropole. Here the soldiers clicked their heels, saluted me, and with unabated high spirits, disappeared into the night.

Africa was my next port of call. Flying to Zurich well wrapped up against the freezing February weather, I only just made my connecting flight to Johannesburg. At midnight as the engine was revving up, I was literally hauled into the plane, the doors clanging behind me. Almost immediately I fell into a deep sleep, without even removing my warm outer garments. The plane touched down in Brazzaville in the Congo some hours later, when I awoke in a fearful sweat. Looking out the window I was astonished to see bare-chested stevedores on the tarmac. Was there not still snow on my boots?

Darling daughters,

I am missing you both & wishing very much that our three lives had managed to flow together at this point in Africa.

Can you picture me this Monday morning seated outside my tiny thatched cottage neath a cascade of the deepest purple jacaranda tree? The sky a formidable blue & just above my head a massive brilliant red bougainvillaea in a paroxysm of bloom – it is all quite heady.

I had felt some trepidation returning to Africa, the scene of so many strong emotions from the past. However, my diary for the

---

[1] Little Mother!

next five weeks was so full and so rewarding, I found little time for tears. My hosts in Cape Town had wasted no time preparing for the dance services which had been planned. Auditions began the very evening of my arrival. As Easter was approaching I chose dancers in Cape Town, Johannesburg and Grahamstown to dance *Easter Canticles*, a piece proclaiming the meaning of Christ's death and resurrection. Two services drew an audience of 1200 at St John's Church, Cape Town.

An unfortunate front page photograph of the dancers in short white tunics, bearing flaming torches brought a scathing comment from one testy gentleman who, it transpired, had not been present at either service. 'I come to church to hear of hell fire and damnation, not to be tempted by women's legs!' he stormed. Fortunately this did not appear to be the attitude of our audience. Only a few weeks later many people were turned away at the church door when the ballet was performed at St Columba in Johannesburg. The minister Dr Jack Dalziel wrote to me of his impressions.

This wonderful service has been the source of numerous conversations since. Naturally everyone did not like it. We have learned you cannot please all the people, all of the time, but the vast majority did, and we all realised that the dance properly used can be a rare tool for proclaiming the gospel. Certainly some dancing would be quite out of place but NOT THIS!

The success we experienced at St Columba was largely due to the dancing of seven young artists I had selected from the Dance School of Audrey King, one time teacher of Margot Fonteyn in Shanghai. They shared a feeling and understanding of their roles far beyond the mere technical prowess usually seen.

My time in Jo'burg was packed with variety and contrast.

The biggest joy was when Anne took me to a Zionist (very pentecostal type) African theological training centre. Bishop Moqulua greeted me warmly & before I knew it, I was facing his students, telling them about my association with Africa – then got them all dancing! I felt the old simple joy being with these people again. Lovedale, the Manse, Donald & you small kids seemed like yesterday...

Although I refrained from joining in on their efforts to beat off any evil spirits lurking in the building with sticks, I was quite certain that the tireless energy of those dancing worshippers would quickly disperse any lurking demon! To their pleasure however, I danced the Lord's Prayer which was spoken by my friend Anne. Again I contrasted the sheer life force of the African Christians with their European counterparts, who seemed anaemic and far removed from a personal encounter with Christ.

In a speech made by the principal of the Seminary, I was made to feel rather ashamed as I heard him say: 'The white men brought us Christianity from across the sea. We are grateful to them, but fear that today they have lost much of it. We believe that one day it will become our Christian duty to bring Christ back to them.'

Between my demonstrations, lectures, and rehearsals for *Canticles* I spent one wonderful morning watching the fantastic energy, humour and power of the tribal dancers of the Witwatersrand Gold Mine of Brakvonstein, and a two hour singing and dancing session in the black township of Soweto. I outlined the story and gave a basic structure of the song 'There is a time and a purpose for everything under Heaven'. The dancers, ranging from tiny children to toothless old women, all danced with enthusiasm and much laughter. They were delighted to be told that it was now considered okay to bring dancing into a church service.

There were two occasions when, in contrast to the above, I was entertained by wealthy Jo'burg society types in barricaded luxury homes with swimming pools attached, and guard dogs to announce the guests' arrival.

*   *   *

Returning to Port Elizabeth 26 years after Donald's death in that city brought back grim memories which I had hoped to forget. Before I could indulge in them however I was whisked 80 miles away to Grahamstown and Rhodes University – one of the main centres of white education in the Cape. The heat that day was incredible. I arrived dripping wet, to be met by a deputation of teachers, dancers, and the press. A tall, oddly familiar young woman rose as I entered and embraced me. To my astonishment I recognised her suddenly as Rosemary Bate, an erstwhile twelve year old pupil from Alice where I had taught dance from 1950 to 1955. Rosemary now ran a ballet school in the city and was eager to have me teach her pupils straight away. I drank gallons of liquid and ate several of the

The MacTavish family upon return to Dunedin, 1956.

Dance of Thanksgiving outside Buddhist temple in Hong Kong.

Silliman University, Philippines

Trina with the Mandaya people.

Shona with Igorot pygmies
in Banawe, Luzon.

Ifugao dancers. Mt Province, Philippines

39 lashes scene, *Jesus Christ Superstar*, Cebu City.

Robyn Merritt dancing *Secular City* at First Church, Dunedin. *M. de Hamel*

Jon Trimmer in *Pania of the Reef.*

On Freedom. Dunedin Dance Theatre, clockwise from top – Jan Bolwell,
Jos Brusse, Trina MacTavish, Marilyn Lusk, Terry MacTavish, and
(centre) Kate Calvert. *M. de Hamel*

Reconstruction of Bodenwieser's *Demon Machine* by Dunedin Dance Theatre. Clockwise from top – Jan Bolwell, Carol Brown, Philippa Laverty, Susie McKewen, and (centre) Terry MacTavish.

While Grandmother Played Bridge

Dance workshop, World Council of Churches Assembly, Nairobi.

Terry MacTavish and Jan Bolwell in *Orlando*.

With senior students, NZ School of Dance. *Alan Knowles*

Members of the Dunedin Dance Theatre, 1992.

With Louise Petherbridge, Auckland Airport.

pineapples we had bought on the roadside, and headed for the Rhodes University Gym. From 150 young girls I selected the six most promising for the ballet I would teach them.

In the midst of rehearsals I escaped one day to a hilltop overlooking the charming little town below where I remembered I had come on a picnic with Donald and the children, years ago. With the familiar smell of Africa strongly in my nostrils I wrote to New Zealand:

Three Xhosa women wearing gay doek have just passed through the shrubbery below me, while a press gang of prisoners in conspicuous white striped cotton suits climbed the road above, an armed warden in charge. Sugar ants are scuttling in and out of holes at my feet, cicadas fill the air, and the sun is very hot. Cathedral spires dominate the horizon which impressive white Rhodes University buildings attempt to match!

Eight hundred students overflowed from the seats and filled the aisles of the Great Hall for our final performance of *Easter Canticles*. This was the ballet's third performance in less than one month and each time with a completely fresh cast. I felt this was quite an achievement. My waist line too was showing the effect of my labours!

But now I had to prepare myself for an adventure of another kind. Eighty miles north from Grahamstown stood the little town of Alice, the centre of black African education in South Africa. Here was the Lovedale Mission where my family had spent five of the most wonderful and most tragic years of my life. It was with mixed feelings of dread and anticipation that I made the journey back to Lovedale. I returned hopeful that I might manage to lay to rest the ghosts which had haunted me all the years since our hurried departure.

Although the scars remained, time had healed many wounds, and it was the love and warmth of old friends – and the discovery that Donald's influence was still to be found there – that finally cured me. Lorraine Matthews, who had lovingly nursed Donald to the very end, threw a party for my return and invited twenty friends, both black and white, to meet me. It was an especially emotional moment seeing again our dear cook Adelaide who, though in her eighties, had walked several miles just to meet me. Her pleasure in seeing recent photos of my three children whom she had cared for when in service with us, and for the various gifts offered, was evident by her constant grin and laughter which said it all.

I first made a pilgrimage to gaze upon our old manse, now inhabited by an African pastor and his large family. Then to 'Under The Oaks', which was still so reminiscent of Donald's voice ringing out from the pulpit beneath the trees. The bird bath which had been erected by the students to his memory had begun to crumble, as had most of the wooden forms in the open church. There was a sad feeling of decay everywhere. Squatters had taken over the dormitory buildings, and gaping holes replaced the windows in the main educational block. Long grass and weeds choked the paths and obliterated the flower beds. Lovedale was no longer a place of pride for the Africans. The full and scholarly education once offered by the missionaries who ran this remarkable training centre was no longer available in the age of apartheid.

My last act in Lovedale was to spend a few quiet moments in prayer in the tiny Bible School Chapel where my Donald's ashes lay – before me a simple altar, a broken vase containing faded flowers and a sacred plaque. The view from the chapel entrance revealed the rolling Hogsback Mountains in the distance, and the brilliant red flowering cactus and aloe plants against the bare African veldt. Africa would call me back, but for now there was the studio and my family to return to.

Chapter Thirteen

The Bishop at last night's gathering said rather archly,
'Now I want your attendance at these sessions, and
not to hear that you've gone off "dancing"...'

I
n 1975 I was invited to be the first ever Advisor in Dance at the Fifth Assembly of the World Council of Churches in Nairobi. I was flattered to be asked, pleased that dance was to be included in this important forum – and of course, thrilled to have an opportunity to visit Africa again. Being away from the children was easier this time, as they were older, and had proven themselves pretty capable and independent in my absence. Terry was teaching in Dunedin, Dugald was now a farm advisory officer in Ashburton and Trina was studying nursing.

I arranged a stopover in Malawi to see my friend Swanzie Agnew who, having been sacked from Fort Hare University for her pro-African sympathies, was now head of geography at the University of Zomba. Travelling further to the capital Lilongwe, I was thrilled to be given entry by the young African Mother Superior to the closed order of the Poor Claires. This French Catholic order had created an indigenous interpretation of the Mass from the amalgamation of traditional European liturgy and modified African dance movements. Undulations at shoulder level represented the Holy Spirit. Their simple dance continued with cupped hands and lifted head to which they added small steps and turns. The playing of the marimba and xylophone also heightened the indigenous quality of the Mass. This had now become an African order, worshipping Christ as Africans. I found it all a moving and beautiful experience.

I had long wished to see two of Rhodesia's national treasures. Firstly to meet the ex-missionary ex-Prime Minister of Rhodesia,

Garfield Todd; and secondly to see with my own eyes the extra-ordinary ruins of Zimbabwe.

Have at last got a pass to go & see Garfield & Grace Todd tomorrow. It's quite a way, so we are to overnight on their ranch. We are stocking up on chocolate which apparently they love...

Garfield Todd was a most impressive figure – tall, handsome, with a warm handshake and a winning smile. At the time of our visit the Todds had already been held prisoner over three years by the U.D.I. on their 16,000 acre ranch. For all the hardships and hostility he had experienced Todd held no bitterness. He seemed to accept his lot with equanimity, and retained great compassion for the Africans. Hippos and crocs sported in the Ngesi River below my little bungalow. Todd took me swimming at midnight in the pool he had built himself. In that remote spot deep in the Rhodesian bush with no other habitation in sight I truly felt I was in the heart of Africa.

I was flabbergasted when we sat down at dinner to a most beautifully appointed table with starched white tablecloth, napkins, cut glass and silver candlesticks. Three African girls in smart blue and white uniforms attended us at table. Considering the shortage of basic household effects and various food items in the country at the time caused by the embargo by many European countries, it was absolutely astounding to find the Todds so well provided for.

Even more astounding however was the next stopover. For over 100 years the Zimbabwe Ruins have been described as one of Africa's greatest secrets. I found it a fascinating place. A brooding atmosphere hangs over all, with a strong sense of the vanished civilisation, which even today remains the subject of scientific controversy. Of the many romantic conjectures regarding the original builders of Zimbabwe I like the theory of the Queen of Sheba and King Solomon best. A more considered opinion is that the ruins are of Bantu origin. Carbon dating suggests the original builders began their mammoth con-struction of conical towers and walls between 1000 and 1500A.D. One argument given for the collapse of this once flourishing city and culture was that high on the Acropolis outcrop above the ruins, young women were held prisoner. In times of poor harvest these girls were sacrificed until the race became extinct. The golden relics discovered give weight to the opinion that Zimbabwe must also have been the religious heart of the land.

I stepped off the plane at Nairobi to find fifteen staff there to welcome one little delegate to the World Council of Churches Assembly. I felt a trifle foolish. As I had several days to settle in I took the opportunity to join a safari to see the villages and the dances of the two main Kenyan tribes, the Masai and the Subaru. The tall slender figures of the Masai, their long hair plaited with rope and plastered with red ochre, crouching beneath mimosa bushes awaiting the start of their dance made a striking impression.

I quickly collected camera, tape recorder, paper and pen as the drummers exploded into rhythm. Young Masai strode gracefully into the dancing area and began to leap into the air, direct as an arrow. There was no visible preparation for these incredible jumps, apart from a deep intake of breath. The leaps were repeated many times until quite abruptly the long body began to keel over. Before hitting the ground the dancer was caught by his comrades, his inert body dragged into the bushes. His place was taken immediately by another young warrior.

I became so intrigued by this display, that I moved closer and closer to the leaping figures, filming and recording at the same time. Suddenly I was struck across the face by a thick mane of hair which I thought to be accidental. However, I felt far less certain when, on my other side, another swish of hair swept across my face. Suddenly I felt afraid. As several warriors began running towards us with raised spears and shields, the answer came to me. 'I have broken a tribal taboo,' I thought. 'I am about to be scalped!' I upped and escaped to a group of Europeans gathered in the distance. When I told them of my experience they laughingly replied, 'Don't panic, they were simply flirting with you – that is their custom.' That made me feel a whole lot better and I returned to the dancing, this time with a smug smile on my face.

The Assembly was an eye-opener for me. Never before had I mixed with so many world leaders representing so many different countries. Two thousand three hundred may not be many for a football match, but when every head was packed into that great Conference Hall in the pagoda style Kenyatta Centre, where each delegate embodied a church, a country, a way of life, a point of view, one experienced an overpowering sense of man's diversity.

The theme of the Assembly, 'Jesus Christ Frees and Unites' remained our hope – that during the next 18 days, some way would be found to hear what the spirit was saying to the churches. We experienced the joy of unity across the barriers of culture, race, sex and class, but we also experienced pain from some deep divisions which kept us from true unity. Bible study and prayer helped in the healing, and brought us closer together. It was ideology and opposing opinions which pulled us apart.

Violation and oppression of the Third World seemed the dominating theme of their representatives whose catch cry was 'The rich must live more simply that the poor may simply live!' One prominent Indian speaker suggested we need a 'spirituality for combat'. Some powerful women at the Assembly spoke of the exclusion of women from God's ministry as being just another form of oppression. They saw women in a changing world, and to a packed plenary session before some startled men, spoke these words: 'You may walk beside me in unity, but we will no longer walk behind you.'

In my official position as 'Adviser in Dance', it was hoped I should bring a visual interpretation of issues discussed, and decisions reached, as opposed to the overworked verbal ones. It was difficult to bridge some real differences, especially when I was fighting my own battles against the old attitudes towards dance in worship.

The Bishop at last night's gathering said rather archly, 'Now I want your attendance at these sessions, and not to hear that you've gone off "dancing", as one of my friends explained she had...'

Nevertheless, the first morning I faced a class of hopeful movers of 17 nationalities. It was hard to know where to start. I began speaking languages I scarcely knew, as well as those I did! Some of my dancers thought we would be performing solemn processions, while others saw it more in terms of abandoned joy. From overdressed clerics, who stubbornly refused to remove their shoes, to a descendent of Henry VIII wearing gym shoes and a faded cotton frock, I also found three in my dance workshop who had studied with me at previous dance conferences at Kuala Lumpur, Singapore and Thailand. I felt heartened to learn that each of them had carried the dance back into their own Christian churches.

Apart from running my workshop I joined a group called 'Community and Ideologies of Other Faiths'. Somewhat to my surprise I was also delegated to a Spirituality Workshop which I was delighted to discover was housed in the original homestead of (*Out of Africa*) author Karen Blixen. The house was beautifully situated with sweeping grounds at the foot of the Ngong Hills.

As this was the first time dance was part of a World Assembly, there was little in the way of practical support. I lost much time hunting down tape recorders, or scrambling up and down the 20 storey tower seeking dancers scattered throughout the building. Communication to say the least was very poor.

Last night I was so mad at the bureaucracy which runs this outfit. They make quite arbitrary decisions which chop into all the plans we might be making – ie: cutting out the last two real workshops for Thursday & turning them into 'business' sessions!

... I am utterly frustrated still – find myself stymied at every turn. Can't get hold of any one or thing. As Boris says, 'Suspended in space'. It's far too big – 400 press men alone, 745 delegates, 800 advisers, 700 visitors etc etc!

At least one adviser to the worship committee returned hopelessly to his own country, because of his distaste for the W.C.C. Geneva staff bureaucracy, who he asserted were stone-walling everything he had hoped to offer the Assembly.

Despite the difficulties, my dance group did achieve a very creditable dance to the conference theme 'Jesus Christ Frees and Unites'. They also danced several hymns to the glorious singing of an African Choir. The most significant dance however was to be part of the final Assembly.

On a free day five of us planned a safari to Tsavo Game Park.

We have been watching the antics of elephant, impala, zebra & giraffe through powerful binoculars. Last night's arrival was made especially exciting as we had got lost in a frightful thunderstorm & upon arrival made our way to see the animals under spotlight gambolling & drinking by the waterhole. Funny to think we saw all this in Kruger Park when Terry & Dug were tiny – in much simpler fashion! If you want a spot of glam, this is it, but I'd prefer the mud hut & sausage on an open fire. You know me!

The variety of wonderful animals we saw made the adventure well worthwhile, in spite of two unfortunate incidents that might well have cost us dear. Firstly by running out of petrol in the heart of the park surrounded by a herd of suspicious elephants; secondly, when we had a blow-out on our way back to Nairobi and our car very nearly ended upside down in a donga. Africa still seemed to me a land full of danger!

Suffering from a wretched Nairobi stomach, I still managed to attend an unforgettable Advent rally where I danced with ecstatic members of the African Church of the Spirit. I was intrigued to see a very relaxed Donald Coggan, Archbishop of Canterbury, affected by the joy of the occasion, singing and clapping with obvious glee.

The miracle for me, though, took place at the closing Harambee Service. Despite early fears we watched three W.C.C. Secretary Generals – Visser T'Hoof, Carlson Blake, and Phillip Potter – join hands with representatives from 100 countries as they sang and danced the conference song, 'Break Down the Walls that Separate Us and Unite Us in a Single Body'. I had devised a simple dance symbolising the breaking down of walls for the combined Assembly. Clapping and dancing in this fashion, everyone moved out of the Plenary Hall and into the black African night. We gathered around the playing fountain to receive the Liturgy of Departure from an African bishop. Then with full hearts we disappeared into the night returning to every corner of the earth. If we had not found unity in all things, we had learned much from one another and felt strengthened in the knowledge that God's work was being carried out in so many nations.

While I was away Dugald came back for summer holidays and again all three of my children were at home for Christmas – without me. I found myself again trying to parent from a distance.

I don't seem to worry so much about you all as I once did. You are all so clever & big enough to cope. However it makes no difference to the love I bear towards you. Please EAT properly Terry & have friends over for the weekend when you can. Get old Trina to come too.

Don't be too fresh with that Graham, Tri – nor Dug with that Liz – nor Ter with that Mike!!!

I planned some interesting spots en route to N.Z. – Athens, Delphi, Pisa, Rome, Venice, Paris – this time with adult eyes and hopefully with greater understanding and appreciation than on my first visit to these places forty years previously. Then suddenly I was home, and back in the Studio, and very happy to see my children and students again, the rest of the world already beginning to seem a dream.

An important turning point in my life came with the return of actor Louise Petherbridge to her homeland after an acting career in the United Kingdom. Our meeting was an auspicious one. I felt ready for an injection of fresh ideas and a new direction. Louise revealed a fertile mind, and a wealth of theatrical expertise, which soon led us to create some unusual theatre pieces together. From instant rapport sprang a deep and lasting friendship.

The first of these collaborations, *Orlando* (1970), was a contemporary masque tracing the story of Virginia Woolf's novel of that name. Louise was largely influenced by the individual talents of the artists involved – the lyrical and humorous musical compositions of Professor John Drummond, the beautiful singing of Honor McKellar, and the dancing and acting of members of my Dunedin Dance Theatre. Jan Bolwell, Terry MacTavish, Jos Brusse and Kate Calvert in the principal roles, danced their way through three centuries of dramatic action covering Elizabethan, Jacobean and Victorian eras, including, along the way, Orlando's dramatic change of sex. The subtly worked narration by Louise and Walter Bloomfield managed to link the various scenes, while detailing the shifting times and mores.

Louise had an uncanny eye for the provocative, the unusual, the outrageous, for the spirit of humanity and the theatrically malleable. Working with her gave me still further opportunity to explore choreography which probed personal eccentricities and behaviours outside the norm. To be part of 'total theatre' as she devised it was a new and inspiring experience. New friends Moli Zisserman and her son Nicholas were the starting point for our next work *While Grandmother Played Bridge* (1981).

Because I had been personally involved in the lives of Jews like Nicholas in Vienna, who had managed to escape the Nazi holocaust, I felt more than happy to be part of a group of artists assembled under Louise's direction to mount this exciting work. The Austrian spirit, with its humour, and famed 'gemutlichkeit' (friendliness), was captured in the sausage dances, waltzes, peasant dances and witty songs interspersed amongst Nicholas's unfolding tale. One by one the players disappear from the bridge table, presumably to the death camps, leaving grandmother alone to observe the breaking up of her known way of life.

Our bittersweet interpretation of these times, presented as it was during the controversial Springbok Tour, succeeded in bringing the full force of the Austrian Anschluss vividly to mind. Inside the theatre, the Nazi Youth paraded. Outside at the same time, young protestors were being arrested for opposing the Springbok Tour. One night the stage manager almost missed curtain up, because he had had to rescue his protesting daughter from the police station. Our relatively mild political comment did not go unnoticed by a critic of the New Zealand *Listener*, so perhaps we made our point.

> The audience identified easily for there was a flavour of what we had experienced on television week after week for those past eight weeks. We all know what it is like to live in a polarised society... It is a story that brings home to us the need to guard jealously human freedom and to be forever vigilant.

Working with the Zissermans recreating the Vienna I had known and interpreting the Jewish spirit had stirred up the past once more. I had long been intrigued by what the Jews had accomplished in Israel since the war and therefore leapt at the chance when I was invited to present a paper in Jerusalem at an 'International Bible and Dance Seminar.'

At the seminar's conclusion I looked forward to having Dugald join me from Egypt, where he was working for an English engineering company. The first of my three weeks I found myself thoroughly immersed in the day to day deliberations of the conference: lectures, panel discussions and films led by experts from many countries by day, dance performances of local and international dance companies by night. Israel was represented by three indigenous dance companies – Inbal, Bat Dor, and Batsheva – and we also saw some vigorous dancing by a Kibbutz Dance Company at Evron. The director of this first Kibbutz dance school in Israel, Yehudit Arnon, still carried a tattooed number on her arm from one of the Nazi camps she had miraculously managed to survive.

For me the most rewarding dance experience was demonstrations by Yeminite and Kurdish groups. The source of their dance movement came solely from their own life experience. The rather hypnotic swaying movement derived from the action of riding a camel, and much of the choreography had clearly evolved from the reading of the Holy Book the Koran. This was demonstrated to us by an elder teaching a young boy how the book should be read. With one forefinger, he traced the letters in a singsong manner, stabbing the important words with a rhythmic flourish of hand. I was fascinated to discover this same finger action becoming the source of the dances which followed. I was also hypnotised by the bowing and bending of the two dancing figures as they revolved around each other.

To unravel the thread of a people's dance is to understand their present as well as their history. The Bible has always been a magnet for the dance, not because we wish to resurrect what is dead, but rather because we want to live what is alive! With the influx of new Jewish settlers, the folk dance of Israel is expanding daily. Israeli dance today (except for the unchanging Yemenites) draws together steps passed down from Central European and pre-Soviet bloc countries. Their dance appears like an ecstatic offering by a people determined to express their depth of feeling in finding themselves once more upon the soil of their forefathers. Variety and style have always added flavour and colour, but the Israeli style should not be regarded as more 'pure' than any other.

Dugald had spent time in Israel previously, as a student at the Hebrew University and later as a worker on En Gev Kibbutz on the shores of Lake Galilee. Upon his arrival he became my tour guide and led me to many of the historic sights. Foremost of these was the Temple of Solomon. In front of what remains of that ancient wall we watched the bobbing and wailing, and the dancing of black clad devotees. There were few women, and those we saw were well tucked away behind barricades. The countless other sacred sights of Jerusalem were equally moving. But the present-day Israel struggling for recognition and a measure of peace with its neighbours seems often to be at war with its own past. Shalom remains an elusive goal.

The ultra orthodox Jews of the Yeshive and synagogue, scrupulously attentive to the prophets' commandments, wage a constant war upon the modern Jews who are increasingly seen to be breaking these laws. We saw a specific example of this. It was Sabbat, the Jewish Holy Day, when Dugald and I watched with horror a carload of young men being viciously stoned by angry Hasidim who objected to their driving on the sabbath.

Bethlehem, Nazareth, Cana, the Garden Tomb, Mount of Olives, the Via Dolorosa, the Shrine of the Beatitudes, Dome of the Rock, Church of the Holy Sepulchre, Capernaum, and Tiberius on the shores of Lake Galilee – all these for me leapt from distant biblical imagery into vibrant reality. Reality too was displayed in other ways. I passed through the Jaffa Gate one hour before a bomb exploded, killing four Arabs. Driving from Jerusalem to Tiberius, we skirted the Jordan River valley, the length of which hummed with the comings and goings of military trucks and personnel.

The inhospitable heat and hazed desert hills around were trying. I felt dehydrated under that merciless sun, and my all-consuming desire was to plunge into the waters of Lake Galilee. Among the many fascinating places we visited, the Fortress of Masada stood out, a searing testimony to the heroic Jewish and Zealot stand against the invading Romans. After three years of enemy attack, the 960 defenders chose mass suicide in preference to defeat. Masada is today a national shrine.

The other unforgettable occasion was the disturbing visit we made to the Yad Vashem Memorial to the Holocaust. The terrible murder of six million European Jews by the Nazis was chillingly documented. Within this stark monument a flame flickers constantly for those who died. Photos and films are on display, but my lasting memory will always be the great piles of spectacles and children's shoes. Long lines of silent spectators as they filed past were testimony to the profound horror and disbelief of the present generation. Dugald and I took our shattered selves from this emotional experience to find balm in the new Israeli Museum's sculpture garden.

I rose at 3am the morning of my departure from Jerusalem, and stood under a starlit sky awaiting the arrival of the sherut[1] which was to take me to Tel Aviv. Beyond lay the Citadel and David's Tower, magnificently spotlit against a black sky. Dropping my eyes to the sombre Valley of Hinnon below, I recalled the children sacrificed there to please the Ammonite God Moloch. I raised my eyes again for a final moment to the spires and steeples of the Holy Mount. The silence of the place at that hour was palpable! For all the love, passion, and human savagery this venerated city has known, the last impression I took with me was sublime and unforgettable. My spirit exalted all the way to the airport.

There it did a dive. For the next couple of hours I was closely questioned by a woman security officer about everything I had done and everyone I had seen in Israel. Younger women than myself found this ordeal too much and were reduced to tears. At 6.30am, the hour the plane was due to take off, my questioner turned to me, smiled, and said very sweetly, 'I'm sorry to have kept you so long, but I have so enjoyed talking to you!'

---

[1] Shared taxi.

Chapter Fourteen

After conducting worship in churches up and down the country for over 25 years, I think I can truthfully say that I do not recall ever having a congregation so rapt in the whole celebration.

On Easter Saturday 1980, my sister Jocelyn and I decided to walk out on the laundry and the kitchen sink and set forth to a friend's bach at Taieri Mouth. Returning from a bracing walk on the beach, I suggested a nice little siesta. 'Oh no,' replied Jocelyn, 'let's not waste time, the blackberries should be out – let's go blackberrying.'

We found a good spot in a bushy valley where the berries seemed plentiful and clambering up a small bank we began filling our billies. Suddenly I heard a cry, and turning round, watched with horror as Jocelyn fell backwards, berries flying in all directions, and with a thud landed head first on the ground below. I rushed to her side and found she wasn't breathing. Desperately I tried – for the first time – mouth to mouth resuscitation, and scanned the desolate spot for any possible help. Finally two small boys came into sight across the field and I begged them to run for aid. The urgency of the situation was very clear. It seemed hours before a vehicle appeared over the horizon breaking down fences to reach us. Their quick-thinking father had phoned an ambulance, and with Jocelyn's inert body lying across my lap, we had to drive as far as Brighton to meet up with it. Already I could not pretend there was still life in my dear sister, but I exhorted the officers to bring out oxygen machines and try reviving her. It was to no avail.

I was devastated.

The Court Inquest I attended with her husband Hubert some days later confirmed the doctor's evidence – Jocelyn had died of a massive heart attack and a broken neck.

We had been working for some weeks on a Danced Eucharist, as a total act of worship, and a 'first' for St Paul's Cathedral, or anywhere else in the country. This service took place just two weeks after the funeral, and at my request, was dedicated to Jocelyn. The shock of her death, allied to the beauty and spirituality of this unusual communion service in an overflowing cathedral, made this occasion one of the most moving in my life.

Bishop Peter Mann retained his central position as celebrant behind the altar throughout the proceedings, while the dancers in simple red dresses expressed in movement the varying moods of the apostles' creed. John Michael Talbot's recorded music, with choir and orchestra, ascended the steep cathedral nave above the congregation. I introduced some genuine ancient Hebrew steps into the dance which were performed by the dancers about the altar, leading up to the final refrain – 'Lamb of God, who takes away the sins of the world, have mercy upon us.' A large number of the congregation came forward to receive the sacrament, including the dancers. Then, holding candles, they led the way along the central aisle to the final words, 'Go out into the world with peace.' I could not have been alone in the universal sense of joy I felt on this occasion, for shortly after I received a letter from the Bishop himself.

> After conducting worship in churches up and down the country for over 25 years, I have not unnaturally developed a capacity for sensing the mood and response of a congregation, and I think I can truthfully say that I do not recall ever having a congregation so rapt in the whole celebration. Spoken responses were superb, and the singing might well have done some damage to a fairly substantial roof! It was however the beauty, the sincerity, the reverence, and the dignity of the choreography, the appropriateness of the music, and above all the total integration of the dance, liturgical word and action, that made the service such a magnificent act of worship, in which all present were caught up in a relationship that transcends time and space and in some wonderful way carried us into the presence of our Lord!

We repeated the Danced Eucharist again the following year, but I was not keen to vie with the beauty of ancient liturgies, as I felt strongly our dance role should be more a catalyst for our time, and a mouthpiece for our generation. I was keen to address issues and problems of the now, not to be an abstraction from the life about us.

The Christian Dance Fellowship movement now operating in almost a dozen countries, owes its existence almost entirely to the drive and enthusiasm of one woman, Mary Jones. Because of the work in religious dance I had begun in New Zealand, I was invited in 1980 to be guest teacher at the first Christian Dance Conference being held at Abbotsleigh Girls School, Sydney – the same school where I had been assistant to Gertrud Bodenwieser thirty years before. The first National C. D. Conference was held in 1988 in Bathurst, New South Wales. Membership had greatly increased, and Mary, having travelled far to promote her vision, had assembled an impressive number of dancers, authors, historians and theologians, even including dancing women pastors. Actors and mime artists also participated.

The New Zealand Dance Fellowship was formed on this occasion by Rosslyn Smaille and David Haddy. I found some kindred spirits at these conferences with whom I have continued a warm relationship. After my early solitary experiments introducing dance into worship, I was now able to share them and compare ideas with others. My new friends were American, Indian, English, French. There were three occasions when young Australian dancers crossed the Tasman and spent several weeks studying dances with me which they took back to perform and pass on to others interested in enlivening and beautifying Australian church services. I was beginning to feel quite useful!

I had always been intrigued by the story surrounding the ancient dance still seen in Seville Cathedral today, *Los Seises* – a dance of great antiquity which is performed by choir boys before the Great Altar. It has survived many centuries, despite several Archbishops beseeching the Pope to suppress it. The Pope however, declared the dances and costumes could only add splendour to the ceremony. As long as the vestments held up, the dance could continue! When Louise and I visited Spain in 1979 with the express purpose of seeing *Los Seises*, we noticed the vestments were amazingly patched and shabby, but the young boys danced for the Holy Spirit with great feeling. I felt heartened by this discovery, knowing my dancers in New Zealand often fell far short of glamour, with patching not unknown.

The Zigeuners who danced for us in the caves of Granada, and the fiery Flamenco dancers in the nightclubs of Malaga, may have danced with more abandon and skill, but the seven little boys who danced for the Lord in Seville tugged at my heart strings.

I had carried an idea for a dance based on the bullfight for a long time, but it was when Louise insisted that Garcia Lorca's poem would give the right dramatic effect in conjunction with the dance that the ballet was finally born. Creating this dance, I tried to recall my impressions of the bull ring in South America. Of all the longer ballets I have choreographed, *Death of a Bullfighter* is the best example of the Bodenwieser style, using dancers with expressive poses and groupings in graceful tableaux. We used the impassioned music of Manuel de Falla, while Louise spoke the evocative words.

NZTV's 'Kaleidoscope' arts programme televised *Death of a Bullfighter* choosing the nearest venue to Spain they could find – Larnach Castle on the Otago Peninsula. The fifteen minute work took the entire day to film. My dancers performed on the rough surface of the stable courtyard without a murmur and I was proud of them. It was a cloudless sunny day, and the tuis, excited by the music, added their song.

My dance studio was thriving and the roll kept increasing. During my overseas trips the classes were conducted by older students, some having returned from further study and performance overseas – Ann Woodhouse and Jos Brusse in particular. I continued to draw the most talented students from the studio into the Dunedin Dance Theatre, and choreographed to my heart's content. I could not expect or wish to remain the sole choreographer, however. In time the dancers began experimenting creatively themselves. Sometimes they delighted, even amazed me.

The first girls to emerge with their own truly artistic works were Jan Bolwell and my daughter Terry. In 1982 they devised a full length piece inspired by nineteenth century women called *No Coward Soul*. Scenes were connected by words taken from diaries and letters of women of the period in New Zealand, America and Britain. This dance was a hit. Aided by the Arts Council, Jan and Terry took their performance to the 1982 Edinburgh Festival. I was to meet them there. But first I had other plans.

For some time I had been contemplating writing a biography of my mentor, Professor Gertrud Bodenwieser. Many of her associates were already elderly, so I had to work fast, and to travel far in my research. Thus a tour was planned starting in Australia, to speak with Viennese and Australian dancers. I also spent many hours in the Bodenwieser Archives which had been created and maintained by Madam's great friend Marie Cuckson and ex-Bodenwieser dancer Emmy Towsey. It was fortunate that visiting Sydney at that time was Bodenwieser's nephew Karl Hecht (whose diplomat father had disappeared in the Anschluss). From him I gleaned some of the more personal aspects of Bodenwieser's life.

Vienna, of course, should have been the obvious and most rewarding place to acquire further information on Bodenwieser's life, and in certain areas this was the case. I was richly rewarded in the Silverding Society of the Theater Sammlung at the Hofburg Palace, where I found some photographs and other artifacts of both Bodenwieser and the entire 'Ausdruckstanz' period. I contacted any early Bodenwieser Ballet dancers I could find, but as Hitler had ordered all documents relating to what he termed 'decadent art' to be destroyed, my task was not an easy one. However I did eventually manage to uncover some important material, chiefly from the lofts and cellars of former Bodenwieser pupils, who had had the courage to hide them.

Returning to Vienna again was a nostalgic experience. I retraced my steps to the favourite places I had enjoyed as a student about 40 years ago. I chose an evening at the Burg Theater, then a rattling tram journey out to the Heuriger at Grinzing. My feet carried me to the Kaffee Hauser I had once frequented with my friends of the Bodenwieser Tanz Schule and from the Vienna State Academy. It seemed a different world.

I was entertained royally by Magda Brunner (now Countess Hoyos) my friend with whom I had danced in Vienna, Paris and in South America. This included two blissful days in her country house in Schauboden on the Danube. Another break to my research work came in the form of Albert Smith, a good friend from my South American days. Now living in Pittsburg U.S.A. he had seen an article I had written for an American dance magazine and wrote to me. Upon hearing of my travel plans to Austria and Scotland, he decided to meet me there himself. No longer the coltish young man I first knew, he had however still retained his boyish charm, despite the greying hair and beard!

Every day I spent hours researching in the Theater Museum, but the evenings were given to a good meal with Smithie, followed by the opera. On one occasion a party was given in my honour by historian Dr Agnes Bleier Brody, an ex-pupil of Bodenwieser. In

1979 she had been instrumental in mounting the 'Tanz im 20 Jahrhundert in Wien' exhibition, where at last the sterling work of Vienna's many dancers was given proper recognition. An entire room was devoted to Bodenwieser, featuring photographs, posters, costumes and excerpts of her work, as well as descriptions and photographs of her most successful pupils from Vienna, Australia and New Zealand.

On to Britain where I was able to see Jan and Terry perform *No Coward Soul* at the Edinburgh Festival and meet Catriona, who was on holiday at the time from studying midwifery in Birmingham. Trina and I took the opportunity to visit the tiny isles of the Inner Hebrides, the seat of early Christendom. In South Africa I had met Dr George McLeod, founder of today's popular Iona community, and had long wanted to see this captivating place for myself. The moment I stepped ashore, I felt a strong spiritual presence and a deep peace. Rarely in my life have I experienced so immediate a revelation. Iona had been occupied by a legendary Druid cult as early as the sixth century, which preceded St Columba's arrival with Christianity. The presence of two such powerful spiritual forces could perhaps account for my state. Through lowering mist I made my way to the rebuilt abbey, the ruined cloisters, nunnery and dilapidated graveyard, all of which increased my sensation of an eerie but holy presence.

In London I was able to interview three of Bodenwieser's dancers, Evelyn Ippen, Bettina Vernon, my sister-in-law Hilary Napier (Dunlop) and most fortuitously, the inimitable 90 year old Marcel Lorber, who before the war had been one of the most sought after dance accompanists in Europe. Marcel had also been Bodenwieser's outstanding musical director in Austria and Australia for over twenty years.

I had a very animated discussion with the three dancers I met in Selfridges store over a cup of coffee. We exchanged affectionate reminiscences of Bodenwieser: her extraordinary creative gift, her innovative teaching style, her little idiosyncrasies.

Trying to extract information from Marcel was much more difficult. 'Setz dich, setz dich' he cried as I entered his room. Looking around I could see no place at all to sit! Piles of manuscripts, books and papers stood feet high on every chair and table. Glass cabinets lined the walls filled with photographs and death masks of the famous artists he had once accompanied – among them singer Maurice Till and dancer Tamara Karsarvina – and the room was dominated by a massive grand piano. When Marcel understood my mission, he dragged more boxes into the room and began hunting for programmes and reviews pertaining to the Bodenwieser years. I was only allowed to look, not to borrow. While Marcel was dreamily playing music he had composed for dances I remembered so well, I suddenly spotted a programme from the Bodenwieser Gruppe Japanese Tour which I greatly desired for the book. I knew it was useless to ask him for it, so I surreptitiously shoved the programme up my jumper. I felt no qualm in resorting to this subterfuge. 'I don't trust you Shoni,' he said as we parted at the door, and he frisked me – without success. After an evening at the theatre, I returned home to find a note awaiting me: 'Du schlimmes Kind, Sofort meine Programme zuruck schicken!'[1] This research business was proving more difficult than I had imagined.

However, after years of playing sleuth hound, of writing and rewriting, in 1987 *An Ecstasy of Purpose, the Life and Art of Gertrud Bodenwieser* was finally published through the united efforts of Les Humphrey and Associates in Sydney.

One year before its publication I attended an Ausdruckstanz Symposium which was held in the medieval German village of Thurnau. This event was held in a charming thirteenth century Schloss. Here a deliberate attempt was made to reinstate the importance of the pre-war dancers who had been ousted under Hitler. Fifty years had passed since their enforced departure, and the time had arrived to reappraise those dancers of the free dance, who had emerged during the great renaissance of the twentieth century.

With this theme and period, I was in my element. I was able to bring the dance fraternity up to date with the life and work of Bodenwieser. It was generally believed that Bodenwieser had died with her husband when Hitler went on his rampage to exterminate the Jews. It was thrilling to discover how deep was the interest of all present when they heard of the strong active dance movement in Australia and New Zealand today, and of the prominent part Bodenwieser played in its growth. At the conclusion of a series of fascinating lectures, it became startlingly clear to all the debt present-day dancers owe to those first pioneers who broke with the traditions of the past.

---

[1] You naughty girl, return my programme at once!

In 1992 I was approached by a German publisher, Zeichen und Spuren in Bremen, requesting the rights to publish *Ecstasy* in the German language. It was particularly gratifying to know that now the German and Austrian people would have the truth about Bodenwieser properly recorded in their own tongue.

While I had been about my business my three children had been very much about theirs. I was overjoyed to see my love of theatre passed on to Terry, equally with Donald's love of books and teaching. She was happily installed at Queen's High School as English and Drama teacher, living with writer Paula Boock and seizing every opportunity to perform in professional theatre.

Dugald, an agricultural engineer (specialising in ground water) had returned from some years of study and work overseas. Like his father he was driven to improve the lot of the indigenous peoples in the countries where he worked, and was involved in implementing several aid schemes in Africa and Asia. After all my fears that he would settle overseas, I was amused and delighted that while away he had married Alison Begg, whose grandparents had holidayed with Dugald's all those years ago on Stewart Island. They built their own home, very different from their first in Swaziland, above the ocean at Moeraki in North Otago, where they rear a number of animals and two children, Jinty and Thomas. Catriona, fired with the missionary zeal first apparent in the Philippines, studied midwifery after graduating as a nurse and married Charles Laurence, an electrical engineer. They live in Lower Hutt and have two little boys, James and Karl.

Outside family, much of my time was spent in creative pursuits with Louise. In 1991 she mounted another work in association with the Dunedin Dance Theatre. *Coup De Folie* (The Fantasy of Sylvia Ashton Warner) was devised and directed by Louise for Writers' Week in Dunedin. Ashton Warner has always been a world-acclaimed though controversial New Zealand teacher and writer. She was an eccentric figure intent upon breaking out from the rather grey society of her time. The complexity of Sylvia's personality and the effect she had on those around her were dealt with as a kind of fantasy, even though the words were Sylvia's own. Louise was less concerned with time and sequence, than with the spirit and contradictions that made Sylvia a creative artist and innovative teacher, particularly of Maori children. Edwin Carr's specially commissioned music for flute, piano and percussion and my choreography completed this slightly shocking, sad and funny production. The role of Sylvia was a very challenging one for Terry who played the demanding part. She showed greater passion and stamina than I had known her capable of, a view shared by the *Otago Daily Times* reviewer who praised her 'range between mental frailty and flamboyant brilliance'. With the assured acting of the two other members of the cast, Bernadette Doolan and Simon O'Connor and two dancers, *Coup de Folie* was a performance to remember.

In between large-scale theatrical undertakings, I continued to create liturgical pieces. I was so inspired on the occasion of the ordination of Dr Penny Jamieson, the first woman Bishop of a Diocese in the world, that I was moved to create a dance for her. *The Call*, a solo danced by Susan Simpson, concerned itself with the dilemma any woman must face called to a religious vocation today. I invited the Bishop to attend the premiere of *The Call* in a Dunedin Dance Theatre programme called *Visions*. I did not think for a moment she would have the interest or take the time to do so, but she came. Shortly after, this dance was performed as part of an evening service at St Paul's Anglican Cathedral. In a letter I received from the Bishop she wrote the following:

> I didn't have a chance to see you or Susan last Sunday to tell you how very much moved I was by the dance. I think somehow it moved me much more this time round. I don't know whether you've changed it, or whether it was the setting which changed my perception of it, but it seemed to be extra spiritual in content. Perhaps too it was the fact that it was taking place right on the spot where I was ordained. Thank you for sharing it with the wider congregation and for making it truly a prayer...

The very idea of dancing in a church building is still somewhat distasteful to many Christians. They consider the church as a building set apart exclusively for worship – as a holy place not to be profaned by secular activities. 'Oh yes,' they say, 'do enter our church, but remember to leave your bodies in the porch!' This seems a presumption which, when analysed, would seem to mean that firstly the Holy is quite separate from everyday life, and secondly that one *can* distinguish between the one and the other, and thirdly that dancing belongs to the profane. None of these, I believe, finds a sound basis in the New Testament.

I continued, and continue, to choreograph for the church. In

1994 I choreographed J.S. Bach's *Magnificat* for the Christchurch Cathedral as part of the city's Arts Festival, with Bronwyn Judge taking the part of the Madonna. It proved to be one of the most dynamic and fully energised pieces I'd made in years. The *Magnificat* was also seen at St Pauls in Dunedin before several of the dancers left the country for further study overseas.

And in 1996, when I was asked to create a dance for the recent 'Living Theology' Ecumenical Conference in Dunedin, I chose the controversial theme of homosexuality. At the recent Presbyterian General Assembly, the remit to accept the ordination of gay men and women was refused. I felt this was a very sad decision. My dance, *A Question of Love*, became part of the opening service of the conference. Two lonely women appear from either side of the chancel. They discover love and acceptance from each other, which they dance in a moving duo. Three masked figures, Hate, Fear and Prejudice, then make an angry entry. First they denounce, then break up the happy relationship, calling out angry words as they dance their rejection. The lovers are forced apart, and tragically return to their lonely search. The final words from Christ himself are spoken on an empty stage: 'A new commandment I give unto you, that you love one another as I have loved you.'

The dance was received in utter silence, most people hurrying away. Some I am sure left in perplexity, or embarrassment, and some in anger. I was told however, that much heated discussion followed in the morning session. At least the subject came under debate. My dancers and I felt proud to be part of an artistic enterprise of significance which managed to hit home, to engage thought and discussion for some time to come.

I was still occasionally invited to overseas conferences and usually took the opportunity to meet fellow dance in worship friends and to revisit countries I had become fond of. 'An Artist's Experience in Bali' was one of the more memorable gatherings I attended, held at Dyana Purna (Place of Meditation), a Christian cultural centre by the sea. Delegates from many countries came together to share cross-culturally our vision and experience. Artists were encouraged to use their gifts towards a more holistic approach for both church and witness. The Protestant Balinese Church believes that if a church is not presented by the culture of its people it cannot grow. This I agreed with, but was most disturbed by the sight of ever increasing tourists invading the country and demanding hotel displays of

Barong, Legong, Kris and Kechak dances. These dances are spiritual expressions of a Balinese way of life, of their humanity and their heritage. They belong in temples, not hotels.

Returning home after adventures in other lands and from other cultures, I often felt inspired to begin new works of my own. It came as a pleasant surprise therefore when Bronwyn Judge approached me with the request that this time she would like to choreograph on me! Bronwyn, with dance partner Anna Holmes, had cut her teeth at the Edinburgh Fringe with the provocative *Oh What a Song and a Dance* in the eighties. Since then she had enjoyed great success as a solo dancer, and with partners Sudha Rao and Carol Brown. The exciting water performance art work she described won me over. So I became one of five dancers portraying the three ages of women, from childhood to the wisdom of old age in *Angels Born at the Speed of Light*.

This extraordinary show was devised by Bronwyn with poet Cilla McQueen and composer Gillian Whitehead. I might not have agreed had I any idea just what it would mean dancing in a triangular pool of water, which deepened almost to waist level as I moved downstage! A porthole cut out of the backdrop acted variously as a golden moon, a secret window, or a birth canal for writhing figures who curled their way through or hung perilously from its edges. The fluid quality achieved where light changed with mood and music combined with a stark dramatic text was most effective.

Two years later, Bron and I decided to share a programme where our two choreographic styles could evolve side by side. I choreographed three solos for Bronwyn, including *Jeptha's Daughter* and *Transfigured Night*. At the conclusion of each of these items, headed under the title *Resinging the Song*, Bron echoed my works with her own emotional and choreographic response in her unique dance style. Mine and Bron's dance eras are there to be compared, indicating that modern dance is no institution, but rather a ladder which each generation ascends to make its own statement, in the style of their time. Bronwyn's third solo, and the main work of the programme, *Wellsprings to Isadora* dealt with the life and art of the first great pioneer of modern dance, Isadora Duncan. After much research I choreographed a dance in what was, I believe, a style close to that of Duncan's herself. In a way therefore the programme stretched right back to the very beginnings of modern dance, through to contemporary New Zealand expression.

Encouraged by the growing interest in dance history and roots, I decided to remount some of the Bodenwieser dances I still remembered so well. The strong/lyrical expressive technique of the early modern dance has been superseded by today's more analytical and detached style. I taught some original Bodenwieser pieces first to my Dunedin Dance Theatre, then to students of the National School of Dance in Wellington, where I have on several occasions run Bodenwieser workshops. I felt quite elated to see again *Demon Machine, Dance with the Golden Discs, Slavonic Dance, Snake Charmer, Russian Peasant* and *The Blue Danube* performed with such spirit.

In 1993 I took a bigger bite, in order to leave a permanent record of Bodenwieser's work for future generations. This time I not only reconstructed but had recorded the *Trilogy of Joan of Arc*, which Bodenwieser had choreographed for me in the 1940s. Carol Brown fitted my original costumes perfectly, but because of their fragile condition, we had them faithfully copied by Charmian Smith. Pianist Terence Dennis learned and recorded the music, from which the Audio Visual Department of Otago University produced an excellent video.

Over the last few years, I had been influenced and stimulated afresh by visits to Prague, still labouring under communism, to St Wolfgang in Austria, where songs from *The Sound of Music* kept resounding in my ears. In Indonesia I had watched entranced the dances performed before the temple of Perambenan, and panted my way up the slopes of the wonderful temple of Borabadur. I had travelled to the outlying island of Ulong Kujong, off the coast of Sumatra, searching for the fabled one-horned rhino. I explored the ruins of Santorini (the lost Atlantis) and travelled to Turkey hoping to see the mesmerising Whirling Dervishes. I had sought out Brecht's House in Augsburg, and Kafka's House in Prague, been offered a seat in the box for the ballet *Orpheus* in the Vienna Opera House – all these, yet back in my own country, rather to my surprise, my next choreography did not spring from any of these wonderful experiences, but out of something new and exciting within New Zealand itself.

The whole country was acclaiming Janet Frame's autobiography *An Angel at my Table* and the film based on the books. When Deirdre Tarrant, artistic director of Footnotes Dance Company, requested a dance from me for her 1994 national tour, I knew immediately what it should be. Inspired by the writing of Frame I created a solo dance, *Two Inches Behind the Eyes*, for the powerful and focused young Christchurch dancer, Raewyn Hill. This dance was a quest which reflects the power of the word and its fusion with the mind. Anthony Ritchie's musical score admirably suited the theme I wanted of panic, doubt, and life inside the head.

My early fascination with tribal dance, the dance of the people, was an unconscious seeking for the kernel of movement. I may not have realised this at the time, but just as tribal dance is both potent and primordial, so I believe should ours be. Dance is about illuminating the spirit. Where it falls short of this I believe we are in danger. Deep inside lies the answer to all our quests, and from that place begins the growing understanding of life's purpose. The dance has the power to speak, to inform, to incite, in a manner we in the sophisticated world today have nearly forgotten. A lifetime in dance is both a growing and a paring down. I feel it is not so much the destination which counts, but the journey itself. All life is a discovery and for me the dance has been my teacher and my guide. Because I am so aware of the power of dance, which apart from the sheer joy of bodily movement, gives one the heightened feeling of being totally alive, I also see it as a kind of living sermon. It is also capable of speaking upon issues of our time with devastating clarity.

Just as I was beginning to feel I had arrived at a time in my life where I might take things more easily, cease to teach dance, and remain content to enjoy my garden, read the books I had long hoped to, listen to my collection of tapes and recordings, and catch up with old friends, I was approached by two former students with a determined look in their eye, and a forceful tread. Perhaps they had guessed my state of mind, and together Gillian Fraser and Bronwyn Judge decided a documentary film of my life and work must be made. Having been impressed by the work of film-maker Halina Oganowska Coates, they engaged her interest, and persuaded her to direct the film.

For the next three weeks, I was subject to an invasion of both my home and my past life. Though exhausting and at times traumatic, it also proved to be a very exciting experience for me, and caused both tears and laughter. The film crew tramped through my home like a herd of elephants, bearing tape recorders, lights and whirring cameras. Halina, who proved to be a warm and humorous companion, taped dozens of interviews of my memories and impressions, and carried away armfuls of photographs, videos and archival movie films made in China, Africa and Australia. I could not imagine how she would ever manage to sort them all out.

Out into the Blue however eventually did become a 35-minute documentary film. I was fortunate in having Bronwyn, with her perception, creativity and energy to dance of the joys and vicissitudes of life in the piece *My End is the Beginning*. In the course of the dance, she learns to accept whatever life has to offer in the belief that beneath all grief the fundamental realities are joy. To commissioned music by Anthony Ritchie, the dance opens before a simple settler's cottage. It also takes place inside a cathedral, in an empty swimming pool, with waves breaking overhead, in a railway station, in a dance studio, in a forest glade, and even barefoot in the snow. The climax of the film is when the dancer scales and appears on the top of a cliff face to open her arms wide towards the great blue sky above. What an affirmation of the richness of life! I felt both humble and proud as I sat with family and friends beside me at Dunedin's Regent Theatre for the film's first private screening.

As I watched my whole life unfold on the screen, my faith that life would be rewarding and exciting, whatever choices I made, seemed justified at last. The only thing that bothers me is the way everyone seems to feel that with the film and now the book, I have done and said it all. Don't you believe it!

Appendix

MAJOR CHOREOGRAPHIES OF SHONA DUNLOP

AUSTRALIA, from 1945	Music
The Moving Finger	Horst Graff
The Lady of Shalott	Schumann
Pavane for a Dead Infanta	Ravel
Slavonic Dance	Dvorak
Temple Dance	Cyril Scott
Will o' the Wisp	Maurice Reger
The Spider	Moeran
Occupation of Japan	Apologies to Puccini
Two Souls Alas Reside Within My Breast	Goethe, W. Baer

NEW ZEALAND, from 1956	
The Exile (three Acts)	Antony Elton
My Skin Is Black My Skin Is White	Antony Elton
Spanish Fiesta	Moskovski, de Falla, Albeniz
National Dances (*Czech Polka, Russian Peasant, Austrian Peasant, Shoe Clapping, Ear Boxing, Round Dance, Viennese Waltz*)	Traditional
Pictures From An Exhibition	Moussorgsky
Prater Cafe (Austrian Traditional)	J. Strauss, Moussorgsky
Wedding Day	Grieg
Torch Tango	Stravinsky
The Other Side of the Wall	William Southgate
Fugitive Vision	Rachmaninov

Dances of the Spirit	Negro Spirituals
Harvest Dance	Maunder
Spatial	Stockhausen
Liberation (Dance Drama)	Various
Encounter (Dance Drama)	Gustav Holst
Hunger	Dvorak
Visions By Painters	Granados, Gershwin, Bartok
Pania of the Reef (three Acts)	William Southgate
Easter Canticles (four Acts)	Britten, Messiaen, Bartok
In the Beginning, God	Duke Ellington
The Rock	Miriam Palmore, words T.S. Eliot
Three Images of the Lord's Prayer	Gothic, Ancient Hebrew, West Indian
The Prodigal Daughter (three Acts)	Penderecki, Faberman, Stravinsky
Dances for *Jesus Christ Superstar*	Rice Webber
The Journey	
On Freedom	Carl Orff
Death of a Bullfighter (with Louise Petherbridge)	words by Garcia Lorca
Pollution	Subotnik
Godspell (excerpts)	Rock opera
Two Spirituals ('He's Got the Whole World in His Hands' and 'Standing in the Need of Prayer')	Traditional
Metaphysical Dances ('Knocking on the Window' and 'This Train Goes on to Glory')	Carter, L. Armstrong
Lest Ye Be My Enemy	Gillian Bibby

Crucify That Man	Geoffrey Ainger
Flight	African Drumming
Secular City (Rock Mass)	Yivisaker
Orlando (A contemporary masque, devised by Louise Petherbridge from the book by Virginia Woolf)	John Drummond
Loneliness (Multi media montage, devised by Louise Petherbridge)	Music Concrete
China Dances (based on book by R.A.K. Mason)	
Danced Eucharist (in memory of Jocelyn Ryburn)	Michael John Talbot
While Grandmother Played Bridge (with Louise Petherbridge)	John Drummond
Bars (For prisoners of conscience and Amnesty International)	Chris Cree Brown
Historic Suite (Rustic Breugelian, Basse and Pavane)	Byrd
Cubist Dance	Satie
Requiem For The Living	Penderecki, words by Kirkup
Dances for The Mozart Harlequin (with Louise Petherbridge)	Mozart, arranged by John Drummond
K.M. (Three facets of Katherine Mansfield's inner life)	Chopin
Don't Fence Me In	Szabo Ferenc
Joy in the Morning (Easter work)	Bolling, Rampahl
Between Two Fires (on the Brontë family)	
Transfigured Night	Brahms

Jeptha's Daughter	Bernstein
The Call (On the ordination of Penny Jamieson, the first woman bishop of a Diocese)	Villa Lobos
Ecstatic Curves, Angular Lines	Ennes, Vivaldi
Elusive Vision	B. Britten, poems A. Rimbaud
Wild Time (an absurdist work)	Russell Scoones
Joan of Arc (A video reconstruction for Carol Brown of the Bodenwieser dance first created for Shona Dunlop)	Marcel Lorber
The Traitor	Szolloy
Nkosi Sikilele Afrika (God Bless Africa)	Mustapha
Greening (An environmental dance drama)	R. Vaughan Williams, Chant of the Navajo Indian, words W.B. Yeats
The World Is Your Neighbour (A contemporary parable of the Good Samaritan)	
Two Inches Behind the Eyes (Inspired by the writings of Janet Frame)	Anthony Ritchie
Wellsprings to Isadora (for Bronwyn)	Chopin, Tchaikovsky, Brahms, Beethoven
The Magnificat (for Christchurch Cathedral)	J.S. Bach
Fragmentations	B. Britten
My End Is The Beginning (The unfolding of a creative life. For Bronwyn)	Anthony Ritchie
A Question of Love (In response to the Presbyterian General Assembly of N.Z.'s refusal to ordain gay men and women.)	Anthony Ritchie